Social Values and Poetic Acts

Social Values and Poetic Acts

THE HISTORICAL JUDGMENT OF LITERARY WORK

JEROME J. McGANN

HARVARD UNIVERSITY PRESS
CAMBRIDGE, MASSACHUSETTS
LONDON, ENGLAND
1988

This book is printed on acid-free paper, and its binding materials
have been chosen for strength and durability.

Library of Congress Cataloging-in-Publication Data

McGann, Jerome J.
  Social values and poetic acts.

  Bibliography: p.
  Includes index.
  1. Criticism.   I. Title.
PN81.M49   1988   801'.95   87-14649
ISBN 0-674-81495-9

To my children
Geoffrey, Christopher, and Jennifer

'Tis not too late to seek a newer world

Preface

THIS BOOK IS the fourth part of a project which I began with the publication of *The Romantic Ideology* and which includes *A Critique of Modern Textual Criticism* and *The Beauty of Inflections*. The project will be finished—I do not say completed—when the fifth part in the series appears: *The Literature of Knowledge*. In these works I have tried to sketch a theory of historical method for Euro-American literary studies which would be grounded in the practice of a critical hermeneutics. Of the four, this book is by far the most general and perhaps therefore the most problematical, since it argues the critical relevance of the "canonical" literary archive for a radical and non-canonical approach to literary studies. It argues as well that a peculiar critical function has devolved upon literary work during the past two hundred years—the period when legitimation in the disciplines of knowledge came to be measured by certain utilitarian and pragmatistic criteria. One hesitates to call these criteria "useful" or "practical" since their legacy has been, at best, an equivocal one.

Part of that legacy has been the so-called legitimation crisis in the human sciences, a crisis registered with special acuteness in literary studies. To the degree that the human sciences have become the ideological organs of our age, to the degree that poetry (in its production and its reproduction) has agreed to take on part of that institutionalized responsibility, to that extent have these disciplines lost their truth functions. The purpose of this book is to argue that poetic discourse has other obligations than to speak for the orders of the state, however liberal and pluralistic those orders may be; indeed, to argue that poetic discourse, perhaps more than any of the other human sciences, has special resources for carrying out this critical and antithetical role, a role which is, in my view, now sorely needed.

In order to operate antithetically, however, "literature" will have to reconceive—and reacquire—its performative characteristics. Theory of Literature since the late eighteenth century has emphasized the representational dimensions of its texts, and hence has set a privilege upon criticism as a process of hermeneutics. But our texts (originary and reproductive alike) will escape us if they are not understood as part of a *process of writing* even as they are also embedded in their *fields of discourse*. We need to do more than explain what our texts are saying (or what we think they are saying); we need to understand *what they are doing in saying what they say*. And the same necessity falls upon ourselves in carrying out our own literary work.

Equally important is the need to preserve the resources of our literary archive—that notorious "canon" which has lately been taken to embody so many fearful and self-destructive values. We must of course continually judge and revise that body of work, but no one can afford to give it up—or, least of all, to consign it to the possession of those who would use it to propagate retrograde ideas and social values. Our literary inheritance must be incorporated into a current literary practice which is committed to the critical examination of society and culture and to the promotion of what corresponds to that critical examination: fundamental change, both social and imaginative.

So much by way of introducing the subjects of this book. But I must add a word or two here about the form. It is constructed around the four Alexander Lectures which I delivered at the University of Toronto in the fall of 1986 (they appear in much augmented versions as Chapters 1, 3, 4, and 11), and two other lectures (Chapters 2 and 5) which I wrote but did not deliver. These six pieces are not so much an argument as a set of interconnected explorations into the nature of an adequate, historically based hermeneutics. The organizational core of the book is therefore relatively loose—deliberately so—and I have tried to loosen it even further with the addition of five other chapters (in Parts II and III) which take up a series of topics closely related to the material in the lectures. Although all but one of these five chapters were written at the same time as the lectures, and although the subjects overlap, the pieces are self-contained investigations, and therefore formally discontinuous with the rest of the book. But they are crucial to my purposes here for two reasons.

In the first place, these chapters carry out a series of more detailed and scholastically rigorous treatments of the book's principal topics than were available to me in the lecture format. Second, because they execute shifts in the formal continuities of the book, they reopen its subjects from a set of slightly altered perspectives. Indeed, the critical virtue of certain disciplined discontinuities in literary work is a recurrent concern here and is specifically developed in several of the chapters. In this respect the book consciously goes over the ground I first tried to explore in *Swinburne: An Experiment in Criticism* (1972). Critical discourse must be able to sustain and develop an intellectual rigor, but if it is to preserve its critical edges it has to avoid the structural inertias of its own formalities. A dialogic or interruptive principle ought to be included in the structure of expository, forensic, and narrative modes of discourse. Hugh Kenner's study *The Pound Era* (1975) would not have achieved its critical depth had it not discovered an expository form to rhyme with the complexities of its subjects. Plato, Montaigne, and, in our own day, Adorno have always seemed to me far more interesting *critical* thinkers than, say, Aristotle, Aquinas, or Kant.

In such a context I should note Blake's centrality to this book. The structural parody of *Jerusalem,* which organizes Part I, is an index of the overall form and content. Blake's habit of returning to the same topics from slightly altered perspectives seems to me one of his most impressive rhetorical moves. The recursive procedures of this book are therefore to be taken as strategic features of the argument. Furthermore, Blake's historical position, in particular the antithesis to the line of Kant which his theory and practice represented, is a constant focus of attention. Blake's work—its major themes, forms, and polemics—has thus had a significant directorial effect on the way I have managed my materials.

Furthermore, the fact that Blake's intervention was literary and artistic rather than, like Kant's, philosophic and theoretical, is an exponent of what separates the work of these two important cultural figures. In a sense their work is not comparable, of course, so the opposition of Kant and Blake, which recurs in this book, might be thought inappropriate. But it is precisely in their different modes of addressing the legitimation crisis of art in their own day that I find the comparison useful, and the example of each instructive for our own time and its special legitimation crises in cultural studies. These problems are normally addressed today as a crisis of theory. But in truth they represent a crisis of cultural practice, not theory, though the practice of theory has been recently thought the best ground on which to engage the issues. In this book, as elsewhere, I have not avoided theoretical discussion, but I do think that the central problems are best seen as practical and, most of all, pedagogical rather than epistemological or theoretical. Kant's work therefore functions in this book as a cautionary tale in several respects; if my own work shows any "resistance to theory," it is only in the sense that one might choose to resist, *on practical grounds,* a certain method for dealing with particular problems. The chief problems facing literary studies today do not seem to me theoretical ones; they seem, rather, social, institutional, and methodological. "Theory" in literary studies has itself become such a social and institutional problem that its continued vigor will depend upon its ability to reflect upon itself more deeply and define more clearly its social and institutional objects and goals.

Much of Parts II and III has already appeared in print: Chapter 7 in *Critical Inquiry* 11 (March 1985), Chapter 8 in *Studies in Romanticism* (Fall 1986), Chapter 9 in *Criticism* 27 (Summer 1985), and Chapter 10 in *Critical Inquiry* (Spring 1987). Chapter 6 is a much revised version of "A Point of Reference," printed in *Historical Studies and Literary Criticism* (Madison, Wis., 1985), and the "Conclusion" was published in *Sulfur* (1987).

The lines quoted from *The Cantos of Ezra Pound* (copyright © 1934, 1962 by Ezra Pound) are reprinted by permission of New Directions Publishing Corporation. The quotations from John Hollander, *Reflections on Espionage* (1976) are reprinted by permission of Atheneum Publishers. The page from Hans Walter Gabler's *Ulysses: A Critical and Synoptic Edition* (Garland Publishing, 1984) is reproduced by permission of the editor and publisher. The poetry quotations from Ron Silliman and Charles Bernstein are reprinted with the permission of the authors.

For help, advice, and encouragement I am grateful to Marilyn Butler, Nick Dirks, Robert Essick, Cheryl Giuliano, Jon Klancher, Cecil Lang, Marjorie Levinson, Tom Mitchell, Marjorie Perloff, Mac Pigman, David Simpson, Jeff Skoblow, Robert von Hallberg, and Lindsay Waters.

Contents

Introduction 1

PART I
A New Jerusalem: The Historical Work of Imagination

1. *Plato and the Dialectic of Criticism* 13

2. *Blake and the Aesthetics of Deliberate Engagement* 32

3. *The Dawn of the Incommensurate* 50

4. *Poetic Ideology and Nonnormative Truth* 73

PART II
Adverse Wheels: Literature and the Work of Knowing

5. *Beginning Again: Literary Studies and
   the Crisis of Legitimation* 95

6. *The Scandal of Referentiality* 115

7. *Some Forms of Critical Discourse* 132

8. *The Idea of an Indeterminate Text:
   Blake and Dr. Alexander Geddes* 152

9. *Ulysses as a Postmodern Work* 173

PART III
Literature and the Future of History

10. *Contemporary Poetry, Alternate Routes*   197

11. *The Third World of Criticism*   219

Conclusion: The Loss of Poetry   241

Notes   251

Index   271

If I forget thee, O Jerusalem, may my right hand
forget her cunning.

Psalm 137

Introduction

In the name of Annah the Allmaziful, the Everliving, the
Bringer of Plurabilities, haloed be her eve, her singtime sung,
her rill be run, unhemmed as it is uneven!

James Joyce, *Finnegans Wake*

FOR LITERARY STUDIES since the Korean War, the most impressive
as well as the most troubling figure was surely Paul de Man. This is
certainly the case for my own work, but it seems to be equally true
for literary studies generally during this period, at least in the United
States. Unlike the coming of, say, Harold Bloom, de Man's influence
took some time to develop, but it has proved far more inexorable—
grinding slowly, like the mills of God, but grinding very small.

De Man's work is, therefore, my point of departure in this book,
as it has been in most of my work for the past twenty years. For me,
his special importance lies in his having exposed so clearly the crisis
which intrinsic conceptions of literature developed for themselves in
the aftermath of their victories over the previously dominant historicist and empirical programs. Here I begin by sketching the crisis
precipitated in de Man's work, for it is the history and form of that
crisis which is now driving literary studies back into various types of
sociohistorical work.

DE MAN'S SIGNIFICANCE as a deconstructionist can be traced to a
pair of important factors in his background as a scholar. In the first
place, his early training took place in an institutional framework still
dominated by the traditions of European philology, along with their

literary-historical methods. Against that foundational grain, however, he would later brush those techniques of close reading and thematic criticism which we associate with Anglo-American New Criticism.[1] Derrida's work seems to have been the catalyst which ultimately brought these two strains of philological and immanent studies into their most fruitful relation.

De Man's initial insights—they would prove to be seminal—evolved through a set of essays which were eventually collected in the book *Blindness and Insight* (1971; reprinted in an important augmented edition in 1983). At issue was the truth-content of literary work, in particular the apparently incommensurable relation between the "meaning" and the "structure" of literary texts. De Man came to the conclusion that criticism commits an "error" when it attempts to find (or "see") a commensurable relation between literary meaning and literary structure. The thematic "truth" of literature, he argued, lies not in some articulable "meaning" (the best that has been known or thought) but in what he called "the systematic character of a certain kind of error" (17).[2] To the end of his life de Man continued to demonstrate that antithetical structure which informs the production of all literary texts. The reading/writing of literature is an "insightful" activity which produces meaning and truth, but all those meanings and truths are inevitably accompanied by—indeed, are built upon— a reciprocity of various "blindnesses" and "errors." To de Man, however, these errors are "fruitful" because of the function they serve in maintaining that unfinishable process of dynamic reflection which literature *is*.

In the first part of his career de Man concentrated on the ways this dynamic functioned in the work of reading and criticism. Toward the end—and paradigmatically in *Allegories of Reading*—he worked to show in detail that the same dynamic informs the texts which are the object of hermeneutics. He had always maintained that this was the case, but his later work went more deeply into the structure of the blindness/insight dynamic, which he developed as a specifically textual antithesis between "cognitive and performative language" (*AR*, ix) in literary works, or what he saw as the "radical estrangement between the meaning and the performance of any text" (*AR*, 298). All literary works *dramatize* or execute this antithetical process, according to de Man, but some carry it out so systematically as to become allegories of the process itself. And the "meaning" of such allegories is that "the truth-value of literature (is) a negative one" (*AR*, 113) in the sense that truth is revealed as the object of a permanent desire which is always being satisfied unsatisfactorily. De Man expresses this view in an unnerving proposition: because the "aim" of art "is precisely *not* to deceive, it is therefore *true*" (*AR*, 113).

De Man's discussion of the Second Preface to *Julie* (*AR*, 195–210) is by now one of the most celebrated illustrations of the content and method of his argument. This reading of the Second Preface, which explores the truth-function of Rousseau's writing, is founded on the assumption that "by truth we understand the possibility of referential verification" (*AR*, 204). De Man shows how the Second Preface—a dialogue between the text-figures R. (who is made to stand in for "the author") and N. (who interrogates R. on the relation of Julie's letters to actual persons)—undermines both the possibility *and* the impossibility of "referential verification" (see *AR*, 202). What de Man sets out to show is that Rousseau's text, including the Second Preface, cannot maintain a firm distinction between an "inside" and an "outside" of itself. In this way the text suffers a "loss of faith in the reliability of referential meaning" even as it also institutes "the persistence of the referential moment" (*AR*, 208).

This brief schematization of de Man's subtle commentaries, though it inevitably leaves out much of importance, may indicate the blind areas of his characteristic insights. One notes, first of all, his acceptance of referential verification as the norm of truth. Furthermore, de Man conceives that such verification relates to some fixed or given "reality" which not only preexists textualization, but—more crucially—*preexists it in a certain specific form*. De Man never considers the possibility that, if *Julie* is taken to have a model in actual history, that model might be as unstable, problematic, and multiplied as the model's textualizations.

This difficulty is allied to another, related one. De Man takes the distinction between what is textual and what is actual to be a *real* (not merely a formal or logical) distinction. He does this because "textual" for him does not mean any single (or several) materially and institutionally generated products. The de Manian text is a purely linguistic, rather than a social, structure of relations. This fact about his textual understanding appears most graphically when he discusses the figures N. and R. in relation to "Rousseau." De Man of course knows that R. is a fiction, and he also knows that "Rousseau" is a fiction; but whereas he *always* conceives R. (and N.) as fictional, he speaks of "Rousseau" sometimes as a fiction and sometimes as an actuality—that is, as the historical author of the work we call *Julie*.

This ambivalence about what is actual and what is figural in the book appears again, even more dramatically, in relation to the initial, nondialogic Preface, which de Man thinks of as "the actual, first Preface" (*AR,* 196), that is to say, as the work of the historical Rousseau. But such a conception undermines the figural argument, for an "actual" Preface (unlike the dialogical and fictive Second Preface) has to fall outside the instabilities of de Man's "text," has to be conceived, in fact, as what de Man calls here a "document." And this "document" has as well an actual, determinate "author," Jean Jacques Rousseau, a person conceived and discussed by de Man as a historical rather than simply a nominal or virtual being.

But by de Man's own logic—a logic that was also pursued by Barthes and Foucault—all these voices are in a certain respect "fictional," or what de Man calls "figural"—literary constructions which serve a semiotic system that generates "meaning." That should be clear enough. What we tend to forget, however, is that this literary system is also in permanent and particular respects (these are not the same as "fixed" and "univocal" respects) "actual": actual in the sense that the system operates (and continues to operate to this day and beyond) in concrete social space and conditions which can be specified. The ambivalence in de Man's argument shows that he has not forgotten the "actuality" of Rousseau's work, but it also shows that he has not been able to accommodate what he knows to his own critical procedures. The work we call *Julie* is inadequately conceived when it is represented—as de Man tries to represent it—merely as a "text," just as the "truth-function" of literary work is inadequately conceived as a matter of "referentiality" in the sense that de Man proposes (a sense taken over from positivism). Reciprocally, if Rousseau may (and indeed must) be thought of as in certain important respects a "figural" being like N. and R., the latter may (and must) be conceived in their turn, and in equally important respects, as material and historical actualities: *not,* of course, as coded names for certain real people, but as a particular means for executing certain literary operations which the institution of letters, in Rousseau's day, provided for its individual practitioners.

The problem in de Man's conception of "the text" occurs, I think, because he wants to resist the pressure of his own critical logic, which inclines to turn the literary event into "the mere play of a free signifier" and the "disinterested play" of a Kantian-type aesthetic (*AR,* 208).

De Man insists, in his reading of the Second Preface, that literature—and this text in particular—is "not free . . . from referential and tropological coercion" (*AR*, 208). Texts have their "ethical" dimensions, which de Man calls their "rhetorical" or "performative" aspects. These make up the text's desire to impose or institute some determinate meaning. But de Man's "textual" (or "readerly") conception of literary activity prevents him from being able to develop anything beyond a purely formal category of "rhetoric" and "performativity." That is to say, his idea of textuality forecloses the possibility of his being able to show that "literature" is as much a "communicative action" (to borrow Habermas's term) as it is a discipline of "reading."

DE MAN'S WORK is typical of the general turn which literary studies took in the early twentieth century, away from sociohistory and the traditional methods of philology and into various types of formalistic, text-centered, and language-based programs. That movement, which culminated in deconstruction, was a broad-ranging critique of the narrowly empirical and even positivist directions which had come to dominate history-based literary studies. Today this situation is in a process of significant change, but the influence of empiricism on historical work in the human sciences continues to be very great (for good and ill alike).

De Man is, however, also *un*typical—and in this respect his latest work is especially significant—because his philological background seems always to have haunted his work, pushing it finally into the crisis I have already noticed. The most dramatic evidence of this lies in his deep concern with the problem of referentiality for all "intrinsic" and language-based programs of criticism. His attempt to characterize the "rhetorical" and "performative" aspects of literary work is a conversation between the ghosts of his philological training (the referentialists) and their renegade inheritors (the intrinsic "readers")—in fact, an effort to accommodate these two ways of thinking about literature. But it is a conversation between figures who share empiricist and positivist conceptions of history and referentiality. As a consequence, when de Man tries to theorize or describe the "performative" aspects of literary work, he is forced to move in the narrow circumstances of personal reflexivity where literature is understood as psychomachy. The "referential moment," which de Man, troubled deconstructor, insists upon, is a singular experience in every sense: it is a moment that takes place in a system of dynamic changes, true, but it is also a moment which only occurs in the unified field of a single "reader."

To bring about the accommodation which de Man was seeking, however, we will have to reconstruct a theory of the text, and a practical criticism, that follows sociohistorical and materialist lines which are not, at the same time, positivistic. This entails an opening of the field of "reading" beyond what is now called "the text" to include that whole range of materials comprehended by the disciplines of history, sociology, and anthropology, as well as traditional philology. Thus, to study, say, *The Marriage of Heaven and Hell* would involve a "reading" of that work in terms of its entire productive and reproductive histories along the vertical axis of their temporalities as well as the horizontal axis of their socioinstitutional structures. This reading would be carried out, however, in the understanding that it is fated to have certain partialities and blindnesses, and hence in the understanding that it must remain open to changes and revisions. In this respect it is necessarily a Nietzschean, a de Manian, a "deconstructive" reading.

It differs from intrinsic and "readerly" approaches in its understanding of the literary work as intersected by many structures and many histories which are not only the creation or invention of immediate readers. These readers may invent new ways of seeing or new "approaches," but their readings will be constrained by the work's accumulated inertias. More often than not, what happens in the histories of reading is that the full and dynamic reality of the works is dismembered by the uses to which they are put by their later readers. The recent work in feminist criticism has shown us all, quite dramatically, how such dismemberments take place. In this respect we have to see that all literary works, including the texts of those works, are inhabited by lost and invisibilized agencies, and that one of the chief functions of criticism is to re-member the works which have been torn and distorted by those losses.

No one was more aware of that necessity than Walter Benjamin, the antiquarian Marxist. His truly mythic career was a scene of memorial devotion directed toward the future, an attempt to save those lost and forgotten agencies from the oblivion which every victorious "history" condemns them to. If it is important, as Shelley said, to "imagine what we know," it is equally important to remember what we have forgotten or otherwise known—not because there are others who comprehend the best that has been known and thought in the world, but because we can never be certain at any moment what "the best" might be. "There is a time for every purpose under heaven."

The "truth" of the past, then, is not simply the Truth, nor is it only of the Past; it is multiplied through time as a body rather than a system of ideas or eventualities. As a body of ideas the truth is more like a collection of proverbs than anything else—a shifting network of "eternal truths" which, if they wake to perish never, constantly contradict each other ("Too many cooks spoil the broth," "Many hands make light work," or, as in Proverbs 26:4–5, "4. Answer not a fool according to his folly, lest thou also be like unto him. 5. Answer a fool according to his folly, lest he be wise in his own conceit"). As an eventual (performative) history, the truth comes to us in a form that Milman Parry once called "a picture of great detail," which the West's first great historian, Herodotus, captured so memorably in his *Histories*. We now might call that picture a "duck-rabbit" because we know that its appearance changes. But in fact it is far more complex than the latter, for the picture holds, even before we ever look at it, more images and stories than we can imagine. The truth *is* stranger than fiction.

But it is also less eloquent, more secretive. And this is one important reason why we require the agencies of literature, where those changing truths are held out to us in reliable (but not unchanging) forms. The forms are reliable because we can always count on them to preserve, often (it can seem) in spite of themselves and their peculiar ideological interests, details and prospects which are at odds or in tension with other details and prospects. What is central and what is peripheral, even what is present and what is absent, all make their appearances and shift their positions in relation to each other. Moreover, the reader is likewise involved in this network of eventualities, and not merely as an individual facing the enigma of "the text." Individuals face their texts in the context(s) which define them, and these are as diverse and enigmatic as the poems which reflect them back.

But, as we know, the contexts are far less coherent than the poems. Yet we tend to forget—it is a legacy of the Kantian tradition—that while imaginative work is more coherent than the world, it is no less exigent and performative *in* the world. Literature is not simply a symbolic or aesthetic structure, it also—and simultaneously—functions as a structure of signification.

This "performative" aspect of literary work was recently brought to a dramatic focus by D. F. McKenzie in his paper on the Treaty of Waitangi. Though centered in a controversy over a legal "document" rather than a poetic "text," the issue involved not merely a conflict of interpretations, but a misunderstanding of the powers and use-values of written work.

Only one aspect of this fascinating story is my immediate concern: the efforts, about 1820, by British missionaries in New Zealand to establish local printing operations in order to introduce literacy into the oral culture of the indigenous Maori people. Along with literacy went, of course, an introduction to western ideology, and in particular to Protestant Christianity, for the texts initially printed and distributed among the Maori were excerpts from the Bible. Because the Maori were eager to obtain copies of the books, and because they appeared to learn to "read" them with some facility, the missionaries were initially pleased and surprised at the success of their efforts.

In fact, however, the Maori had been receiving these novel products of western society almost wholly in terms of their own oral culture. In the first place, most of their "reading" was memorizing—an eventuality one might have expected in the case of an oral culture. Second, the Maori typically treated the much-desired books as fetish objects. Indeed, the Maori's inclination to fetishize the western book was merely one aspect of their overriding tendency to emphasize the executive power they found in these written (or printed) works. Consequently, while the missionaries were teaching the Maori to "read" and assimilate western ideas, they were also—wholly unbeknownst to themselves—giving the Maori an important weapon which they would soon employ against the British colonizers. As McKenzie observes: "The main use of literacy to the Maori was not reading books for their ideas, much less for the access they gave to divine truths, but letter writing. For them, the really miraculous point about writing was its portability; by annihilating distance, a letter allowed a person to be in two places at once, his body in one, his thoughts in another. It was the spatial extension of writing, not its temporal permanence, that became politically potent in gathering the tribes and planning a war a decade and more later."[3]

The Maori seized upon an important use-function of materially produced literary work of which "letter writing" is merely the exponent or symbol. It is a literary power which our theories tend to neglect or forget about altogether. But through Maori eyes we may see that texts have a "rhetoric of temporality" far different from what was described by de Man. The Maori find a "pleasure of the text" in the fact that texts are material agencies, and that part of their "meaning" is always involved with their socially instrumental powers. The oral culture of the Maori throws this aspect of textualization into bold relief, and while the poetic theory of literate cultures has recently tended to obscure that agenting function, it continues to operate through the texts we produce and reproduce. Indeed, it operated with—or rather "was operated by"—the missionaries as much as by the Maori. The difference was that one group worked the texts in order to obtain political power over another group, while the other turned what Blake called an "adverse wheel" in an effort to define their independence.

Poetic is one form of discourse by which personal and social interests are framed and executed. About this there can be no question. The real questions are: how do these operations get carried out, to what end, by whom; and what are the special agenting functions of literary discourse (as opposed, for example, to legal, or psychoanalytic, or religious discourse)?

That last is an especially important question in an age which has seen the development of a major "legitimation crisis" in literary studies. Dealing with it will require a "social studies" of poetry which focuses on its distinctive character: that poetry is a discourse deploying a form of total coherence—and thereby a hope of coherence—within the quotidian world, which is dominated by various forms of relative incoherence. No other form of human discourse manages to do this, which is paradoxical since poetic forms are in another important respect fundamentally unstable and incommensurate. Texts governed by memory and imagination—poetic texts—display networks of human interests which are massively heterodox. They are not merely open to various "readings," they are inhabited by long histories of complex and often conflicted self-understandings. In this respect they hold a mirror up to the human world. But the mirror is held up as a challenge—like Ahab's doubloon—and not simply as a picture to be observed. That challenge is to imagine more than you know, and to understand the imperative of such an act of imagining. Those who do not grasp this, who do not carry out the task of poetry, put their lives and their histories in the hands of men like Cyrus and Xerxes, whose modern equivalents are Captain Cook, Napoleon, Ezra Pound. They are all great men and they all produced great works. They are equally, all of them, figures of disaster—for themselves and for count-less others besides. None understood the meaning of their own lives and actions because each one "read" by the light of his imagination alone. Yet the disasters which they precipitated have been saved for us (they can never be redeemed) in discourses of literature, where they acquire the possibility of new and nondisastrous meanings and uses.

PART I ⟨∽⟩

A New Jerusalem: The Historical Work of Imagination

And I heard the Name of their Emanations: they are named Jerusalem.

William Blake, *Jerusalem*

1 ⌒

Plato and the Dialectic of Criticism
To the Deconstructionists

> Everything changes if one considers that society is presented
> to each man as a *perspective of the future* and that this fu-
> ture penetrates to the heart of each one as a real motivation
> of his behavior.
>
> Jean-Paul Sartre, *Search for a Method*

NORTHROP FRYE'S *Anatomy of Criticism* first appeared in 1957.
Historically considered, this work was a response to the reigning New
Critical practices, which Frye saw as excessively subjectivized and
"aesthetic." In their place he proposed a synthetic critical program
based upon four *a priori* narrative categories which constituted the
fundamental "scientific" ratios of all literary objects.

Any criticism which aspires to a programmatic comprehensiveness
must transcend the immediate activity of reading, must find a way of
totalizing both the artistic and the critical experience. Frye's project,
which is founded on a "subject-object model drawn from nineteenth-
century science,"[1] establishes such a totalization. Initially, in the climate of emerging structural programs, Frye's *Anatomy* gained enormous circulation and influence, but its authority has waned somewhat
with the coming of poststructuralist ideas. The greatest challenge, in
this respect, came from the deconstructive arguments which sought
to undermine every hermeneutics founded on the innocent subject and
the innocent object.

There is no need to rehearse these matters, which have been widely
discussed throughout the academy. Nor do I instance Frye's work as
a special case of what Hartman has called "criticism in the wilderness";[2] the fate of our reading the *Anatomy* has been entirely paradigmatic, and criticism is now dispersed into various competing

"schools" and "strategies." Frye's work remains attractive, however, because, on one hand, it has never compromised its demand for critical comprehensiveness, and, on the other, it has always understood clearly that literature is a social and an institutional practice. What lays his work open to the critiques of poststructuralism is its neglect of the historicality of literary practice: in fact, his resort to certain conceptual categories which are assumed to be transhistorical.

Frye's holistic imperative can be reinstituted, however, if his ahistorical "anatomy" is replaced by a dialectical model of critical and literary practice. The point of departure, in such an approach, would be located, historically *and* methodologically, in the genealogical procedures which our traditions of philological inquiry established between approximately 1780 and 1930. It was this line of critical work which was evaded, and then supplanted from its academic dominance, by the sequence of critical endeavors which rose between 1930 and the present day in England, the United States, and Europe (especially Russia and France). Although this is not the place to analyze in detail the shape of the historicist movement and its several immanentist successors, I must at least sketch out those ideas which locate the main issues and the principal areas of conflict.

Historicism is a general term we now apply to those nineteenth-century genetic methods whose subject was ancient texts and whose avowed purpose was to interpret them on their own terms. Thus Eichhorn, on the study of the book of Genesis, tells the student to "forget . . . the century in which you are living and the knowledge which it gives you; and if you cannot, do not dream that you will be appreciating the book in the spirit of its origin." Only a reading carried out in that original spirit will yield the truth about the past: "The youth of the world . . . requires that one sink into its depths. The first beams of dawning intelligence will not bear the bright light of the intellect" if it is to be understood; consequently, the student of ancient culture and its texts will devise a way to alienate himself from his own culture and to think of the past "objectively," on its own terms.[3] In *The Spirit of Hebrew Poetry* Herder outlined this kind of project in a startling way. "If our time and nation has a desert," he declared, "it is in this cool effort, unintoxicated by glosses and strange interpretation, to approach the simple original meaning of those poets, and to hear their own god-like utterances in the historical context of the earliest times."[4] Eighty years later Nietzsche would also see historical scholarship as a "desert," but whereas to Herder such a figure suggested a place populated by the simple and clear imaginations of poetical and godlike souls, to Nietzsche it merely suggested an arid and fruitless badlands. And Nietzsche's critical turn on historicist scholarship soon became a commonplace, not to say a cliché, in twentieth-century immanent criticism.

Anyone now interested in historical scholarship will be impressed by the achievements of the critical tradition which stretches from Wolf to Parry. On the other hand, no one who has experienced those other critical traditions stretching from Kant to Abrams, or from Hegel to Derrida, will fail to understand the profound difficulties which historicist programs eventually had to contend with. Historicism itself raised up its own Nemesis in "its affirmation of knowledge as perspective."[5] If the book of Genesis reflects a historically particular culture, and if the texts of that book are equally the product of particular contexts and interests, the same is true of the new historicist procedures for studying the past and its texts. Historicist studies do not reveal the past, they construct it out of their own (often mystified) present interests. Correlatively—and this is the second part of the critique of such programs—in the pursuit of an identification with the past, the philologians tended to lose sight of the relation which the past, and the study of the past, always has for the present and the future.

The most typical assumption in such reconstructive programs was a Romantic ideology of organic and continuous development which, it was believed, was incarnated in our cultural remains. Equally clear was the objectivity of the subjects to be studied and the methods to be followed. Neither of these key assumptions was able to survive the searching criticisms mounted from various quarters within and without the historical tradition, some positivist and some humanistic. All this antithetical work was first fully articulated by Nietzsche in his *Untimely Meditations,* and particularly in the second of them, *On the Use and Abuse of History* (1874).

That the critique of philology and historicism had seized the day is patent from our literary experience of the past fifty years. During this period, serious theoretical work in historical criticism virtually ceased, and Nietzsche's critique of philology—it was a philologian's attack, we should remember—seemed to have achieved its definitive success. Yet in our day, in the decadence of the period of immanent criticism, we are witnessing a revival of interest in historical theory and criticism. This is due, it appears to me, in no small part to the work of Nietzsche's contemporary avatar Michel Foucault, a historian and poststructural theoretician who sketched a model for a revived program of sociohistorical studies in the human sciences, including literary studies.

I want to extrapolate here my understanding of Nietzsche's and Foucault's work. This will involve a reconception of certain key philological positions and ideas. For although one neither can nor should revive the historicist program, one should and must reincorporate its work into literary studies. Empirical and archival work has not ceased to be part of our literary *institutions,* yet our reigning *theories* of criticism and interpretation—those we have fashioned for ourselves in this century—have never been able to restore the connection, which the early historicists certainly maintained, between "intrinsic" and "extrinsic" literary investigations, between hermeneutics and scholarship, *verstehen* and *erklären*. The best literary scholars have always practiced as if the two were not theoretically disjoined; nevertheless, to the degree that such practice was grounded in an incomplete theorization, to that degree the practice itself suffered, and continues to suffer to this day.

What is it that we want to regain from the philological tradition and its storehouses of empirical fact and positive knowledge? That is one of the main questions we have to consider. Dealing with it will require the articulation of a fairly comprehensive program in sociohistorical literary criticism. That program will have to determine the status of literary work (both the particular work and literary production in general) as well as the tasks of those who read, write, and promote literary discourse.

Furthermore, since the question is being posed in a very particular (academic) context, it presupposes a theory of pedagogy which must also be articulated. One of the worst aspects of advanced academic studies in our day is the gap that has opened between the study and the classroom, the scholar and the teacher. The metaphor of the human world as a "text" has proved a useful one in our day, but its disadvantages are sometimes forgotten: for it is not "texts" which act in the world, it is the men and women who formulate and deploy those texts and who have assented to the textualization of their lives. This process is neither to be deplored nor to be reversed, but it must be clearly understood. In this respect it is important to see the human faces and the particular social structures which constitute the texts of the world.

These are large subjects. But the topics are pressing ones for everyone involved in cultural studies, and they must be confronted. Furthermore, I believe that our cultural experience of the past thirty years—the period dominated by structural and poststructural work—has created the conditions which have made it possible to reconstitute literary studies (and cultural studies in general) on a footing that is both positive and critical, concretely and textually centered but also with a conscious sociohistorical focus.

I BEGIN by sketching briefly Paul Ricoeur's view of the hermeneutical project. Ricoeur is important partly because he is a distinguished representative of the interpretive tradition, and partly because his work has embraced the legacy of twentieth-century semiotics and language theory. As a consequence, his views about texts and their interpretation, grounded in an idealist conception of the philological program, overlap and accommodate many forms of contemporary critical ideas.

Hermeneutics "concerns the rules required for the interpretation of the written documents of our culture."[6] This formulation distinguishes, quite properly, spoken from written discourse, but that distinction is based upon a prior conception of the relation between these two forms of discourse. I shall quote Ricoeur at length on this point since his view has become a widely dispersed commonplace which my own argument shall be contesting:

> Here is the place to recall the myth in Plato's *Phaedrus*. Writing was given to men to "come to the rescue" of the "weakness of discourse," a weakness which was that of the event. The gift of the *grammata* . . . was just that of a "remedy" brought to our memory. The Egyptian King of Thebes could well respond to the god Theuth that writing was a false remedy in that it replaced . . . real wisdom by the semblance of knowing. This inscription, in spite of its perils, is discourse's destination. What in effect does writing fix? Not the event of speaking, but the "said" of speaking, where we understand by the "said" of speaking that intentional exteriorization constitutive of the aim of discourse . . . In short, what we write, what we inscribe, is the *noema* of the speaking. It is the meaning of the speech event, not the event as event.[7]

Reading this, we understand where Ricoeur differs from the deconstructionist program. For Ricoeur, "a text is a whole, a totality," and the "relation between whole and parts—as in a work of art or an animal—requires a specific kind of 'judgment' for which Kant gave the theory in the Third Critique."[8] Ricoeur's stable and autonomous text "fixes" the unstable and fleeting "event" of immediate spoken discourse, and that fixation establishes the *meaning* of all that is past and passing and to come. For Derrida, however, there is no point of fixation. For Derrida, the inscribed text has "priority" over the oral text, not because it is more stable, but rather because—unlike the oral text—it can dramatize its instability in the play of its illusory stabilities.

This important difference between these two paradigmatic interpretive positions underlines as well their common agreement: that a distinction must be made between text and event, and that "meaning"—whether ontic or illusory—is a textual and not an eventual function. Their manner of distinguishing text from event produces a shared inclination to "textualize" experience, and to see the reasoned disposal of experience—its manipulation and its interpretation alike—as an exegetical operation. In this approach to the human sciences, the total field of knowledge is assumed to be in place when the act of inquiry begins. More than that, the field is assumed to be the locus of what is "true" in the important sense that it *is* in place, it has the authority of its existence (even if that "existence" is understood as the construction of the interpreter's eye).

I would point out that this assumption operates in nearly all forms of contemporary hermeneutics and that it is taken over from the philological tradition. Deconstruction is often thought to be an exegetical method that works against the authority of the received texts, that undermines or displaces them from their centered or self-centered positions. But while deconstructive exegesis does operate a critical investigation of certain types of textual "meanings," it remains in basic agreement with the traditional hermeneutic program, which treats its "texts" as self-referential discourse structures and which fashions a corresponding form of exegesis. Literary criticism today no longer sees either its texts or its own operations "innocently"; nevertheless, the texts it does see and the criticism it still deploys remain philological in this sense: it is all taken as a play of words, *langue* structures and *parole* discourses, intertextual fields where "meaning" is aesthetically or academically dispersed. Pierre Bourdieu's work is important in this context precisely because it has exposed the uncritical dimensions of this hermeneutic practice in both its deconstructive and its reconstructive (philological) modes.[9]

There is, however, an alternative procedure for dealing with texts which was first clearly adumbrated by Marx but which traces its roots to Plato's *Republic*. Nietzsche was the earliest critic to elaborate and deploy it in a comprehensive way, and in our own day Foucault has been its master tactician and theorist. In what follows I shall be trying to redevelop certain parts of this alternative tradition. Let me observe in advance, however, that although I shall be using categories we associate with Nietzsche and Foucault, my own views sometimes run against the grain of their conscious purposes.

In fact, I want to begin at just that antithetical point. In *The Genealogy of Morals* Nietzsche deconstructs the ethical history of philosophy in order to free human action from its self-destructive conceptual limits. It is a drama in which "the will to truth" is made to bend before the human lives which encompass that will.[10] In the course of the argument Nietzsche reverses the traditional relation of Apollonian and Dionysian authorities: "Art . . . is far more radically opposed to the ascetic ideal than is science . . . Plato felt this instinctively—the greatest enemy of art Europe has thus far produced. Plato vs. Homer: here we have the whole, authentic antagonism; on the one hand, the deliberate transcendentalist and detractor of life, on the other, life's instinctive panegyrist."[11] When Nietzsche chooses Homer's side he is recalling Books 2, 3, and 10 of the *Republic,* where Plato denounces the poets when they tell lies about the gods and heroes. Today—indeed, since Kant at least—no one who has thought in interesting ways about poetry has stood with Plato on this matter.

A well-known essay by the speech-act theorist John R. Searle brings the issues into sharp focus. He begins by alluding to what he calls Plato's "common misinterpretation" of the status of fictional discourse, and he then asks: "Why would such a view be wrong?"[12] His essay goes on to explain, in the familiar argument now given speech-act terminology, that it is wrong because Plato has not properly distinguished fictive discourse from nonfictive (or illocutionary) discourse. "In the terminology of *Speech Acts,* the *illocutionary act* [in poetry] is pretended, but the *utterance act* is real."[13] In poststructural terminology, poems are self-referential discourse systems which use language in nonpositive formats, whereas "ordinary language" discourse involves speech *acts* which have reference to the "world."

Searle's philosophy of language follows Austin's original insights into the so-called "performative" dimensions of discourse. For both, words are not simply reflectors of meaning, they are themselves the agents of meaningful *actions*. In "the logical status of fictional discourse," however, according to Searle, discourse does not "perform" either propositional, referential, or transitive ("illocutionary") acts. In Auden's famous poetic version of this view, it "survives in the valley of its saying," it "makes nothing happen."[14] Yet at the end of his essay Searle makes a sharp critical turn on his own argument by raising the old problem—which he had bracketed out at the beginning when he dismissed Plato—of how one can speak of the "moral" or "didactic" functions of literary works if they are all to be subsumed under "the pleasure of the text." "Literary critics have explained on an ad hoc and particularistic basis how the author conveys a serious speech act through the performance of the pretended speech acts which constitute the work of fiction, but there is as yet no general theory of the mechanisms by which such serious illocutionary intentions are conveyed by pretended illocutions."[15]

Searle does not attempt to deal with this problem, which amounts to asking not only "Why are Plato's ideas about poetry wrong?" but also "Why are those ideas right?" In effect, this is what I want to do here. What should result is the fulfillment of Searle's call for a "general theory of the mechanisms by which . . . serious illocutionary intentions are conveyed by pretended illocutions."

Searle himself has made an important contribution to such a theory in his philosophy of speech acts, which effectively undermines what Foucault has called "the sovereignty of the signifier."[16] Foucault's work carries this critique one step further because he follows Nietzsche in regarding human discourse structures as systems by which societies deploy their illusions and their ideologies, to the detriment of human life and human living. Under these illusions discourse structures are seen not for what they are—deeds, acts, performatives—but rather as signifiers and intertexts, the intermediaries by which one arrives at "the truth." Foucault means to break down such an understanding of discourse, to "restore to discourse its character as an event."[17] Discourses do not reflect, or reflect upon, reality, they actively constitute it in particular (and specifiable) ways.

Like Nietzsche, however, Foucault sees Plato as the villain who deposed Homer and the poets and thereby substituted illusory for "true discourse." In the transition from the poetic sixth century to the rational fifth, "the highest truth no longer resided in what discourse *was*, or in what it *did:* it lay in what was *said*. The day dawned when truth moved over from the ritualised act—potent and just—of enunciation to settle on what was enunciated itself: its meaning, its form . . . A division emerged between Hesiod and Plato, separating true discourse from false . . . And so the Sophists were routed."[18] That this view is a travesty of Plato should hardly have to be said; one need simply point to Plato's myth of the life of Socrates which is dramatized, even enacted, in the dialogues. Nevertheless, Foucault's misrepresentation of Plato, and especially of Socrates, is important and consequential. First, as we have already seen, it reemphasizes the Nietzschean critique of the illusions and bad faith of the purveyors of discourse. Second—and more to the point of my present concerns—Foucault's distinction between the "true discourse" of poetry and the false discourses of ideology is gained by suggesting that poetry does not traffic in ideology—at any rate, poetry before the coming of Plato (which presumably means, for subsequent periods, "authentic" poetry, or poetry as such). Whatever in poetry is ideological is *ipso facto* not poetry.

If we step back from Searle and Foucault for a moment we shall see a remarkable thing: both are interested in restoring a conception that words are acts or events, constitutive operators (what E. D. Hirsch has recently called "stipulatives").[19] But for Searle the model linguistic performative is what he calls "serious" or nonfictive discourse, whereas for Foucault it is the opposite—it is poetry and "the literature of power." Correlatively, Foucault designates poetry as the "true" eventual or performative discourse because it is not concerned with ideas or the Nietzschean "will to truth," whereas Searle sets nonfictive discourse as the standard performative because it *is* concerned with those things.

"Plato vs. Homer: here we have the whole, authentic antagonism." Thus Nietzsche distinguishes between those who operate on a "will to truth" and those who are driven by the "will to life," and in *Untimely Meditations* he focuses on the philologians and scholars of his own day as the true descendants of this Plato, the "detractor of life." Foucault's critique of current scholarship, in which speech acts and discourse events are reduced to a spectacle of textualizations, explicitly carries forward Nietzsche's critique.

My own argument will follow the line indicated by both Nietzsche and Foucault. Nevertheless, I shall make two important departures from their positions. First, I want to show that Plato is badly represented as the villain in this story told by Nietzsche and Foucault. Plato's work has some deeply puritanical elements, but it is entirely false to think that his commitment to Ideas involves a programmatic of what is correct and "the truth." The famous dictum—that Socrates is the wisest of men because he knows that he knows nothing—is ironical only with respect to those who pretend to some greater understanding. Indeed, the method of the Platonic dialogue anticipates in the most striking way Nietzsche's and Foucault's efforts to develop critical systems which will resist and even dismantle the reifications involved in the use or study of discourse systems. This line of argument will carry us to the heart of Plato's hostility to rhetorical and textual formations, and his insistence upon preserving language as living social interchange, as dialectic.

My second argument involves a departure from Plato and Nietzsche rather than from Foucault. Having reconstituted the heart of language in dialectic, or what Habermas calls "communicative action,"[20] I shall nonetheless argue that the necessary tools for promoting a correspondent view of poetry have to be sought in the philological tradition. For however much we may deplore the *ideology* of the text and of *textualité*, the *fact* is that current discourse is deeply textualized. In particular—since my main subject is poetry and imaginative discourse—the entire tradition of poetry comes into our hands in textualized forms. The problem then becomes: how are we to preserve and encourage a dialectical understanding and engagement with imaginative work that descends to us in those profoundly nondialectical forms we call texts?

I SHALL BEGIN the argument proper, then, by turning to Plato. The crucial question here will be the question that Searle did not ask (but that Iris Murdoch, in *The Fire and the Sun*, did): what *insight* (not what *error*) led Plato to banish the poets from the Republic?[21] The simple answer we all know: poets tell lies and misrepresent reality. Searle thinks this view represents a "common misunderstanding" because, in his mind, poetry does not deal in matters of truth or error. But Plato's argument assumes that poetry does deal with such matters, that art has commitments to the truth.

In Book 10 of the *Republic* Socrates returns to the theme initially raised in Books 2 and 3 concerning the status of poetry in the well-ordered state. He completes the earlier arguments that poetry deals in fictions and even falsehoods, and affirms that "we really had good grounds then for dismissing her from our city . . . For reason constrained us" (607b).[22] Socrates reaches this conclusion reluctantly, however, for "we ourselves are very conscious of her [poetry's] spell" and "would gladly admit her" to a place in the city. "Do not you yourself feel her magic?" he asks Glaucon, "and especially when Homer is her interpreter?" Glaucon assents, and Socrates declares that poetry can "return from this exile after she has pleaded her defense." Once again the accommodating Glaucon agrees, as Socrates states the requirements for a defense of poetry. It can be cast in prose or meter, and it can be made by the poet or the lover of poetry. Its essential task is to "show that [poetry] is not only delightful but beneficial to orderly government and the life of man. And we shall listen benevolently, for it will be clear gain for us if it can be shown that she bestows not only pleasure but benefit" (607c–d).

Whatever else one may say about these passages, their attitude toward poetry is clearly equivocal. Socrates does not *want* to banish poetry, and he is not led to his conclusion simply by his "reason." Socrates banishes poetry because, although its function is seen as a social one, its benefit to society has never been demonstrated by the poets or the friends of poetry. In the context of the Platonic corpus generally, this equivocalness is appropriate. The *Ion* is only the most famous text in which poetry is associated with the highest orders of knowledge. Furthermore, Socrates and Plato are themselves notoriously poetical in their discourse, as we see in their frequent use of myths to explain the most difficult and complex matters.

In fact, Socrates' position here recalls those numerous passages in the dialogues where poets are represented as saying things which, though perhaps true, are obscure to the poets themselves. "Poets," says the Athenian in the *Laws*, "singing as they do under the divine afflatus, are among the inspired and so, by the help of their Graces and Muses, often enough hit upon true historical fact" (682a). But Plato's and Socrates' idea is that because the poets do not understand the character of their own knowledge, they are unreliable guides and educators. The whole point of associating poetry with divine inspiration connects with this (critical) view of poetical discourse.

By the time Plato came to write the *Laws*, his judgment about poetry had narrowed considerably from what he had written in the

Republic, not to speak of the even earlier works. In fact, the *Laws* answers Socrates' injunction by working out a defense of poetry. This defense, in *Laws* II, argues that poetical work must be produced under the guidance of appropriate "judges," those who—unlike the poets— are socially responsible. Clinias and the Athenian agree that the present state of poetry is debased—indeed, that the very structure of the relations between the poet and his audience is the source of that debasement. No reliable judgment about "the good" of poetry can come from such a social formation. What is needed is "a true lawgiver [who] will persuade . . . the man of poetic gifts to compose as he ought, to employ his noble and fine-filed phrases to represent . . . men who are pure, valiant, and, in a word, good" (660a).

Plato had not yet imagined such a commissariat for poetry when he wrote the *Republic.* As a consequence, "the old quarrel between poetry and philosophy" noted in Book 10 of the *Republic* (607b) remained to that point as problematical as ever. We see this most dramatically—I should perhaps say, Plato dramatizes this for us most clearly—in the *Republic*'s culminant resort to poetical discourse. For at the end of Book 10 Plato and Socrates offer their implicit defense of poetic feigning in the myth of Er. Coming as this does after Socrates has banished the poets and their fables until they have demonstrated their usefulness, the myth of Er clearly lays itself under an obligation to Socrates' own imperatives.

I do not wish to give a reading of this great passage but merely to indicate one of its salient aspects. Socrates introduces the fable with a series of poetic flourishes: an allusion to Homer that invokes a parallel between the tale of Er and *Odyssey* Book XI (the Nekuia), a witty paranomasia on the name Alcinous, and a self-conscious reminder that the hero of his myth—"Er, the son of Armenius, by race a Pamphylian" (614b)—is a fabulous creature.[23] His otherwordly adventures are therefore presented to us as events that never "really" happened. The final mythic text in the *Republic* appears to be what Plato earlier called a lie: a representation, deliberately advanced, that is not in accord with the truth and that is known to be untruthful.

In fact, of course, it is no such thing, and what Plato is doing here is suggesting a line of defense for poetry, as well as an illustration of the way poetry ought to work. The "argument" of the myth moves via a typically Platonic inversion of the common ideas about the nature of reality. The great error of the poets, in Plato's view, is that they take the world of appearance, as well as their (second-order) representations of those appearances, to be "reality," or the measure of what is true and false. But in Book 10 Socrates carefully sets "reality" as the world of the forms, so the eventual and factual world stands at one remove from reality. In that case, poetical discourse will stand at two removes from reality—*if* such discourse is taken as an imitation of reality, either noumenal or phenomenal.

The wit of the myth of Er—it typifies the way Plato uses myth in his dialogues—lies in its peculiar pretensions. Unlike other poets, who do not understand the nature of their own knowledge, and who do not practice their art self-consciously, Socrates carries out through the myth of Er an exemplary poetical discourse. In the event, Socrates (and Plato as well) represents the poetical as a certain type of activity and not a particular form of truth. He does not imagine or suggest that his myth is an imitation or a coded version of truth. The fable is deliberately set out as a fiction, as a myth and a poetic tale.

This insistence upon the fictionality of the discourse glances ironically at the prevailing ideas about poetical truth. Socrates' position recalls that taken earlier by Thucydides, who instituted, at the outset of his great *History*, an alternative method for establishing the kind of truth which poetry traditionally pretended to. Thucydides presents his *History* as a reliable guide to historical knowledge, and he dismisses the claims of the poets—Homer in particular—as well as those of "poetical" historians such as Herodotus. These are writers who invent and exaggerate, and they repeat all sorts of unfounded and superstitious materials as if they were empirically true. What is worse, people generally still read poets like Homer as if they could be depended upon for reliable historical knowledge.

For anyone who understands poetry in the conventional way attacked by Thucydides and Socrates—that is to say, for the majority of Athenians—the resort to myth at the end of Book 10 must appear contradictory, a resort to untruth. It must appear so because no one—not even Socrates—has yet offered a model by which one could understand poetry as a discourse of truth.

Socrates' use of the myth of Er is itself that needed model. Not the myth itself, but Socrates' deployment of the myth, the actual event of his discourse. In that event Socrates is pretending to offer an untruth, pretending to be telling the falsehood he has already associated with the fables of the poets. The discourse is a test. In the narration of the myth Socrates issues an ironic invitation to Glaucon and his other listeners to seek the "truth" which is disguised and misrepresented in the "lie" of the myth. The actual *un*truth embedded in Plato's text is the traditional idea that poetry (or any other discourse for that matter) can *contain* a form of truth—for example, that it can give an "imitation" of truth, as if the real were an object which could be faithfully represented by a secondary object. The world of the forms is beyond such acts of representation. What poetry *can* do, however, is sponsor or induce reality and the truth. The myth of Er is not what it might appear to be. It is a pretense. Its function is not to imitate, whether truly or falsely, but to install a pretense of imitation in order to generate critical thought. And the most immediate object of critical thought, in this case, is the traditional set of ideas which sees poetry as a fixed and secondary form requiring an exegesis of its determinations.[24]

What Plato does at the end of the *Republic* is more explicitly presented in the *Protagoras* when the poem by Simonides is subjected to interpretation, and Plato's position is perhaps even clearer at the end of the *Phaedrus*. There he tells the story—its purely fantastic basis is remarked upon by Phaedrus—about how the god Theuth introduced written characters into Egypt. Written characters offer, Socrates says, only the semblance of wisdom and the appearance of reliability and permanence. They have nothing to do with the truth because they are not human. They are simulacra, and entirely "analogous to painting": "The painter's products stand before us as though they were alive: but if you question them, they maintain a most majestic silence. It is the same with written words: they seem to talk to you as though they were intelligent, but if you ask them anything about what they say, from a desire to be instructed, they go on telling you just the same things forever" (275d).

This critique of writing recalls Socrates' preference for dialectic over extended and oratorical discourse, and it repeats the position, dramatized in the *Protagoras,* that poems—and, by extension, myths—have nothing to do with the truth, but are open to endless interpretation. At the beginning of the *Phaedrus,* when he is asked if he believes the myth of Boreas and Oretheia to be true, Socrates refuses to answer yes or no. The truth-function of poetry is not of that order; if it were, hermeneutics would produce interpretations which corresponded to the "truth" of the texts. To Socrates, however, poetry and its interpretation are specific kinds of social practices. Their "truth" is a function of what they do, and the investigation of their truth will have to be, therefore, an investigation of their praxis. This view is what carries Socrates into dialectics and away from rhetoric: the point of the latter is to establish a certain view or perspective, whereas the aim of the former is to interrogate perspectives. Socrates' attitude toward the myth of Boreas and Oretheia, therefore, is critical and anthropological: "I . . . accept the current beliefs about" mythical stories and poems, Socrates says; he does *not* say that he assents to their truth. His position will carry him toward his critical inquiries into the grounds of his and other persons' beliefs. It will also carry him to his trial and death.

When Socrates, in narrating the myth of Er, thereby pretends to deal in untruth, he calls attention to a crucial function of all the mythic texts imbedded in the *Dialogues,* including the legend of Diotima set out in the *Symposium.* The myth of Er is in part a critical reflection upon the social function of poetic discourse. Most immediately, it tests the reader's (or the audience's) understanding of the place of such discourse in the state. Although Socrates' narrative may be the occasion of misunderstandings, whatever false conclusions are drawn from it cannot be charged against Socrates. For there is no act of deception here, only the pretense of one. In setting out the myth of Er, Socrates acts like a true poet—far truer, in Plato's view, than poets who work through inspiration—because he aspires to a full consciousness of the meaning of his actions. No gap is meant to exist between his text and his consciousness of his text. As Wittgenstein might say, the meaning of his text is its use.

We may understand Plato's text better if we recall Socrates' somewhat scandalous defense of voluntary or conscious deception set out in the *Lesser Hippias.* The point of that dialogue is to expose the intellectual poverty of the braggart sophist Hippias. After distinguishing voluntary and involuntary deceptions, Socrates argues (correctly) that only a man of knowledge can carry out a voluntary deception, whereas involuntary deceptions are a consequence of ignorance. This general point is used to expose the weakness of Hippias' particular and initial contention, that in Homer Achilles is a truth-teller and therefore good, whereas Odysseus is a deceiver and therefore bad. The dialogue ultimately shows that Hippias' mind is confused, indeed, that Hippias is not the man of wisdom and knowledge he pretends to be.

The dialogue also shows, however, that Hippias does not carry out a voluntary or conscious act of deception. Like Euthyphro and so many others we meet in the dialogues, Hippias truly thinks he is wise.

Socrates, on the other hand, consciously practices an art of deceit in the dialogue. That is to say, he consciously plays the part of the sophist by driving a conclusion which he knows to be false. At the end of the dialogue Socrates snares Hippias in the idea that "he who voluntarily does wrong and disgraceful things . . . will be the good man" (376b). Hippias does not agree with this conclusion, but he is incapable of resisting it.

This conclusion assumes the form of a proposition, but it is something far more important. Socrates offers it to Hippias as a test of his ability to deal with sophistry. Hippias fails the test. But Plato offers the scene to us because he wants to demonstrate that truth is a pursuit and an eventuality, that it has to be understood in a context of human actions and interests. From the point of view of Plato and *his* audience, then—as distinguished from the points of view of Socrates and Hippias—the proposition is the focus of a test for Plato's reader/audience. Let me explain this further.

The most immediate point of Socrates' sophistry is to expose the truth about Hippias and his pretenses to wisdom. But more important still—and this is the case in all the dialogues—is the revelation that truth and falsity are not abstract contents or functions of otherwise concrete things or particular ideas. Knowledge is a process and cannot be abstracted or objectified. Hippias thinks he "has" knowledge, whereas Socrates demonstrates, from his own *example,* that wisdom is a praxis, a discipline of thought and conscious pursuit of the truth. To Hippias, who does not understand these matters, Socrates "appears to be dishonest" (373b) when he reasons to outrageous conclusions. But the conclusions are not Socrates' conclusions, they are the consequents he draws out of the ideas and positions held by men like Hippias.

In this way Socrates arrives at the truth. Negatively, the truth consists in the revelation of the illusory character of various traditional conceptions of what is true and what is untrue. Positively, knowledge and ignorance appear as activities rather than as ideas or abstractions—as ways of being, "forms of life." Thus Socrates "appears to be dishonest" only to those who are ignorant of the actual truth: that this appearance is, like his deployment of his poetical texts, a conscious pretense which he may, under certain conditions, assume.

Finally, the dialogues argue, through artistic representation, that the Socratic conception of knowledge-as-praxis is not itself an abstraction. At this level we read the dialogues as texts designed by Plato to pull the reader into a struggle for truth. For example, the proposition that the good man is he who voluntarily does wrong, though abstractly absurd, expresses a fundamental truth. Uttered by Socrates, and embedded in a text which connects to the entire Platonic corpus, this proposition glances at that life in which Socrates continually and deliberately did what was judged to be wrong and disgraceful. The "meaning" of the proposition will be very different when we weigh it in the framework of Plato's myth of Socrates' life: that is, the central drama of his trial, conviction, and death. Socrates is charged with corrupting the minds of the young and disbelieving in the gods of the state.

The *Lesser Hippias* glances toward this crisis in Socrates' life at several points, but most clearly in Socrates' final remarks when he ironically chastises himself for "always changing my opinion" about what is true. "Now, that I or any ordinary man should wander in perplexity is not surprising, but if you wise men also wander, and we cannot come to you and rest from our wandering, the matter begins to be serious both to us and to you" (376c). The passage distinctly echoes both the *Euthyphro* and the *Apology*. It thereby suggests the precise sort of "serious" consequences which lie ahead for people who live like Socrates and people who live like Hippias. To Plato, nothing less is involved here than the safety of the entire social corpus.

The conversations of Socrates, like the dialogues of Plato, establish knowledge as a function of one's daily life in a particular community of people, a personal and a social interchange. The myth of Socrates gives a structure to these social interchanges such that we are forced to see that truth must be understood in relation to one's social investments. Thus we observe that Socrates' conversations are not merely intellectual games. His sophistical appearance, like his proverbial ugliness, is just that—merely an appearance. He will die for, and as part of, the way of life he lives. We also understand that the charges brought against him may reflect no fault in Socrates, but rather a weakness in Athenian society at large. The youth "corrupted" by Socrates are those who have learned to question the accepted wisdom of their fathers. Included here is the supposed wisdom of authorities like Homer and "the poets," whose texts have become the "forms of worship" of Athenian society rather than their store of "poetical tales."

Socrates' pretended sophistry in the *Lesser Hippias* is analogous to his pretense of lying when he deploys poetical discourse such as the Myth of Er. In each case he demonstrates that poetry (like so-

phistic) is a form of social practice whose "meaning" can be determined only in relation to its social determinants. Ultimately, the
"meaning" of poetical discourse emerges in the ways it is carried out,
both in its initial immediacies and, later, in its subsequent redeploy-
ments (its so-called critical or reception history). Poetical discourse
may deal in mythical and fictive materials, but its appearance of
deception, like its modern, Kantian, appearance of autonomy and
disinterestedness, is *merely* an appearance—is merely a function of a
socially grounded determination to set poetical discourse apart from
the daily praxis of communicative action in society.

Finally, then, the truth of the great myth of Socrates is not that it
reflects empirical realities, which it does, but that it provides a structure within which we are to understand the "truth" of those realities.
This is a social and a critical truth because it is a function of how the
myth is deployed. The content of the myth is neither allegorical nor
empirical, it is functional. The myth cannot be decoded because its
meaning (whether in the history of Athens or in the texts of Plato)
resists hermeneutical translation and abstract reduction. Meaning in
this case—that is, the meaning of "Plato's text" as well as the meaning
of "Socrates' life"—is something that is carried out. As with the
parables of Jesus or the Confucian mode of teaching, meaning here
is revealed as the execution rather than the content of language.

In the end, Plato's dialogues do not "tell" us that Socrates was
right and his detractors were wrong. Socrates, their central figure,
would never have sanctioned such an approach to truth. Just as he,
in his conversations, put his interlocutors to the test of their thoughts
and their convictions, so Plato forces his audience into similar engagements. If the context of Plato's work is academic—literally, a
pedagogical world and institution—it is on that account no less socially imbedded than Socrates'. Indeed, one of the principal issues in
Plato (it is not an issue for the peripatetic Socrates) is precisely the
shape and the aims of truth when it is carried out within an academic
framework.

That issue is urgently before us today. The truth-functions of the
academic production of poetic discourse are by no means clear any
longer. The Coleridgean and Arnoldian versions of Kant's program
of aesthetic autonomy have become a part of history. The revisionist
Kantianism known as deconstruction has recently asserted a strong
claim to take over their cultural authorities. Much of what I shall be
proposing here draws upon the insights we associate with deconstruc-

tionism. My own view, however, is that deconstruction has in general evaded the central issue of the truth-function of poetical discourse, including the reproductive phase of such discourse known as literary criticism.

This evasion is epitomized in that commonplace deconstructive line—picked up from an uncritical reading of Nietzsche—that it is Plato and not Homer who should be expelled from society. In fact, we can afford to lose neither. But the academic may well be especially troubled at the loss of Plato, who is not merely our ancestor, he is ourselves. Like ourselves he has many things to answer for, and he requires—as we all require—the kind of searching criticism to which Derrida has subjected him.[25] But if we, in the shadow of that event, merely take Derrida's work as established and even propositional truth, we shall have lost all that he—like Socrates and Plato before him—has gained. We shall have become, at best, the Alcibiades of our culture.

Nor is this simply, in our epoch, a metaphoric danger. Plato set the scene of the *Symposium* at a specific place and time—in Athens, on the eve of the departure of the Athenian fleet for Syracuse. It is a moment of awful portentousness. Anyone today who reads the *Symposium* without an awareness of this setting will, quite simply, miss a framework of understanding we can ill afford to lose. For that social and political context lifts Plato's work out of abstraction and thereby provides a model for a present encounter which might avoid the danger of a similar abstraction.

For his logocentrism, such as it is, Plato has no doubt much to answer. It is the academic sin *par excellence*. But of course God—far more logocentric than that erring mortal Plato—never laid this sin under prohibition. Indeed, logocentrism is a divine error, not a mortal sin—the error of those entities St. Paul called thrones, principalities, powers, and dominions, who always seek to transform human truth into abstract forms and to expel what is demonic. This error I shall try, however vainly, to avoid. I shall try to stick to the human rather than the divine truths, and in the process persuade you that poetic discourse—both original and reproductive—has chartered these attachments.

2

Blake and the Aesthetics of Deliberate Engagement
To the New Historicists

The Eastern Gate fourfold, terrible and deadly its ornaments,
Taking their forms from the Wheels of Albion's sons, as cogs
Are formed in a wheel to fit the cogs of the adverse wheel.

William Blake, *Jerusalem*

BETWEEN OCTOBER 1984 and January 1985 the Hirshhorn Museum presented an exhibition of visual art from the previous ten years. The exhibition, called "Content," took as its topic "the reaction to formalist art,"[1] which had marked so much of the most innovative work between 1974 and 1984. The immediate point of departure, on the negative side, was that late modernist style known as minimalism; on the positive side the exhibition displayed a number of startling developments from that other important form of late modernism, conceptual art.

Conceived and put together by Howard Fox, the Content exhibition involved a critique of the project of modernism from a postmodern perspective which most students and observers of the postmodern have neglected. That is to say, the exhibition displayed postmodernism as a movement conscious of its political commitments. Central to that consciousness has been the work and career of Robert Morris, who, around 1968–1970, broke from his early minimalist work to develop a more capacious and specifically political artistic expression. Reflecting on the modernist experience, Morris in 1981 asked: "Have we become less concerned with absolutes, with our place in the universe and our individual mortality? In some sense I believe we have. It has not been just a matter of the exhaustion of modernist forms. An emotional weariness with what underlies them has occurred."[2] This critical attitude toward modernism characterizes the thought and work of all the Content artists. "The most pertinent kind of art practice today," Douglas Huebler remarks, "began to surface in the late '6os. It is the issue about whether or not 'association'—referencing to worldly matters—will be permitted back into art."[3] And Neil Jenney: "I don't think the artist should deal with space or think about dealing with space. He should think about adjusting culture . . . meaning the significance of the items depicted."[4]

Such ideas form part of the core of the postmodern attitude in the visual arts, an attitude which moves against that modernist style of self-referentiality epitomized in Frank Stella's famous remark: "What you see is what you see."[5] Thus Philip Guston contradicts the entire modernist project, and Stella's formulation in particular, when he says: "The painting is not on the surface, but on a plane which is imagined. It moves in a mind. It is not there physically at all. It is an illusion, a piece of magic, so what you see is not what you see."[6] In a trenchant introduction to the Content exhibition, Howard Fox calls attention to postmodernism's return to art's traditional dual function of instruction and delight. He speaks of "art's function as a moral agent, and . . . obligation to something beyond the aesthetics of the object."[7] "The post-Modern art object," he observes, "is *not* a complete manifestation in and of itself."[8] Indeed, the postmodern experience carries out a revisionary understanding of all art practices. Just as "the 'purely optical' theory is inadequate to account for the [visual] art experience,"[9] so the entire conception of art as a self-contained "aesthetic" moment is being rejected. As Thomas McEvilley says: "the artwork exists . . . not as an isolated absolute or an end in itself, but as a rounded cultural object which relates to philosophy, politics, psychology, religion, and so forth."[10]

Later I shall have occasion to suggest that these postmodern critical formulations obscure their significance somewhat when they refer, as they often do, to the art "object." They have carried this term over from the vocabulary they wish to avoid—the spectral vocabulary and stationist decorum of viewers and things to be viewed. Postmodernism is notorious as a kind of nonmovement in art, so undefined, various, and shifting are its manifestations. The scandal of its frequent faces, however, is a function of its solicitude toward the polymorphous and the heteroglot. It is a house of many mansions, and one enters its heavens by an adherence to the spirit rather than the letter of an artistic practice. Indeed, in the postmodern perspective art is primarily understood not as an object at all, but as an activity; and the activities of art, in this view, are not the sole prerogative, or obligation, of the artist alone.

The significance of the Content exhibition emerges even more clearly when we reflect on its relation to other forms of postmodern expression. The work of Morris and Huebler calls attention to an important feature of all types of the postmodern: that is to say, its roots in the period of the Cold War, and in particular its relation to the socially volatile period of the late sixties. Literary postmodernism emerged during the same historical moment. The epitome of its poetic formation—the (now so-called) L=A=N=G=U=A=G=E Writing projects—began in the margins of the dominant discourses early in the seventies, and in conscious response to the sixties and their immediate social aftermath.

At first glance, however, literary postmodernism may appear to differ fundamentally from its visual counterpart. This appearance comes from the frequent attacks upon "referentiality" which one finds in the discourse of literary postmodernism, and its placement of "textuality" and the textual *physique* at the center of the poetic event. But the critique of referentiality is not a defense of the self-contained poem. When Charles Bernstein attacks the idea "that knowledge has an 'object' outside of the language of which it is a part,"[11] the point is to emphasize two ideas about poetic discourse: first, that it is an event localizing a quest for true knowledge, for knowledge in and of the world; and second, that poetic discourse is itself an activity or event in the world. Like all the L=A=N=G=U=A=G=E writers, Bernstein sees poetry as a *practice* of discourse rather than as a scene of representations. The attack on referentiality—far from meaning to separate the poet or the text "from the world"—intends to expose and destroy inveterate habits of conventional signification. L=A=N=G=U=A=G=E Writing *carries out* its discourse. Hence Bernstein says, in another essay, that the goal is "not [the] 'death' of the referent—rather a recharged use of the multivalent referential vectors that any word has."[12] Bernstein's "object" is, first, to restore poetic discourse to the world by refusing to accept the distinction between the moment of "art" and the moment of "experience"; and, second, to institute this "object" as a program of discourse, as a practical—indeed, as an everyday—set of events. Bernstein's postmodern writing imagines and executes its work in a space that is self-consciously social and political.

These directions in the artistic practice and poetical discourse of postmodernism contrast sharply with the ways in which postmodernism has normally been translated in the academy. The postmodernism practiced and theorized by figures such as Jameson and Lyotard runs along lines that coincide with the artistic and literary work I have been sketching.[13] But academic postmodernism—in the United States especially—is most closely associated with the Yale school of criticism. In that school, of course, the social and political dimensions of artistic work are generally bracketed from consideration. Yet academic postmodernism is no less socially and politically situated for those acts of exclusion; and in fact Yale criticism emerged during the same period as its artistic and poetical counterparts. But the Yale school was established by a group of men whose intellectual roots are deeply driven in the ground of modernism and New Criticism. As a consequence, their emergence during the seventies—their interpretation of the sixties along with the Cold War it had exploded— generally followed a disengaged, apolitical line. Academic postmodernism is an effort to maintain Kantian and modernist forms below those structures of social instability which have emerged through the postmodern experience. In this respect, academic postmodernism gives, quite literally, a reactionary expression to the postmodern experience.

To the degree that postmodernism, whether engaged or reactionary, imagines itself simply as a cultural happening—a rural debate carried out by marginalized social figures—it would have to be regarded as a relatively local event, a blip in the graph of twentieth-century ideas about poetic and artistic style. But postmodernism represents, I believe, a far more important social phenomenon. In order to understand this better, we will have to make a considerable retreat from the present—to the moment when the aesthetic norms that would dominate western art and poetry for more than one hundred and fifty years were first set in place. We have to go back to the revolutionary epoch of the late eighteenth century, to the same epoch when Kant tried to shore up the ruins of traditional metaphysics.

IN CHAPTER FOURTEEN of the *Biographia Literaria* Coleridge set out his famous dictum that a poem proposes "for its *immediate* object pleasure, not truth." The pronouncement stands at the pivot of his chapter, which is a variation upon Kant's novel- –and, subsequently, normative—discussion of art and its operations in the *Critique of*

Judgment. This modern tradition of thought takes as its point of departure the commonplace notion, grounded in classical theory, that art is an emotionally expressive vehicle, but it works an important sea change in that idea largely because of the intervention of Locke's *Essay* and the new tradition of empiricism. The opening sentences of Part I of Kant's treatise illustrate the situation quite clearly:

> If we wish to discern whether anything is beautiful or not, we do not refer the representation of it to the Object by means of understanding with a view to cognition, but by means of the imagination (acting perhaps in conjunction with understanding) we refer the representation to the Subject and its feeling of pleasure or displeasure. The judgement of taste, therefore, is not a cognitive judgement, and so not logical, but is aesthetic—which means that it is one whose determining ground *cannot be other than subjective*. Every reference of representations is capable of being objective, even that of sensations (in which case it signifies the real in an empirical representation). The one exception to this is the feeling of pleasure or displeasure. This denotes nothing in the object, but is a feeling which the Subject has of itself and of the manner in which it is affected by the representation.[14]

Two remarks are immediately in order. First, we should note that, following Locke, Kant's *Critique* will psychologize the discussion of the experience of art by confining it to the categories "the Beautiful" (art in the objective point of view) and "pleasure and pain" (art in the subjective point of view). Art in the objective point of view, moreover, is not to be understood in terms of the "art object" itself, but rather as an *ideal* of art formulated intuitively by the judging subject. Second, we must understand that Kant performs this act of rationalization because he is primarily interested in defining not the experience of art, but the ground of critical judgment.

According to classical tradition, poetry's ends were to please and instruct; Kant's aesthetic deliberately counters that position by removing instruction, or truth, from the realm of art and poetry. The modern uneasiness with "didactic" and "moral" poetry takes its origin in the Kantian view, which, as is well known, was formulated as a response and solution to the epistemological crisis generated by the rise and development of positive science. Kant's aesthetic is an effort to establish, in a noncognitive sphere of reality, an accessible Form of ultimate order. This noncognitive Form, in its realized state, Kant called the aesthetic; and through its operations human beings could apprehend, under the "Form" or experience of pleasure, the ultimate Forms of Order which Kant had shown, in his first *Critique,* to be beyond the grasp of human cognition.

Two general problems in Kant's analysis must be faced. First, when Kant discusses the initial "Moment" of aesthetic pleasure[15] and argues that it is "disinterested," we recognize a troubling diminishment in the expressive sphere of poetry as we actually experience it. Kant distinguishes between "sensation" and "feeling" in his analysis, but he has no category for what we call "emotion," that is, for "feeling" conceived in a social dimension. As a result, the aesthetic experience becomes encapsulated in a subject-object dialectic; it is characterized chiefly, if not wholly, by what has become known as "the aesthetic experience" (Kant's "feeling"); and the rich emotional dimensions of art fall into critical (and theoretical) neglect.[16] Tolstoy's famous attack upon the Kantian tradition in "What Is Art?" vigorously (if unsystematically) exposed this theoretical weakness.

The radical turn which the Kantian idea of aesthetic pleasure gave to the understanding of poetry can be seen if we retreat from Kant to Dryden, in particular to his "Ode on St. Cecilia's Day," where he presents some classical commonplaces about the affective dimensions of poetry. Dryden's ode gives a picture of the aesthetic experience which is very different from Kant's.[17] "What passion cannot Music raise and quell!" For Dryden the emotions proper to art are by no means to be graphed on the sensationalistic pleasure/pain coordinates. When his ode presents art's power to evoke a religious sense of wonder, martial enthusiasm, the sorrow felt by "hopeless lovers," jealousy, or passionate indignation, this illustrative set of generalizations emphasizes his principal point: that an indefinite range of human emotions exists and that art has the power to display them all.

Dryden's work postulates a human experience marked by some considerable richness and diversity—"all the compass of the notes." This plenitude in Nature is, however, ordered by its relation to what Dryden calls "harmony," the controlling music of the spheres uttered (ultimately) by God: "The tuneful voice [which is] heard from high." This Master Musician sets the universe in tune, and part of his tuneful numbering is that final untuning of the sky announced, Dryden wittily observes, when "The trumpet shall be heard on high."

In contrast to Kant's, Dryden's idea of a general and ordering harmony is not *a priori* but cognitive. The difference is clear when we recall this famous passage from Kant: "There can be no objective rule of taste by which what is beautiful may be defined by means of concepts. For every judgement from that source is aesthetic, i.e. its determining ground is the feeling of the Subject, and not any concept of an Object. It is only throwing away labour to look for a principle of taste that affords a universal criterion of the beautiful by definite concepts; because what is sought is a thing impossible and inherently contradictory."[18] But Dryden has in his possession a whole set of "definite concepts" which enable him to articulate the harmonic Idea which lies behind natural diversity. When Kant tries to discuss the "objective" ground and standard of Beauty, he resorts to what he calls a "psychological explanation" of the aesthetic Idea.[19] Furthermore, in this discussion he admits that he is dealing with a faculty— Imagination—whose movements are "quite incomprehensible to us" because of its unconscious—its noncognitive—mode of operation.[20] Coleridge's "Aeolian Harp" represents a Kantian approach to aesthetic harmony, and its position is equally opposed to Dryden's.

The patently "didactic" or cognitive aspects of Dryden's excellent verse expose the other major problem in the Kantian tradition of modern aesthetic Idealism, which has few means for dealing critically with the substantive components of poetry. This weakness does not appear, however, when a particular set of conditions prevails: that is, when the critic shares with the work its fundamental and ordering structures of cognition. In that case the critic's task becomes hermeneutical rather than analytic, and the effort is directed toward discovering "new" or "deeper" levels of meaning.

The tradition initiated by Kant, then, breaks with classical theory to embrace the following notions about poetry. First, poetry is an experience of subjectivity in which an imaginative object (the "poem itself," the "text," the focus of the reader's attention) enters the experience of an individual reader who has engaged with the object on previously agreed conditions of subjectivity. Second, the experience of subjectivity is by definition "autonomous"; that is, it is a formal event whose otherwise objectively relational elements (emotions, feelings, historical references, ideology) are turned inward and made purely self-reflexive. Third, the poetic experience occurs as a noncognizable event registered as a "feeling of pleasure" or sense of harmony; this pleasure principle, which is poetry's nonrational or irrational sign of a noncontingent Idea, is the special Form of Reason which poetry undertakes.

The proper tasks of literary criticism follow from these premises.

Because the cognitive aspects of poetry are believed to transcend the experience of poetry, hermeneutics—or the science by which hidden meaning is reflectively constituted—becomes a privileged critical activity. Because the poetic experience is taken to be formal and subjective, poetry's historical and social relations are regarded as peripheral ("extrinsic") concerns of criticism. Because poetry is thought to be autonomous, either as "the poem itself" or as the self-infolded intertextual field, stylistic and structural descriptions come to replace the regulative methods of earlier literary criticism.

KANT'S AESTHETIC has dominated western attitudes toward art and poetry for more than a hundred and fifty years. To appreciate the full significance of his work, however, we have to understand the way this aesthetic functions ideologically. We have to expose, that is to say, the social significance of the aesthetic as it operates in its characteristic forms.

Kant's "aesthetic feeling" lies at the ground of the Romantic idea of Imagination. Coleridge's discussion (in *Biographia Literaria,* chapter fourteen) of the harmonizing powers of Imagination extends and elaborates the Kantian analyses of the aesthetic experience. The following celebrated passage from "Tintern Abbey" contains Wordsworth's paradigm report on the nature of those "pleasures of the imagination" which Kant had called aesthetic.

> that blessed mood,
> In which the burthen of the mystery,
> In which the heavy and the weary weight
> Of all this unintelligible world,
> Is lightened—that serene and blessed mood,
> In which the affections gently lead us on—
> Until, the breath of this corporeal frame
> And even the motion of our human blood
> Almost suspended, we are laid asleep
> In body, and become a living soul;
> While with an eye made quiet by the power
> Of harmony, and the deep power of joy,
> We see into the life of things.
>
> (37–49)

Wordsworth is memorializing certain private and intensely subjective moments of imaginative insight which he has known "oft, in lonely rooms, and 'mid the din/ Of towns and cities" (24–25). At such moments "the burthen of the mystery" is lifted, and we experience a deep peace, a serenity which is associated with the conviction that human life is governed by an unseen and benevolent order, by "the power of harmony." The central point of "Tintern Abbey" involves the celebration of that power and the discovery that it is latent in the human imagination.

Kant and the critical traditions he fathered declared this special concept of Imagination to be a universal feature of poetry and of the "aesthetic experience" in general. Coleridgean Romantic theory followed this line by making imagination a "synthetic" faculty, the special power that brings "harmony" into being and, with it, the pleasure that one takes in experiencing harmony. These two consequences are functions of each other, since a psychological artistic theory like this one radically interiorizes the affective experience of art. Poetry thereby becomes a locus not of emotions but of feelings.

Kant's *Critique* and Coleridge's formal criticism do not offer explanations for this shift in emphasis initiated by Kant. But the passage from Wordsworth calls attention to the reciprocal relation which exists between a crushing sense of the "weight/ Of all this unintelligible world" and the renovating experience of "harmony, and the deep power of joy." Wordsworth's famous "Preface" recurs to this relationship—for example, when he says that the "pleasure" generated by poetry is "an acknowledgement" of the "beauty of the universe" and when he goes on to add, of the poet: "He is the rock of defense of human nature; an upholder and preserver, carrying everywhere with him relationship and love. In spite of difference of soil and climate, of language and manners, of laws and customs, in spite of things silently gone out of mind and things violently destroyed, the poet binds together by passion and knowledge the vast empire of human society, as it is spread over the whole earth, and over all time."[21] Shelley's great "Defence" speaks to the same point, but more eloquently and emphatically. Poetry "returns to potable gold the poisonous waters which flow from death through life"; it "defeats the curse which binds us to be subjected to the accident of surrounding impressions." When Shelley associated poetry with the imaginative capacity to "reproduce and arrange [knowledge, and power, and pleasure] according to a certain rhythm and order, which may be called the beautiful and the good," he called attention to the unhappy conditions of his own age which, in his view, placed a special demand for a redemptive and transforming artistic practice. "The cultivation of poetry is never more to be desired than at periods when, from an excess of the selfish and calculating principle, the accumulation of the materials of external life exceed the quantity of the power of assimilating them to the internal laws of human nature. The body has then become too unwieldy for that which animates it."[22]

The aesthetic pleasure associated with poetic imagination, then, is a concept which has special reference to the cultural formations which began to emerge in Europe in the late eighteenth century and which were especially typical of England. The art and poetry of the period is characterized, stylistically, by this sort of imaginative quality. How quickly this artistic ideology came to dominate the thought of the period can be seen in Hazlitt's *Spirit of the Age,* especially in the contrast between his remarks on Wordsworth and his essay on Crabbe. Wordsworth, of course, exemplifies the Spirit of the Age in a profound way, not least because "he elevates the mean by the strength of his own aspirations."[23] Crabbe, on the other hand, although he treats many of the same sort of humble and mean subjects as Wordsworth, seems almost deliberately to avoid an elevated effect. "Mr. Crabb's Helicon is choked up with weeds and corruption; it reflects no light from heaven; it emits no cheerful sound; no flowers of love, of hope, or joy spring up near it, or they bloom only to wither in a moment. Our poet's verse does not put a spirit of youth in every thing, but a spirit of fear, despondency and decay. It is not an electric spark to kindle or expand, but acts like the torpedo's touch to deaden or contract."[24] Although "one of the most popular of our living authors," Crabbe is "repulsive" to Hazlitt for his unloveliness, for his positive refusal to generate an experience of aesthetic pleasure of the sort we noticed in "Tintern Abbey," and for his insistence upon depicting "unwelcome reality": "and while he desolates a line of coast with sterile blighting lines, the only leaf in his books where honour, beauty, worth, or pleasure bloom, is that inscribed to the Rutland family."[25]

Despite Hazlitt's strictures, few who have attentively read Crabbe's *Tales* (1812) or *The Borough* (1810) or a great narrative like "Delay Has Danger" have failed to see the stature of this poet. Hazlitt's troubled judgment of Crabbe is important, however, because it exhibits the dominant aesthetic criteria of the age struggling with the actual practice of a poet who does not operate according to such criteria. "Infancy" (1816), Crabbe's autobiographical poem, declares his characteristically antithetical position:

> For what is Pleasure, that we toil to gain?
> 'Tis but the slow or rapid flight of pain.[26]

The importance of Crabbe's work lies in that mordant quality. As Hazlitt rightly saw, Crabbe's poetry refuses to declare that "the deep power of joy" can transfigure "all this unintelligible world," so no experience of "aesthetic pleasure" emerges to reorder experience. What his poetry does do, however, is to reveal, more graphically than most writing of the period, the power of the world's adversative elements. In doing so it highlights what *in reality* underlies the Romantic program generally, as well as the special privilege which that movement gave to imaginative experience in particular. Crabbe's severe and factive narratives illustrate that necessary reciprocal of any Romantic experience—a reciprocal which Wordsworth's "Peele Castle" also brings to light. The "Fenwick note" to "Lucy Gray" is interesting in this respect because it contrasts the "spiritualising" quality of his lyrical ballad with the "matter of fact" style of Crabbe in "treating subjects of the same kind."[27]

What Kant analyzed as a crisis in human knowledge, then, appears in the poets, in more comprehensive and revealing terms, as a general crisis involving European culture at large. "Our life is a false nature," Byron says, because " 'tis not in . . . harmony" at the social, or even at the personal and psychological, level. The age, marked throughout by terrible dislocations, nurtures its doctrines of Imagination and aesthetic pleasure as a final position of cultural and psychic resistance. At such liminal points one encounters a figure like Byron's Egeria, the visionary beloved of a legendary philosopher king. To Byron's deeply critical mind, the experience can only be "the unreached paradise of our despair," a nympholept's dream of a historical order which exists only by desire, and in the mind. In history the dream must become a nightmare.[28]

Implicit in Byron's despair, and the unhappy consciousness of Romanticism in general, are the critical problems and instabilities which the Kantian aesthetic sought (vainly) to overcome. Yet even as this approach was establishing itself, an alternative poetics began to develop. I think that this alternative line has recently, in nonacademic postmodern practice, begun to move out of its position of cultural marginality. Like the Kantian program, this line is also properly characterized as a "critical" tradition. Unlike the Kantian line, it emphasizes the social and political centrality of artistic work and insists that art carry out its work within the complex spheres of competing social interests. In this view, art is an engaged set of social practices.

BEFORE TURNING to consider directly the chief initiating figure in this alternative poetics, let me summarize what I have tried to show up to this point. The Kantian program makes a sharp departure from traditional poetic theory and practice, as we have seen by glancing back at earlier traditions. The example of Dryden is only one of many that might have been adduced. Earlier analogues could be found for Kant's central ideas of poetic autonomy and disinterestedness, but no one before Kant theorized, in positive terms, the social isolation of poetic practice. For Kant, of course, this isolation supplied poetry with its special power and social usefulness. In the space of aesthetic disinterestedness poetry would nurture a "feeling" of fundamental harmony and order. Poetry's social function, then, was precisely to supply a ground for the Idea of fundamental order. On the one hand, Kant argued that such an Idea was an imperative of Reason; but on the other, he showed that it was an Idea which neither Reason nor Understanding could deliver as conscious knowledge. The aesthetic functioned as the arena within which this necessary Idea came into human experience: that is, via the sensational and nonconscious orders of art.

As important as the antinomy of traditional poetics is, if we wish to see the historicality of the Kantian aesthetic, even more important is the antinomy of William Blake. For Blake's work emerges in the same epoch as Kant's, and indeed represents an alternative response to the same kinds of sociohistorical pressures which lie behind the Kantian programmatic. In face of various, often radical, dislocations within the social and cultural orders, Blake—unlike Kant, Coleridge, and their many later interpreters—developed an activist and contestatory poetics. Where the Kantian aesthetic moved to save the appearances of the social and cultural orders as given—to find Reason in the status quo—Blake argued that the social given was precisely what it appeared to be: a chaos of war, self-interest, and widespread social fragmentation. The function of art was not to display the harmony in such circumstances—to rationalize and justify what he would call "the wastes of moral law"[29]—but to work against the entire machinery, which he perceived as an illusion of the human and the social.

The consequences of this stance are profound. In the first place, the separation of "subjective" and "objective" artistic orders is canceled at the level of artistic practice. The point is that, insofar as "meaning" is involved in his work, the poetry does not deploy a set of "images" which "have reference to" a secondary order of ideas. The Kantian idea of a disinterested art standing apart from social practice, within its own sphere of autonomy, is the antithesis of everything Blake believed and made.

The *Marriage* illustrates the situation very well and is in addition a useful, because reasonably familiar, example.[30] One of the work's dominant tropes is printing itself, and even more particularly, Blake's printing and production processes. This trope is most dramatically presented in plate 15, the so-called Printing House in Hell episode, but readers have noted its presence throughout the work. Blake's use of this trope demonstrates the intimate relation between his artistic practices and the social/religious preoccupations of his satire. Thereby does the *Marriage* reveal itself as a specific deed of imagination— mind not in meditation but in action, and with its acts located in a particular sociohistorical frame of reference.

As a consequence, the horizon of the *Marriage* is unusually immediate and imperative. In the first "Memorable Fancy," for example, Blake recounts his descent into the regions of hell where he makes a collection of their proverbs to bring back to "the present world":

> When I came home, on the abyss of the five senses, where a flat sided steep frowns over the present world, I saw a mighty devil folded in black clouds, hovering on the sides of the rock, with corroding fires he wrote the following sentence now perceived by the minds of men and read by them on earth.
> How do you know but ev'ry bird that cuts the airy way
> Is an immense world of delight clos'd by your senses five?   (plates 6–7)

Because the passage equates the act of that "mighty devil" with Blake's engraving processes, the temporal disjunction between Blake's work and the devil's is collapsed. What the devil wrote and what Blake engraved *and* what is "now perceived . . . and read" by the audience of the *Marriage*—any and all audiences, it should be noted—is the same, and takes place at the same "time."

The poem enforces its grammar of immediacy at every turn and in the smallest details. In plate 5, for example, Blake refers to "the Devil or Satan" as "the Original Archangel, or possessor of the command of the heavenly host." In plate 14 he recalls this text to work one of his typical effects. Referring to "the ancient tradition" that the New Jerusalem will be established "in fire at the end of six thousand years," Blake writes: "For the cherub with his flaming sword is hereby commanded to leave his guard at tree of life, and when he does, the whole creation will be consumed." Note that even the verbal text forces one to see Blake as "the Original Archangel, or possessor of the command of the heavenly host," forces one to take it that the command which brings about the apocalypse is being given even now, in this very text. The critical and imperative nature of the passage is underscored in the rest of the plate and in its immediate successor, the famous plate 15: Blake's work "hereby" carries out the fiery consummation anciently foretold. The *Marriage* is itself the execution of the original archangelic command.

The *Marriage* is in these respects typical of Blake's engraved works, which are executive—"illocutionary" is the word, from Speech-Act theory, which we now use—rather than expository in their rhetorical structures. "Rouze up, O Young Men of the New Age"[31] is the imperative sign under which Blake begins *Milton,* and the poem is organized as an overlapping set of dialectically related acts of imaginative vision and revision. That Blake understands imaginative vision as an active rather than a receptive event is explicit in the poem—for example, in the attack, announced at the very beginning, on what Blake calls the "False Tongue! vegetated/ Beneath [Beulah's] land of shadows" (plate 2). This Tongue, Blake's version of the Blatant Beast, is the figure standing for every sort of negative or false communication: not "communicative acts" but the parodic and illusory opposites of such acts.

Blake's poem imagines that human life in an unredeemed condition is effectively tongueless. He expresses this figuratively in plate 29, at the end of Book I, when he says that in fallen Man "the Nerves of the Tongue are closed"—but not the nerves of the other senses. Those senses are preserved in generative form through the creative acts of Los, Blake's figurative artificer, so that through these portals of the fallen body Man may receive intimations of the Eternal worlds his imagination requires. All this is Blake's way of presenting his idea of the difference between imagination conceived as a set of receptors— the tactile, visual, and auditory senses—and imagination conceived as an active agent: the speaking tongue. Thus the poem's consummation involves a series of actions by the interacting figures of the Bard, Milton, Blake, and finally Albion—that is to say, publishing actions, prophetic deeds whose character is that they provoke and reciprocate other prophetic deeds. Blake's prayer, in plate 20, that his "gross tongue" be able to "tell of the Four-Fold Man" not only alludes to this entire structure of thought, it participates in the execution of the event. In Blake's work, authentic communication is performative communication; just as to give is to receive in Blake's world, so to ask is to answer, and to speak is to act. In *Milton*, speech is the representative figure of a true human life, a life of social action. So when Blake wishes to represent a world evacuated of effective social action, he shows it as a world in which "the Nerves of the Tongue are closed." It is a world in which speech is a passivity, involuted and self-regarding, speech without the will to act or interact. It is the world of the "False Tongue," a world—despite its many words—of silence.

Blake's position on poetics—it has much in common with Shelley's and Byron's—was not to prevail over that of Kant and Coleridge. The complex of ideas which holds that poetry neither affirms nor denies anything, that it erects a virtual and autonomous world of its own—in short, that art is not among the ideologies—came to dominate cultural thinking until late in the twentieth century.[32] Blake's work itself was eventually interpreted within the general Kantian/Coleridgean framework. But there is no question that Blake saw poetry very differently. He believed, for example, that poetry's world is not a virtual reality separated from the quotidian order; on the contrary, it is engaged with that order—engaged in an adverse and critical relationship. One of his favorite ways of expressing the relationship appears in the following passage from *Milton*:

> This Wine-press is call'd War on Earth, it is the Printing-Press
> Of Los; and here he lays his words in order above the mortal brain,
> As cogs are formd in a wheel to turn the cogs of the adverse wheel.
>
> (27: 8-10)

The lines are quintessential Blake. In the first place, they illustrate the Blakean principle that everything is as it is perceived: War on Earth—for Blake, the single greatest evil visited upon the world—is a death-machine which Los's imagination will turn to human gain. He turns it by reversing that machine's direction by engaging the cogs of the wheel of life with the cogs of the wheel of death. This engagement of the imagination with the destructive inertias of the natural world and its moral orders reveals the truth about "life" in the "real" world we (falsely) imagine—that such life is really misery and death—and it simultaneously carries out, or executes, a form of true life. In the present passage, the figure of the printing press calls attention to Blake's immediate activity as an example of the forms of life which Blake and Los seek to promote. Blake's printed works carry out a form of what he called "Mental Fight," the commitment to telling and revealing the truth about the world, both in its deadly and in its liberating aspects.

We must realize that for the tradition which Blake epitomizes, poetic discourse is ideological, and is therefore capable of both truth and error. The whole point of a poem like *Milton,* for example, is to expose and correct the ideological errors in Milton's works. This involves a rereading of those works, in particular the poetical works, along the lines first set down in *The Marriage of Heaven and Hell.* In *Milton,* however, the rereading is carried out not in the early 1790s but during the height of the Napoleonic Wars. *Milton* is a denunciation of those wars, and especially a denunciation of England for its hypocritical righteousness. In *Milton* Blake brings back the great Puritan to pass a judgment on England's righteousness. Himself an epitome of such holiness, Blake's Milton is delivered over to reprobation and sin as a model to the English who take their deluded, "patriotic" part in the Napoleonic Wars—that most recent manifestation of those "wastes of moral law." This judgment on the English is not, needless to say, an exculpation of France.

Blake's rereading of Milton does not involve producing a "correct" reading, the True interpretation or meaning of Milton's work. "Truth" for Blake is not something one can acquire; Truth is a function, not a possession, and it emerges in the dialectics of serious intellectual commitments. In every case these commitments are made under particular circumstances, and they take specific forms. Those forms live on and undergo multiple transformations in other circumstances. *Paradise Lost* for Blake is a work which is formed and transformed repeatedly, for good and ill alike. This is why Blake takes Milton's ideas seriously: he takes them as social acts, works which continue to act in the world of men, either to enslave or to liberate. This is also why, for Blake, there is no such thing as "disinterested" thought. "Disinterestedness" is itself a social commitment which carries, under different specific circumstances, different consequences.

THESE IDEAS of Blake were at the periphery of cultural thought for a long time. They have emerged once again in certain important aspects of postmodernism—specifically, in that promoted, for example, by the world of L = A = N = G = U = A = G = E Writing and the artists represented in the Hirshhorn's Content show. In the field of critical discourse—literary and cultural criticism—this alternative tradition has been slower to develop, but today it does seem to have at last established a solid foundation even within the academy.

At the heart of this tradition in poetics, however, lies an important paradox which has to be clearly seen. In Blake and the Content artists, for example, we recognize it as a doubled set of commitments: on the one hand, to an art which promotes productive diversity and formal experimentation and, on the other, to an art with sharply focused ideas and social goals. Nietzsche—one of the chief precursors of postmodernism—represented this as an antinomy: as a choice that had to be made, "either Homer or Plato." And in our day, under the continuing pressure of the Kantian program, the academic tradition of postmodernism has reified that choice and has gone on to urge that discourse, both critical and creative, should pursue an aesthetic line.

Blake is important because, while he accepted that antinomy, he refused to be compelled to that choice. He developed a postclassical mode of artistic expression—an "aestheticism"—which remained ideological. Work like Blake's demands critical procedures which will correspond to that engaged salient. More than this, however, we may see that the cases of Blake, or Byron, or the Content artists and L = A = N = G = U = A = G = E writers are merely dramatic instances of a truth about all artistic practice. Even the most private and meditative poets—Keats, Rossetti, Dickinson, say—have their characteristic and significant ways of engaging with their worlds. The retreat of Emily Dickinson is eloquent with social meaning, and her poetic methods— the refusal to publish, the choice of album verse forms, the production of those famous manuscript fascicles—are all part of a complex poetic statement which is explicated in the context of her world, and which carries significance into our day when we are able, not to enter, but to face and come to terms with that world.[33]

In a framework where everything is as it is perceived—and all modern theories of artistic work rest on such a premise—the problem of art becomes that of the relation between artistic perception and social engagement. Criticism formulates that problem in the question: how does "interpretation" acquire its social meaning or significance? Marx expressed the same problem, for philosophy, in his famous eleventh thesis on Feuerbach: "The philosophers have only *interpreted* the world in various ways; the point, however, is to *change* it." What Blake showed, however, was that there could be an ideological production, even in the modern world of capitalized productive fragmentation, where gaps would not be fostered between an artistic interpretation and its social reproduction. In a capitalized world, all work may be abstracted and objectified. But some works resist the process more vigorously than others, and may offer positive alternative forms of communicative action, may suggest these forms even to criticism.

3

The Dawn of the Incommensurate
To the Formalists

In its ideas about itself and about society, as in all its other
endeavors, the mind goes from mastery to enslavement. By
an irresistible movement, which imitates the attraction death
exercises over life, thought again and again uses the instruments of its own freedom to bind itself in chains. But when-
ever the mind breaks its chains, the liberty it wins is greater
than the one it had lost, and the splendor of its triumph sur-
passes the wretchedness of its earlier subjection. Even its defeats strengthen it. Thus, everything in the history of
thought happens as if it were meant to remind us that, although death lasts forever, it is always the same, whereas
life, which is fleeting, is always something higher than it was
before.

Roberto Unger, *Knowledge and Politics*

"HISTORY WITHOUT FOOTNOTES" was the brief and brilliant subtitle which Cleanth Brooks gave to his famous essay, almost forty
years ago, on Keats's "Ode on a Grecian Urn." The phrase glanced,
most immediately, at the tradition of philological criticism, which had
dominated literary studies for more than a hundred years; but it
captured as well that long-standing antipathy which the common
reader has always felt for the pedant and the professor, with their
dusty minds and intrusive backward looks. A happy thought to imagine a historical text free of all footnotes, but happier far to imagine
that a poem might be such a text and that it could be handed over
to the reader in a book unencumbered with learned notes, commentaries, glossaries, or related scholastic materials. *The Well Wrought
Urn* (1947) is a sizable book (270 pages); it has just fourteen footnotes,
and these are all decidedly unscholastic: leisurely, self-referential, or
digressive discussions or brief cross-references. This book is a very
learned study, of course, but it is also a book which has studiously
removed all traces of the learning and pedagogy in which it is immersed.

What's in a footnote, that it should have achieved such a bad eminence? Why does "History" use them or need them, and why should poetry, that immortal thing, also find itself, from time to time, covered with their dust? These may appear trivial, dare I say pedantic, questions. Raising them, however, brings one directly to the central issues of all literary work and literary study.

Brooks's subtitle is a shorthand way of telling his readers that he understands these things. It is also a coded declaration about the nature of poetry and criticism: that poetry is important precisely by virtue of its ahistoricality, its divorce from everything factive and circumstantial. Just as for later critics like de Man and Stanley Fish, for Brooks poetry is an intertextual system. In consequence, literary criticism is a hermeneutic quest for the wholeness which poetry, as organic system, sets forth. Unlike his postmodern inheritors, however, Brooks is confident that the wholeness of the poem can be effectively mirrored in the action of the critic. That correspondence between poetry and criticism has broken down in de Man and Fish, who typify the programmatic lines of most contemporary criticism.

Brooks's interest in a history without footnotes is connected to *his* experience of the legitimation crisis—that is, to the epoch of modernism rather than to its aftermath. Brooks is a typical ideologue of modernism in his attempt to solve the legitimation crisis by separating poetry from history. In poetry one enters a realm where historical relativities do not operate—a realm of moral values, not exchange values, a realm of the normative rather than the circumstantial. The erosion of that modernist ideal is now an accomplished fact, as I have already observed. Fallen is Brooks's belief, which he inherited from his philological past, in the necessary interdependence of poetry and criticism. That relation is now seen as either arbitrary or purely (that is, relatively) conventional. But though part of Brooks's program has been dismissed, the idea that poems operate autonomous and intertextual systems remains generally in force. The poem as a history without footnotes is, therefore, still a cherished imagining.

I shall begin my critique of this line of thought by turning briefly to Ezra Pound, who is in certain ways the prototypical modernist poet. Many people—I am decidedly one of them—regard the *Cantos* as the most important English poem of this century. It is, however, a tragic poem, a work which is finally ensnared in its own illusions. Setting out to erect a monumental synthesis of human history and human knowledge within a poetic endeavor, the *Cantos* ends in bits and pieces. *Drafts and Fragments* is not merely the poem's conclusion, it is its revelation: the failure of its ideological pursuits immortalized in the triumph of its art.

In an important sense the *Cantos* ends as it began, in a swirl of cross-currents and cross-purposes. "So-Shu churned in the sea." Pound attempts to construct a transtemporal form of cultural order on the ruins of the failed attempts of the past (the Tempio, Dioce, and so on). The form must be not merely the *idea* of such an order but its concrete and material embodiment. Pound's conviction is that this order must be unearthed, that it lies buried and hidden in the ruins. His view is analogous to that of the synthetic mythographers of the late eighteenth century, like Jacob Bryant, who glossed and deciphered the texts of antiquity. Out of that scholarship came the image of a unified historical field—the single story, the tale of all human history.

The *Cantos* extends that project by arguing, or showing (which is the way poetry argues), that it is part of that unified historical field. Like all parts of the field, however, the *Cantos* intersects with the field at a particular moment and vantage. Consequently, its understanding and participation in the field is necessarily confined: it is not just liable to obscurity through error, it is radically limited to a specific horizon. Its task, therefore, is to find ways of breaking out of its immediacies to make contact with the larger, the totalized, historical field.

In a Romantic poem like *The Prelude,* totalization is established through a visionary experience generated in the so-called spots of time, extraordinary moments of grace which cannot be consciously determined or prepared for. They are also ineffable moments in which totalization comes as an *aesthesis,* or feeling. In the *Cantos,* by contrast, totalization is the goal of research and work, and its emblem is not the spot of time but the footnote. The *Cantos* is a poem replete with glosses, footnotes, found material of every sort. Its quest for totalization is always carried out in a text of gaps and absences and in a context comprising what is piecemeal, or fragmented, or lost.

Such are the fundamental characteristics of the *Cantos,* and the Poundian footnote is its epitome. Toward the conclusion of Canto I, for example, when Pound launches his poem into and out of Book XI of the *Odyssey,* the following passage occurs:

> Lie quiet Divus. I mean, that is Andreas Divus,
> In officina Wecheli, 1538, out of Homer.[1]

I would like to remark on many aspects of these two lines, and those surrounding as well, with their brilliant use of pronouns and phrasal positioning to achieve multiple levels of statement and voicing. But I shall stick to my main point and ask you to notice that the lines represent a kind of footnote in Pound's text. A major function of Pound criticism to date has been given over simply (simply?) to glossing his dense epic, his "poem including history." In the present case, Pound supplies us with an introductory or preliminary gloss. He means—among other things—to identify the text of Homer he is using. It is the Renaissance Latin translation done by the scholar Andreas Divus. The actual *book* he is using is also identified: the edition from the Paris printing house of Christian Wechel. And Pound might have added, as he tells us elsewhere, that he acquired this volume in a bookstall in Paris in the early years of the century, probably in 1908.[2]

Dryasdust? Well, a meditation on this passage and others like it in the *Cantos* would go a long way toward restoring the consequences of doing history, or poetry for that matter, with or without footnotes. The crucial point was made extremely well some time ago by D. S. Cairne-Ross: "It is a cardinal principle of [Pound's] poem that the materials it presents must be presented exactly as they are or were. A man's actual words, and as far as possible even the sound of the words, must be reported, the date, location, etc. must be given."[3] Pound adheres to this position because he understands that "history" is a continuous process, and preeminently a continuous process of transmission. The text (any text) of Homer that we read today is embedded in a particular and explicable *history,* and we cannot even begin to read with intelligence and clarity the books we hold in our hands unless we understand the history those books incorporate. It makes a difference if we are reading Homer in a Greek or a Latin text, or some modern vernacular, and the character of the book in which the text is transmitted is equally crucial. The importance of such things is not an abstract matter, it relates to—is in fact only explained by—the immediate moment(s) at which these various pasts are intersected.

Every act of reading is a journey to the dead and the underworld, especially in the case of works which are not our contemporaries. Pound is evidently quite conscious of this situation, and the *Cantos* is in many ways a philological and archaeological epic—an epic for a world in which these modes of incorporating knowledge and culture are central. The book which Pound bought in Paris in 1908 was for him both vortex and epiphany, and it represented an epochal event in his life. Its effect was, he suggests in this passage, an immediate and shocking one—an effect registered not gradually, as he read the text of Divus's translation, but immediately, when he first looked into Wechel's edition of Homer. "In officina Wecheli" reproduces part of the imprint he saw on the book's title page: "Parisiis, In officina Christiani Wecheli MDXXXVIII." What has struck Pound is the strange hidden history of human beings, whose second voyages are as complex and important as their first. The second voyage of Ulysses is the voyage of Andreas Divus and of Christian Wechel and—of course—of Ezra Pound. In certain ways it is more the voyage of Elpenor than it is of Ulysses, as Canto I of Pound's poem strongly insists. From the line "A man of no fortune but with a name to come," Pound wants us to see not only that Elpenor and Ulysses are companionable forms, but that those who are "to come" later are also companions on the voyage, and that all must descend to the underworld. The chief function of these "later" companions will be to communicate with their dead fellows, and ultimately—for the good of all the living and the dead, as well as the future generations—to save their names and their deeds.

When Pound addresses Andreas Divus, urging him to lie quiet in his grave, he is telling us at least three things: that Divus was anxious about his own duty to the quick and the dead; that Pound has determined to share his voyage, as Christian Wechel had done; and that Divus may be comforted with the knowledge that his work is being carried on.

One of the principal functions of the scholar's footnote is to elucidate the transmissive character of the (so-called) superior text. The footnote historicizes what the scholar is doing. It alerts the reader to the fact that what we call knowledge is not a corpus of information but a series of knowing acts that have been and are carried out under particular circumstances. A "history without footnotes," then, is not a history, it is and must be a mythology—a story displaced out of time and circumstance, a narrative set in the never-never land of what is now called "the text."

Poems often represent themselves as just this, as histories without footnotes. Urging us to accept this representation, Brooks speaks for all those who treat literary works as self-sustaining acts and self-consuming artifacts. Enter the footnote, and a world of relative creatures is ushered in. Pound's text is arguing not merely that there are no histories without footnotes, but that poems are historical artifacts, and that when poems lose their footnotes they are threatened with extinction. This is not simply to say that poems are the constructions of those who use, transmit, and interpret them; it is also to say that this sociohistorical dialectic which *is* poetry must be experienced and defined in the concrete, the material, and the particular. The footnote is an emblem of differentiation. It initiates a will toward connections by laying out a network of separations and discrete things.

We who were taught to read literary works as intertextual fields, and who therefore had to learn the actual *truth* later (perhaps too much later), used to imagine that whatever in a poem needed a foot-note was certain to be of little importance. Poetry did not build its temples in the excremental places of the local, the topical, the circumstantial, or—least of all—the biographical. I would be embarrassed to say how long it took me to begin to get free of such ideas. (In any case, that history can be traced—is a matter of record—though I did not footnote it, or even note it, at the time.) The subject of poetry is what humans share in common, what transcends temporal and cultural boundaries. We all understand the wrath of Achilles. We do not need history, or footnotes, for such things.

And indeed it is true that poetry deals in the communal experiences of human beings. But a poem stands to its materials in a certain way, with a specific set of interests and methods of self-presentation. As a consequence, a poem will either center or marginalize what it represents, and certain matters salient to the work will be left out of its accounting altogether. In this respect every poem is an action, and the text is its residual form. This special character of "the poem itself" is reciprocated in the equally specific condition of the reader of the poem, who is also engaged from a vantage of certain conditions and interests.

The footnote is, therefore, the exponent of a differential. It localizes the inevitable fact of the poem's estrangement from its readers. It may also call attention to the poem's self-estrangement by lifting into prominence some feature which the poem has presented only in a glancing way. In this respect the footnote will emphasize a crucial feature of all poetic discourse: although it expresses the common experience of human beings, it does so in a context of particular and often sharp tensions and estrangements. Of course the passage of time and cultural differences account for much of the fragmentation in the

community of human experience. Less apparent, but equally significant, are the processes by which—in a single culture and cultural
moment—the unity of experience undergoes the conflicts of interest
which produce arrangements of domination and marginalization.

The inertias of art—as poetry and as philology alike—operate to
preserve and illuminate these processes of domination and repression,
of the (un)certain fracturings which are the prerequisites of all the
(un)certain orderings. Works produced in the various disciplines of
knowledge commonly avail themselves of these artistic inertias, and
the most important of those works—Plato, for example, or Herodotus, or the Bible—acquire much of their transhistorical significance
from their deployment of poetic method. This is why the literary
experience is now so crucial for the consciousness industries in general. A network constructed to maximize contradictions and incommensurability, literary work (poetry and philology) marks an antithesis
to forms of normativity and dominance.

FOR WESTERN PEOPLE, the work which most graphically displays
the form of poetical discourse I have been sketching is undoubtedly
the Bible. Biblical texts exhibit three important social characteristics:
first, they are ancient and hence incorporate a long and complex
historicity; second, they are widely dispersed culturally and geograph-
ically, and hence develop complex filiations along various, often discontinuous, lateral axes; and third, the Bible—unlike the Homeric
epics, for example—maintains to this day a moral and cultural authority which functions through numerous ideological institutions
(principally the churches and the academy). The Homeric texts, on
the other hand, though they may be used for ideological purposes,
no longer exert that kind or degree of moral authority. The authority
of Homer is now largely cultural and is maintained by scholarship
and the institution of literature.

The ideological voice of the biblical texts is important because it
always argues that the value of these texts in the present is continuous,
perhaps even coterminous, with their past value and significance. The
work, that is to say, exhibits a permanent meaning (as "the Word of
God") which infuses all the diversities of the texts and transcends
their historical peculiarities. The permanent meaning is originary, but
it is displayed—or obscured—in the transmissive adventures which
the documents have undergone in various times and places.

This textual self-conception, whereby "meaning" and "value" are deployed in a context of permanences and commensurabilities, is what we understand as the ideological dimension of literary work. In this respect, the ideology operating in the biblical texts stands as the domination-form of the particular investments—what Habermas calls the "human interests"—which every reader brings to every textual event. But what is especially useful about the Bible—as opposed to the literary works we deal with more frequently in our modern national scriptures—is that its formative and transmissive histories are so richly dispersed and documented. No Word has ever been more textualized than the Word of God, none is more surrounded by, and immersed in, human words. In fact, its permanent and originary meaning is one that had to be constantly maintained in the face of various forces— the Bible calls them "strange gods"—which exercised alternative authorities and meanings. Reading the Bible, therefore, one may observe—in socially and historically particularized contexts—the struggle by which a "permanent" and transcendental meaning is deployed: the drama—set down monumentally and as a form of domination— of the conflicts of various human interests.

At the time Wordsworth was writing "The Ruined Cottage," certain biblical scholars, especially in Germany, were laying the foundations of modern literary criticism. Their object was to develop systematic procedures for elucidating the texts of antiquity. This new scholarship came to the "common reader" of Homer and the Bible as the voice of the old man in Wordsworth's poem. Scholars like J. G. Eichhorn looked at the book of Genesis in the light of their researches and were led—indeed, were forced—to say: "I see around me here / Things which you cannot see."[4] What they saw was the historicity of the biblical texts, their cross-cultural characteristics, and the basic structure of discontinuity and fragmentation which lay— half-invisibilized, like the ruins of the Capitoline—under an appearance of wholeness and uniformity. That appearance, they came to understand, was itself the consequence of a long and discontinuous historical process.

Some of what they saw had been observed before—for example, the famous discrepancy between the two accounts of creation in the first two chapters of Genesis. Comparative ethnography and textual studies revealed other, theretofore unnoticed details which tended to undermine many of the most traditional ideas about the Bible. In the end, classical and biblical studies were completely revolutionized and set upon the sociohistorical footing which remains, to this day, the basis of our understanding.

Anyone who has inquired into these matters, even in the most perfunctory way, is aware, for example, that the first account of creation, as well as a number of other important parts of Genesis— especially the story of the flood—draws heavily upon certain pagan material best known from the Babylonian epic *Enuma Elish*.[5] This material, however, has been variously transformed in the process of its incorporation into Genesis, and sometimes these transformations are of secondary importance from a hermeneutic point of view. For example, in the famous text commonly rendered "and darkness moved upon the face of the deep" (1:2), the word "deep" translates the Hebrew word *Tehom*, a corruption of the *Enuma Elish*'s *Tiamat*, the name of the Babylonian goddess identified with the salt ocean.

This detail is an index to the numerous fragmentary remains of non-Jewish materials which lie half buried in the biblical texts. Some of these materials are part of the formative history of the texts—as is the case with what has been taken over from the *Enuma Elish*— and some of them are part of the transmissive history. The division of the Bible into chapters is a medieval deposit in the text which calls attention to its "edited" character. Such continuity and order as it has—the organization into "books," the division of the text into verses, the sequencing and choice of the various materials—all these reflect a process of construction, stretching over several thousand years, which continues to this day.

That process of construction can and should be seen as a cooperative attempt to bring all these heterogeneous materials and interests into a unified order. Indeed, the incorporation of the *Enuma Elish* into Genesis may be taken as an emblem of this quest for bringing vast amounts of diverse and often conflicting materials under a single authority and monomorphic order. The Babylonian creation story is fundamentally polytheistic and centers in the struggle of cthonic forces, Tiamat and her consort Apsu, against the emergent forces of a different cultural order, represented as a group of second-generation gods under the leadership of Marduk. In the Jewish texts this material is taken over only to be subjected to a radical process of further transformation. Nor is there any doubt that the Jewish authors understood exactly what they were doing. Genesis turns the *Enuma Elish* on its head in order to give an account of the origin of the world which contradicts, *at the essential ideological points,* the account given in the *Enuma Elish*.[6] Most obvious, of course, is the substitution of a monotheistic order for a polytheistic one but numerous other transformations are made. The Genesis account, for example, represents the creation as a single act of divine benevolence, whereas *Enuma Elish* sees it as a product of dynamic tensions between conflicting forces and authorities; the cultic form of the pagan myth equally asserts that this dynamism is recurrent. In *Enuma Elish* creation is viewed in an anthropomorphic form: it takes place in the orders of sex and politics. In Genesis creation is viewed as a divine event: it is solitary and unique, an act of fission.

Genesis pretends to tell the whole and "true" meaning of the creation story that is (if the pun be permitted) bound up within the *Enuma Elish*. The latter represents, from the Jewish point of view, a confused accounting of a true event. Of course, what is false and what is true in Genesis and *Enuma Elish* are relative matters. In original Babylonian culture, *Enuma Elish* was a central text expressing a dominant set of truths. With the demise of Babylon, however, that text assumed a marginalized existence within the hegemonic texts of Jewish culture, and the process was replicated, in a variant form, with the institutionalization of the texts of Christianity.

Unlike the Old Testament with respect to the texts of ancient pagan cultures, the New Testament did not submerge the received Jewish texts into the new scriptures. The New Testament marginalized the Old Testament by declaring it to be a text full of truths which were, however, only partially known to itself. The Old Testament is represented in the New Testament as a set of proleptic documents whose full and true meaning is achieved, and revealed, in the life and death of Jesus, and in the various interpretations of that life and of the Old Testament scriptures which are preserved in the New Testament. A formula like "Then was fulfilled that which was spoken by the prophet" (Matthew 2:17) appears throughout the New Testament. It implicitly declares that the Old Testament scriptures possess an authority which the Old Testament did not give to work like the *Enuma Elish*. In this respect, the text *as such* of the Old Testament is not marginalized in the text of the New. Rather, one Jewish interpretation marginalizes another, and eventually establishes this differential in a decisive way— at the programmatic and institutional level known as Christianity.

With the advent of modern textual studies, this entire process began to be systematically revealed. The consequence has been a new disposal of authorities and an overriding sense that what is marginal and what is central, in textual and cultural matters, shift with time and circumstance. What is last shall be first and what is first shall be last, always and recurrently: this is the ironic message of these anthropological methods. The very recovery of a lost text like the *Enuma Elish* is a hermeneutical event which may shift the categories of marginality and centrality in textual studies. The event highlights the polytextuality of western religious scriptures and supplies the silenced voices of a great pagan culture with a forum for speaking in their own right. This more humanistic and democratic way of dealing with powerfully hegemonic texts and institutions is the foundation of modern critical studies.

The status of the biblical texts, therefore, as well as the modern scholarship which elucidates those texts, provides criticism with a model case history, on the one hand, and an exemplary methodology, on the other. The Old Testament is particularly useful because its procedures for reinvesting alien and antithetical materials do not call attention to themselves, as is often the case in the New Testament. Indeed, the long and dispersed textual history of the Old Testament generated some dramatic examples of texts which have reproduced themselves as a nexus of fruitful incongruities. A signal instance is offered by the (now so-called) Wife-Sister narratives in Genesis (12:10–20; 20:1–18; and 26:6–11). The three passages contain variant versions of a single story in which a patriarch (twice it is Abraham and once it is Isaac) visits a foreign country and represents his wife (Sarah or Rebekah) as his sister. According to each story, this representation is seen as a subterfuge undertaken to protect the patriarch. The beauty of Sarah and Rebekah is seen as a possible source of danger to the husband.

This anomalous textual situation has motivated numerous interpreters over a very long period to try to make sense of the texts. An important advance came when nineteenth-century scholars showed that two of the passages (in chapters 12 and 26) are J texts, whereas the other is an E text, and that the two textual lines worked, in this case, from independent sources. Clearing the documentary lines did not, however, remove some of the greatest difficulties in the passages. In particular, the deceptions practiced by the patriarchs presented obvious ideological problems, especially since the deceived party in two of the passages, Abimelech, is represented as a wise and good ruler.

E. A. Speiser brought important new light to the problem when his researches into Hurrian society—the land from which Abraham set out, and Rebekah's native land—revealed certain legal arrangements by which a husband would, on marrying a woman, make her legally his sister as well.[7] This was a practice peculiar to Hurrian culture. "There is not a trace of such usage among the Akkadians, and it was expressly stigmatized by the Hittites . . . Nor can the institution be compared with the brother-sister marriages of the ruling houses of Egypt . . . for the Hurrian practice extended also to women who were sisters by law but not by blood."[8]

The biblical passages, in other words, embody a complex process in which certain originally Hurrian cultural deposits were preserved by Jewish compilers of the biblical text. These men, however, no longer understood the meaning or practical operation of certain details which their records preserved. In Speiser's words, "Tradition had apparently set much store by these incidents, but the key to them had been lost somewhere in the intervening distances of time and space. In such circumstances, an interpretation was bound to be improvised, one that would be in keeping with more familiar conditions and with common human understanding. It is not surprising, therefore, that the indicated recourse to half-truth, if not outright deception, was just so much anachronism."[9] Each of these texts contains a hermeneutic intervention (and invention) supplied by later compilers of the earlier materials. The editorial intervention is an attempt to give a (new) meaning to an old set of texts, but a meaning which, from the "new" point of view, is taken to be the "true" and "original" meaning, indeed, the permanent meaning. Serious and obvious discrepancies remained in the composite text that resulted from this editorial intervention, however, as the later controversial history of biblical comment shows. The Hurrian wife-sister customs have been obscured and marginalized in a double process of memory loss and reinterpretation. Nevertheless, the Hurrian material is preserved as an operative element in the texts. Its presence is the principal stimulus for the anachronistic interpretive rewriting by the later Jewish compiler.

These texts exemplify the structure of meaning which operates in every fictive discourse (and many factive ones). Poetical works, in representing and memorializing the human world, carry forward with them a history of contradictions, fractures, incommensurates of all kinds. The very effort to remove these elements often produces only further splinterings and disjunctions. In our day, the most prominent literary commentators have represented this as a process of hermeneusis—a multiplication and complication of meanings laid upon the received documents and texts by generations of critics, interpreters, and readers. What the biblical texts show, however, is that the hermeneutical process is always already preserved in the texts themselves. "New" interpretations are a reflex of what had hitherto remained obscure, or marginalized, in the received texts, a reorganization of all the materials in the light of old but hitherto unperceived—or misperceived—materials.

NINETEENTH-CENTURY POETS were the first to compose their works in a conscious replication of this structure of thought. "The Rime of the Ancient Mariner" is paradigmatic, but all the Romantics—one thinks especially of layered texts like *The Marriage of Heaven and Hell, The Giaour, Prometheus Unbound,* and Keats's two "Hyperions"—follow similar organizing patterns. Blake's *The [First] Book of Urizen* (1794) is an especially pertinent example because it is the first English poem whose structure is consciously modeled on the new biblical scholarship. Along with *The Book of Ahania* (1795) and *The Book of Los* (1795), *Urizen* is produced in double columns and divided into chapters and verses to reflect the traditional Bible format. (These are the only three books engraved by Blake that are formatted in such a way.) The three books comprise the remains of what Blake had projected as his "Bible of Hell," that is, a "Bible" which would stand in an antithetical relation to the received Scriptures of heaven and the established churches.[10]

Urizen and its two companion works are formally related to the fictional reconstructions carried out by Macpherson and Chatterton. The models for the Ossian and Rowley poems are taken from the antiquarian tradition, however, whereas Blake's poems would not have been possible without the hermeneutical work of scholars like Heyne, Eichhorn, and Geddes. Such men, along with their contemporary counterparts in classical philology, like F. A. Wolf, laid the groundwork for a whole new procedure in literary studies. These scholarly advances had a profound impact upon the poetry and fiction of the nineteenth century, especially in the imaginative treatment of historical and legendary materials. In Blake and so many other writers, the new philology served as a tool for revealing—or deploying—the layered and polyglottal text.

Crucial to this new exegetical procedure was the status it gave to the factive dimensions of discursive materials. Dr. Alexander Geddes, perhaps the chief practitioner in England of this philologically based hermeneutic, insisted repeatedly that the function of scriptural interpretation was to deliver *literal* meanings. Allegoresis, or the process of reading moral and thematic forms into the text, was to be scrupulously avoided. More particularly, the critic must isolate the allegorical residues which have been deposited on ancient texts, including the biblical texts. What Geddes and his German counterparts recognized was the historicity of the received materials. Traditional criticism approached the texts of antiquity armed with allegoresis as a fail-safe device: thus, when confronted with a particular passage, especially a difficult one, the text would be brought into a state of orderliness by deploying allegory. In rejecting this method of reading, the new philologians tried to move the texts of antiquity into a condition of extreme alienation—or purity. Homer and the Bible appear to their philological imaginations as texts corrupted by a long line of misguided, if well-intentioned, readers and interpreters. The new philology meant to restore the texts, so far as possible, to a state of (as it were) original innocence.[11]

As a consequence, what had once seemed familiar and transparent to interpretation became remote and exotic. To read Homer or the Bible with these new and Higher Critical eyes became a kind of adventure, a journey to strange places and peoples. "On First Looking into Chapman's Homer" is Keats's late Romantic version of Wolf's *Prolegomena ad Homerum* (1795), and Pound's replication of this form of thought, which we glanced at earlier, continues to deploy the same philological imagination. In this view of the text, the (apparently) irrelevant or incommensurate detail begins to appear everywhere and in abundance. Two great styles are born from this historicist experience, Romanticism and Realism. But they are born antithetically, as ways of establishing forms of order within which the new flood of facticity could be understood and controlled. Organicism and empiricism are what Blake might have called the "limits of opacity" which Romanticism and Realism would set for the proliferation of these minute particulars.

If we remain within the Romantic or the Realist horizons, however, we will fail to gain the full—or at any rate the further—critical potential which is latent in this novel hermeneutic situation. Romanticism and Realism, in this context, are what Benjamin called *Einbahnstrassen*—one-way streets.[12] They interpret their materials, and if their antithetical moves are not met with a corresponding antithesis *located in the materials themselves,* they will tame and colonize them. This antithesis must be sited in the materials themselves, and not in our understanding, because our understanding is as much a function of the materials (objective history and circumstances) as the materials are a function of our understanding. Objectivity and subjectivity are relational conditions, and criticism is the exploration of those relations.

Current dialectical theories of criticism do not usually allow for this kind of objectively based antithesis. To that extent their hermeneutic circles resemble the mirage-dialogues between the rival powers of our first and second worlds, which struggle in a blind night battle for what they interpret as the allegiance (and therefore the "freedom") of the third world. But from the point of view of the third (and alienated) world, the first and second worlds are not in dialogue, they are in hegemony. Dialectic begins when the voiceless speak and the invisible appear—when the godlike Captain Cook discovers, to his surprise, that he is indeed a god and therefore must die.[13] In this way does Benjamin's thesis—that "the critic has nothing in common with the interpreter of past cultural epochs"[14]—reveal criticism as a two-way street where the hermeneut meets his subject coming from the other direction. Homer, like the Bible, has something to say to us that we weren't prepared to hear, and this impertinence localizes itself most dramatically in the incommensurate detail, where the critical limits of interpretation are revealed.

In this respect we can see the special virtue of reading the works of western antiquity. Though they are a part of us as we are a part of them, they reveal as well the discontinuity which makes up the geometry of our relations. A contemporaneous focus tends to obscure odd tangents and diagonals. More removed works accumulate their textual thicknesses in ways that are not easily overlooked. We have glimpsed this briefly in the Bible's strategies of marginalization, but in Herodotus the process achieves a spectacular level. Indeed, Herodotus is a veritable celebration of the marginal and the tangential.

THE *HISTORIES* of Herodotus are a narrative whose ultimate (but not "central") concern is the emergence of fifth-century Greece as an important power in the Mediterranean region. They are sometimes, if wrongly, titled in translation *The Persian Wars* because the climax of the narrative—Books 7–9—deals with Persia's invasion of Greece and the Greeks' successful defense of their homelands. The *Histories,* however, are notorious for their meandering and digressive ways: the whole of the second book, for example, is taken up with Egypt, her geography and ethnography. In this respect Thucydides' tight, tragic narrative is the antithesis of Herodotus. Stephen Usher speaks for many centuries of readers, both devoted and exasperated, when he says of the Herodotean texts: "He solicited and recorded these stories as he proceeded, and their ultimate inclusion in the *History* was determined by one criterion only—that they were worth the telling. To talk of relevance in Herodotus is thus itself an irrelevancy."[15] And yet to put it just this way may be slightly misleading. To talk of relevance is to talk of meaning, so that we might take Usher's comment to indicate a failure of meaning and significance in Herodotus' work. In Herodotus, however, what is relevant and what is irrelevant are precisely the issue.

When Herodotus investigates some event, his theory is always that it can be, and will have been, explained from many different points of view. Rather than trying to find "the meaning" of the event, then, or "its place" in "the historical pattern," he always seeks out the different explanations. His justification for this procedure is given explicitly in Book 7 when he records the fact that the Argives did not join the Greek alliance against the Persian invasion. Herodotus narrates a series of stories involving oracles, Persian accounts, and various tales out of Argos, Sparta, and Athens. For himself, however, he withholds a synthetic judgment: "My business is to record what people say, but I am by no means bound to believe it—and that may be taken to apply to this book as a whole" (7:152).[16] Notice that Herodotus does not say that he has no particular opinion on the matter, or that he is bound to suppress his opinions (in the interests of "objective history"?). He says, rather, that all the stories must be told, that all the accounts are important.

So we *must* talk of "relevance" in Herodotus, for what is relevant is literally everything that "people say." Yet Herodotus' narrative often seems digressive and full of irrelevant details. The first four and a half books of the *Histories* (1–5:27) present materials that far exceed what would be necessary to set the historical and ethnographic context of the Persian invasion of Greece; compared with the brilliant analytical summary of Thucydides' *Archaeologia,* this initial material—more than half of the entire work—seems impossibly overblown from a structural point of view, however interesting it may be in its particular details. It seems tangential to the main object, which is to celebrate great human achievements, in particular the Greek repulse of the Persian invasion. In short, the two parts of the *Histories* seem incommensurate.

But this view of the matter mistakes the structure of Herodotus' narrative units. One cannot properly grasp the magnitude of the Greek success without also grasping the relative position of Greece in the eastern Mediterranean at the beginning of the fifth century. With the defeat of Persia, Greece emerges as an important political and cultural power, but she emerges from obscurity, as it were. From Herodotus' point of view, Greek history before the Persian invasion is relatively inconsequential. The record of human greatness, in the world which impinges on Greece, is written in the histories of Assyria, Babylon, Egypt, Lydia, Persia, and in the related histories—lesser, but sometimes equally impressive—of the Phrygians, the Scythians, and the Massagetae.

What is more important about Herodotus' general procedure is that the Greek achievement is placed in a proper scale. Its grandeur and significance are by no means minimized, but they are situated so that we see them as part of a much larger—a more ancient and more sweeping—set of events. Reading the first half of the *Histories* one is forced to see the Greek victory in a world-historical context; this redounds to the glory of Greece, of course, but it also—and paradoxically—forces us to recognize that the emergence of Greece is taking place in a vast context of events, which has witnessed many shifts of fortune, celebrity, and power, including the appearance and disappearance of entire civilizations. The emergence of Greece to a position of prominence appears, then, as one of the potentials, as it were, of the complex network of circumstances which preceded and surrounded it. For Herodotus, however, the Greek victory was also something more than one of the possible consequences of the given network of forces and elements. It was one of the fates which lay hidden in that complex network, a fate which none could have foreseen (least of all the Persians), but which the Greeks seized, and realized.

Herodotus' greatness as a historian is deeply connected to his belief in a primitive concept of fate. Fate operates in Thucydides' tragic narrative as well, but in Thucydides we know that "character is fate." The fatal outcome of the Peloponnesian Wars is a consequence of the political "character" of the various forces involved, perhaps especially of Athens, Sparta, and Corinth. In Herodotus, however, fate is far more mysterious and impersonal. The difference between the two historians is epitomized in their respective attitudes toward dreams, omens, oracles, and all the paraphernalia through which people seek to understand and master their fates. Thucydides gives little space and no credence to such things, though obviously they figured largely in the actual events. To him the protagonists deploy their oracles and prophecies with deliberate, even cynical, purposes, in order to justify what their reason or their passions have already decided to do.

With Herodotus it is far different. "I cannot deny that there is truth in prophecies," he says, and he dismisses those who refuse to accept their literal authority (8:79). He does not uncritically accept *all* prophetic utterances any more than he accepts all *ordinary* statements about the events he is researching. Nevertheless, he always takes dreams, omens, and oracles into account when he sets out his narratives.

This aspect of the *Histories* locates one of the chief sources of Herodotus' appeal for many contemporary historians, whose work has been drastically altered under the impact of developments in anthropology, ethnology, and the various "horizontal" disciplines in the social sciences. Less theoretical than Thucydides, Herodotus gives his reader large bodies of material which are intensely interesting to the social scientist. As a consequence, Herodotus' narratives tend to be scenic rather than eventual in their structure—like a novel by Smollett or Scott rather than one by Fielding or Godwin. The consequence is that, at the level of *events,* the Herodotean narrative is typically organized as a tangle of complex and interacting forces whose meaning and direction are difficult to ascertain.

The largest pattern which Herodotus discerns is basically reciprocal: in each event or set of events involving the political relations of various peoples, a rise in the fortunes of one group will be tied to a decline in the fortunes of another. This pattern is obviously at work in the presentation of the conflict between the Greek states and Persia, but it is equally plain in the structure of Book 1, where the fall of Lydian power is connected to the advancement of Persia.

The pattern would be simple, not to say simple-minded, were it not for Herodotus' perception of the relativity of all these reciprocal movements. This relativity is presented at the very outset, in Book 1. After a brief general introduction Herodotus takes us to the Lydia of King Croesus, "the first foreigner . . . to come into direct contact with the Greeks" (1:8). Lydia is at the height of her power when Croesus has his famous interview with Solon, the Athenian, who refuses to flatter the unwary and self-satisfied Croesus. "Who is the happiest man you have ever seen?" Croesus asks Solon, but the latter not only does not give the expected answer—that is, "King Croesus is the happiest"—he delivers the oracular advice which will hover over the entire length of Herodotus' *Histories:* "Look to the end, no matter what it is you are considering. Often enough God gives a man a glimpse of happiness and then utterly ruins him" (1:34).

And so it is, as Croesus and his great empire are destroyed by Cyrus and the rising power of Persia. The fact that it is Solon the Athenian who warns Croesus is obviously pertinent in the context of the *Histories* as a whole, especially since, after the fall of Croesus, the Lydian king is then taken into the court of Cyrus to act as counselor and advisor to the Persian king. In Croesus' postlapsarian career he plays the part of Solon to Cyrus and his erratic son Cambyses. According to Herodotus, when Cyrus listens to the wisdom of Croesus he is successful; when he fails to follow Croesus' advice, as in the matter of the invasion of the land of the Massagetae, Cyrus is destroyed. The latter event, which closes Book 1, is presented as a prolepsis of what will happen at the end of the *Histories,* when Persia will be utterly defeated in another—equally unprovoked and unjust—invasion.

Two things are important to notice in this structure of events. The first, which I have already mentioned, is the relativity of the cycles of good and evil fortune. When Croesus speaks with Solon, Lydia appears in the ascendant—in relation to the various peoples recently brought under Lydian subjection. But even as Croesus and Solon are speaking, Persian power is on the advance; in terms of this "Persian cycle" Lydia is on the decline, and Persia in the ascendant. But if we "look to the end" we glimpse as well the "Greek cycle" beginning to turn on its slow axis. Furthermore, within each of these cycles are smaller epicycles, as we see most graphically in the case of Cyrus, who is destroyed even though the larger Persian cycle moves in a generally favorable arc. Because individuals take part in many such cycles, fortune and misfortune await them at every turn. One must not simply "look to the end," one must also try to be clear about all the lines which intersect one's life at every moment.

Thus an incredibly complex network begins to emerge—lines of force and direct counterforce, as well as various tangential, marginal, and distant lines of other forces which may or may not impinge upon each other. This situation highlights the second important aspect of the Herodotean narrative, which tries to teach an important practico-moral lesson to the individual. A fatal order rules everywhere, but from the point of view of the individual this order always remains obscure and impossible to master. Extreme circumspection, attention to detail, is therefore the foundation of all wisdom. Herodotus' *Histories* are, from the most obvious point of view, a celebration of Greece and her coming to a position of power and importance; from another (any other) point of view, they may be taken—especially by the Greek reader—as a cautionary tale and warning, for the cycle of Greek ascendancy occurs in connection with many other cycles and lines of force, and no one can be certain from which quarter danger may come.

The incident involving Persia and the Massagetae illustrates this Herodotean moral very well, especially if we view it from the point of view of Herodotus' reader rather than from Cyrus's point of view. In the former vantage the invasion of the land of the Massagetae is a prolepsis of the invasion of Greece. The parallel is interesting, however, precisely because it is, in certain respects, not easy to see: the Massagetae live at the very opposite end of the known world, in the vast region to the east of the Caspian; they are a land-based people and are not dispersed into separate states, but live under the single rule of Queen Tomyris. Nevertheless, Herodotus observes the parallel and solicits the reader's awareness as well. His purpose becomes clear much later, when Xerxes is on the brink of his invasion of Greece. The incident of the Massagetae is part of the cycle of Persian history and ought to have been in Xerxes' mind, as a warning to him. It haunts the mind of Xerxes' chief counselor Artabanus when he warns the king against undertaking the invasion of Greece (7:18).

Thus, when Herodotus brings that piece of apparently non-Greek history into the narrative of Book 1, he is implicitly telling us that no one can afford to leave any scrap of information, however peripheral it may appear, out of one's accounting. Lydian, Egyptian, Babylonian, Scythian—all these histories, as well as those involving even more remote and minor peoples and events, are part of a vast order, and hence may prove crucially important for anyone to remember at any time.

This is the situation in which Herodotus' dreams, omens, and oracles gain their significance. To ignore such things is sheer folly, for they provide access to the fatal orders which operate at all times. Nevertheless, heeding them is merely the beginning of wisdom, for they are often extremely difficult to interpret. In those riddles where time is a factor, the key to successful divination lies in the ability to recognize which cycle, and which point on the cycle, and finally which point of view on that point on the cycle, is being called to one's attention in the oracular text or event. These are often the most complex riddles presented in Herodotus, though from our later point of view—where oracles and omens have lost all authority—they are not always the most mysterious.

Indeed, from our point of view the deepest mystery lies in the facticity of the omens themselves, and hence in our ability—our need, finally—to plumb their significance, to find what meaning they hold out to us today. Of course we may take Thucydides' course and pay such obviously superstitious material little mind; but if we do we may well be haunted with the Herodotean idea that nothing human can be alien to us, and that we can little afford to lose the significance of anything that has found some place, however remote or small or peripheral, in human history and culture. Is our position so important, so grand, so central, that we can afford to pass such judgments?

The Thucydidean judgment is that omens and oracles do not actually figure into the final accounting. In a superstitious world they operate either as apparitions or as rationalizations; to an enlightened consciousness, on the other hand, they must be either demystified or left out of the reckoning. But this confidence of the enlightened mind, in a Herodotean context, can only remind one of Croesus and Cyrus and Xerxes—of men out of control, with their foolish sense of control and illusions of understanding. We read Herodotus and discover again and again that we do not understand, and that his text undermines our confidences. A small incident in Book 7 illustrates the situation quite well. It occurs at a crucial juncture, immediately after Herodotus narrates the passage of Xerxes' army across the Hellespont: "After the whole army had reached the European shore and the forward march had begun, an extraordinary thing occurred—a mare gave birth to a hare. Xerxes paid no attention to this omen, though the significance of it was easy enough to understand. Clearly it meant that he was to lead an army against Greece with the greatest pomp and circumstance, and then to come running for his life back to the place he started from" (7:59). One scarcely knows what to regard as more marvelous in this text: the fact that Xerxes paid no attention to so bizarre an occurrence, the fact that Herodotus takes the details as given and expects the same from us, the meaning produced for the omen, or, finally, the fact that Herodotus regards the "meaning" as almost laughably obvious. All these things are clear from the text, yet equally clear is that, to us, none of these things makes any sense at all.[17] The text plunges us into a world that is utterly remote from anything we could pretend to understand; what is worse, it does so without any inclination either to apologize for or rationalize the incident, or—on the other hand—to recoil from it in an attitude of romantic wonder or surprise. Herodotus of course acknowledges that the event is "extraordinary," but his narrative and explanation provide a response that is equal to the event itself. As a result, the entire text presents an unruffled surface. The scandal of this passage, to a modern consciousness, is not the event but the meaning with which the text surrounds the event.

A passage like this—Herodotus is replete with them—reminds one of the folly of modern hermeneutics, and of all our proud schools of criticism. We have bred a class of professional diviners and haruspicators whose confidence in their ability to read and interpret is without bounds. And it is indeed the case that, like the prophets and priests paid for and kept in Persian courts and halls of power, we can always be counted on to produce a "meaning" when called upon to do so. This is what it means to be professional. Yet we have our limits, and this text from Herodotus exposes them very well. No one today would be able to venture such a text as Herodotus has given. What this *means* is that in this text we are confronted with a human event which we recognize as human and yet cannot comprehend under an interpretation. The text speaks to us, and we are left with only inadequate responses. In this textual encounter, we learn to judge our interpretive inadequacy by first witnessing it. There is a judgment here which supervenes and measures our own, as well as the judgments of any possible supporting interpretive communities. Furthermore, this judgment is not a function of a de Manian absence or textual emptiness. Of course, interpretation may move along the allegorical alternations of blindness and insight. But if we want a dialectical criticism, the language of the work itself must be heard, even as it will not be comprehended. So it is here in Herodotus, where we see that the gap in interpretation is a function of positivities in the work which anticipate the interpreter.

In this passage one encounters the dawn of the incommensurate—

an event which is not peculiar to Herodotus but which locates the pervasive quality of every literary (that is to say, every poetic) text. Blake saw this as the moment of "minute particulars." As often as not, a scholarly footnote will draw our attention to such moments— moments when, if we are alert, we may begin to glimpse presences we could not have reckoned upon. Nonpoetic discourse, like history and philosophy, discovers these moments frequently. But because poetry is the discursive form proper to the incommensurate, it is in poetic texts that one will find the richest store of the incommensurable.

We are interested in such things because both of "the two cultures" have neglected the knowledge function of poetic discourse. This is a critical function, of course, but not simply a critical function. There is a knowledge through the incommensurate which is a positive knowledge and which has its roots in the ancient understanding of the memorial function of poetic discourse. To understand this more clearly, however, we shall have to explore further the structure of knowledge through incommensurability. We shall find that incommensurates are not "facts"—or what Coleridge called "objects as objects"[18]—they are details which already carry or imply those contexts of competing human interests by which meaning is constituted. At the dawning of the incommensurate we come to understand that the human world is not made up of "facts" and/or "interpretations," it is made up of *events*—specific and worlded engagements in which meaning is rendered and used. Poetic work locates one type of event. Its special function is to display the eventuality of meaning through representations of the incommensurable.

4 ⚬

Poetic Ideology and Nonnormative Truth
To the Marxists

> There is no first or last discourse, and dialogical context
> knows no limits . . . At every moment of the dialogue, there
> are immense and unlimited masses of forgotten meanings,
> but, in some subsequent moments, as the dialogue moves
> forward they will return to memory and live in renewed
> form . . . Nothing is absolutely dead: every meaning will cel-
> ebrate its rebirth.
>
> Mikhail Bakhtin, last written words, 1974

PERHAPS THE MOST INFLUENTIAL TEXT on poetics in English is
Sidney's *Apology for Poetry,* in particular the famous passage where
he distinguishes poetic from historical and philosophical discourse. In
this text Sidney defends poetry from the Platonic critique by deploying
an Aristotelian argument: that poetry is a mimetic discourse and not
a predicative or propositional one. Poetry therefore delivers a kind
of virtual reality wherein nothing is affirmed and nothing is denied.

This argument for poetry later acquired a new and special force in
the context of Kant's third *Critique* and its aftermath, as we have
already observed. Thus, in chapter 14 of the *Biographia,* Coleridge
speaks of poetry and poems as if they were magical structures devoid
of ethical or positive knowledge. Later still, in this century, theorists
would complete the argument that poetry and art, in their essential
features, have nothing to do with ideology or positive knowledge.
Virtual realities and immanent structures, imaginative works came to
be theorized and studied as autonomous realms—textual or intertextual fields, entirely self-sustaining and self-authorizing.

Despite certain areas of agreement, however, these more recent
aesthetic emphases do not simply recapitulate the ideas of their precursors. For example, when Sidney observes of the pagan Greek poets
that they "did not induce [the opinions of paganism] but did imitate
those opinions already induced," he is arguing that poetry is mimetic

and affirms nothing. But for Sidney, it is fundamental that poetic discourse is not simply disinterested imitation, that its imitations are charged with positive knowledge and values. For Sidney, pagan Greek poetry is "not . . . an art of lies but of true doctrine" because its positive content is explained and redeemed in what Sidney calls "the light of Christ."[1]

This ideological ground is important to see because it reminds us of what is and what is not involved in Sidney's and Kant's and Coleridge's theories of poetic autonomy. When Sidney and Coleridge represent the poetic field as noncognitive, they are saying only that poetic discourse does not deal in factual or moral propositions as such. They are most definitely *not* saying that poetry is amoral, however, because each insists upon the theological foundation of poetry: what Sidney calls "the light of Christ" and what Coleridge calls "sacramentalism" or "the symbol." In each case the moral dimension of the poetic is maintained by indirection. The same is true of Kant, although for him the fundament of the aesthetic moment is metaphysical rather than theological.

The issue, then, is not *whether* poetic discourse is involved in topics of value and questions of ideology, but *how* it is engaged. The elucidation of the forms and methods by which the poetic actually involves itself in these matters is the theoretical move which will cut through many of the most vexing problems of current theory.

FORMAL AND IMMANENT APPROACHES to the poetic tend to conceive the discourse system as a verbal or grammatological one. Hence a sharp distinction is commonly made between "the text," on the one hand, and "the document" on the other. The distinction means to bracket out of consideration those bibliocritical and textual-critical materials with which poetic discourse is always and necessarily involved. Such matters are taken to be accidental rather than substantive to the nature of the poetic. Consequently, bibliography and textual criticism are conceived as either preliminary or tangential to criticism and interpretation.

This critical neglect of the documentary aspects of poetical discourse—this failure to incorporate documentary studies into modern hermeneutics—has obscured that horizon of the poetic where the work's ideological dimensions are clearest. The options that writers choose in the areas of initial production, as well as in printing, publishing, and distribution—the options that are *open* to them in these matters—locate what one might call the "performative" aspect of the poetic: what poems are *doing* in saying what they say. A hermeneutic which understands that poetical systems operate simultaneously in both grammatological and documentary modes will go some way toward resolving the two problems which have most plagued twentieth-century literary theory: first, the relation of poetical discourse to ideology and moral/political engagement; and, second, the referential aspect of poetical systems.

When we read poems through their documentary codes, when we read out the meanings embodied in their bibliographical formulations, we confront poetical discourse as a particular deed of language—an institutionalized event in communication which takes place according to certain particular rules and possibilities, and which has particular ends in view. All these things change with time and circumstances, however, so the reading of the performative dimension of the poetic event has to seek the same kind of concreteness and specificity which grammatological readings have always insisted upon. The horizon of concreteness in the performative dimension is social and historical.

Poetical works communicate in performative codes. Juvenal does not begin to produce his satires, whose direct focus is the world of Domitian's Rome, until the reign of Trajan. This is a political and social fact about the satires which was initially coded at the documentary level. The particular significance of this fact—its import for the localized interpretation of line and poem—is not the issue here. What matters is the interpretive frame which is necessarily thrown around the entire corpus of Juvenal's work by the presence of this general fact about the poetry, by the presence of what one might call this Mastercode. And the significance of the Mastercode is preserved even in the absence of those early documentary materials—that is to say, in the later surviving documents and editions, as well as in the grammatology of the poems, where the performative work of the satire is translated and redeployed.

Nor is this aspect of the poetic confined to topical works. The most aesthetic poetry—Keats's, say, or Rossetti's—is produced within certain social contexts, and it does not merely *reflect* the presence and pressure of those contexts, it carries out a positive response to them. To see the illocutionary dimension of a poem like "La Belle Dame sans Merci" or a book like *The Early Italian Poets* (1861) is often difficult because such works have been programmatically generated from a theory which seeks to displace that dimension from immediate view. In *The Romantic Ideology* (1983) I tried to expose some of the mechanisms of such an aesthetic procedure. Here I want to emphasize a salient point of critical methodology: that the acts carried out by such works are often most clearly defined by paying attention to their production rather than to their grammatological codes. This is because, in aesthetic work, the performance sets out to represent the poetry as purely grammatological.

This representation is of course a poetical illusion. It is also one of the characteristic *deeds* of post–eighteenth-century poetics. The illusion is peculiarly manageable because the means and the modes of textual production, between the eighteenth and the mid-twentieth centuries, serve to disperse and depersonalize the work of poetry. In an industrialized structure writer, producer, and distributor are far more alienated from each other—and from their own work—than is the case for coterie poets like Donne and Rochester, or for a patronized poet like Pope. All manipulate performative codes, but in each case the social and institutional circumstances are far different from those of Keats and Rossetti, and the differences are registered at all of the poetical levels.

Writing like Keats's and Rossetti's does not struggle with its productive options in the same way that the writing of Blake and Byron does. In the case of the first two, the autonomous poem accepts, as it were, its alienation and depersonalization, but it simultaneously claims a special privilege for the aesthetic over the social, political, and economic. Byron and Blake, on the other hand, are constantly engaged with poetical production in problematic ways. It is always for them a positive difficulty as well as a positive opportunity. Both poets foreground not merely their acts of writing but their *activities as writers,* the social and institutional horizons within which their work operates. A poem like *Don Juan* discusses its own process of composition, of course, but it also discusses its audience, its publishers, its reviewers, and, in general, the world of its circumstantiality. Thus, while all four of these poets exhibit specific performative operations in their work, Blake and Byron display the form of their production codes—and hence the social dimension of their linguistic acts—most clearly.

In studying specific poems, then, we have to elucidate their productive and documentary forms as fully as possible if we mean to deploy a comprehensive hermeneutic. One of the most salient features of Blake's work lies in its repeated and literal insistence upon the "meaningfulness" of its documentary forms. The fruitful instabilities built into the various copies of the *Songs* and *The [First] Book of Urizen*, the formatting of the three extant books of Blake's projected Bible of Hell—in general, his deliberate and positive employment of materials and modes of production in the construction of meaningful poetic codes—all these things dramatize Blake's clear sense that the poetic functions at the intersection point of the grammatological and the documentary codes. One of the most important arguments in *The Marriage of Heaven and Hell* engages directly with these issues. The Printing House in Hell in plate 15 is the center of gravity for a thematic field which is dispersed across the whole of the poem.

Earlier we saw that application of a poetic method to the construction or elucidation of texts elaborates a poem's network of particular tensions and contradictions. The poetic develops its materials into a state of systematic incommensurability. When we highlight the framing function of poetry's performative Mastercodes, however, we establish the horizons within which textual heteroglossia will be operating in particular cases. These Mastercodes define the poem's communicative system: its parts, their relations to each other, and—ultimately—the object of the system as such (that is, in contradistinction to the objects of other communicative systems—say, predicative or propositional systems). These performative Mastercodes establish the poem's particular set of sociohistorical interests and engagements.

ONCE AGAIN the Bible is a useful source of examples. I begin by concentrating on the performativity of the text as it operates at the grammatological (or "intrinsic") level. But I choose the Bible at this point because it is a work whose documentary (or "extrinsic") performativity is hard to overlook even when our focus of attention is primarily directed at the grammatological level.

Matthew, chapter 13, presents a sequence of famous parables— parables of the kingdom, as they are called, including the famous parables of the Sower and of the Mustard Seed.[2] The chapter as received is beautifully constructed so that a number of crucial and interrelated topics are handled together. Verses 1–8 and 31–33 display Jesus speaking in parables to "the multitude" but in the presence of his disciples. After each of these public performances Jesus goes aside with his circle of intimates and discusses both the meaning of certain parables and the general significance of parabolic speaking.

This formal structuring dramatizes the human and social dynamic which is being represented in the text. When Jesus, for example, tells one of his disciples that "it is given unto you to know the mysteries of the kingdom of heaven, but to them [the multitude] it is not given" (verse 11), he distinguishes between what he calls the man who "hath" and the man who "hath not" (verse 12). This is a hard saying, for it not only separates the men of faith from everyone else, it suggests that this faith is a gift from God—an arbitrary gift, in fact, and analogous to the traditional covenanted relation between God and the Jews.

One other important general feature of the chapter must be noted. When Jesus speaks in parables, the event itself serves to separate two types of auditors: the man who hears but does not understand and the man "who hath ears to hear" (verse 43), who has understanding while he listens. This would be a simple enough distinction were it not for the fact that Jesus is urged by his disciples to explain the parables to them. The multitude and the circle of disciples both hear the parable of the Sower in verses 1–8, and immediately afterward Jesus tells his disciples why he speaks in such a way:

> 13. Therefore speak I to them in parables: because they seeing see not; and hearing they hear not, neither do they understand . . .
>
> 16. But blessed are your eyes, for they see: and your ears, for they hear.
>
> 17. For verily I say unto you, That many prophets and righteous men have desired to see those things which ye see, and have not seen them; and to hear those things which ye hear, and have not heard them.

A startling thing then happens in the text: Jesus proceeds to explain the meaning of the parable of the Sower to the disciples. Thus we are suddenly made aware that when Jesus spoke the parable recorded in verses 1–8, it was obscure to *everyone,* the multitude and the initiates alike. The disciples' relative ignorance is underscored later (verse 36) when they specifically ask Jesus to explain a parable he has just delivered "unto the multitude."

The text supplies its own gloss on these problems in the concluding verses of the chapter (verses 44–53). Here Jesus delivers a sequence of parabolic sketches which illuminate the character of the person glanced at in the famous text: "Who has ears to hear, let him hear" (verse 43).

44. Again, the kingdom of heaven is like unto treasure hid in a field; the which when a man hath found, he hideth, and for joy thereof goeth and selleth all that he hath, and buyeth that field.

45. Again, the kingdom of heaven is like unto a merchant man, seeking goodly pearls:

46. Who, when he had found one pearl of great price, went and sold all that he had, and bought it.

47. Again, the kingdom of heaven is like unto a net, that was cast into the sea, and gathered of every kind:

48. Which, when it was full, they drew to shore, and sat down, and gathered the good into vessels, but cast the bad away.

The point is that the person "with ears to hear" will be actively involved in trying to understand. "True" understanding entails agency and involvement. In general, it means being a disciple—performing the actions that are proper to discipleship—rather than being merely one of "the multitude," or one of those who listen but have no "ears to hear."

At every textual turn we find this message replicated—for example, in those texts which specifically appeal to Old Testament precursor texts:

34. All these things spake Jesus unto the multitude in parables: and without a parable spake he not unto them:

35. That it might be fulfilled which was spoken by the prophet, saying, I will open my mouth in parables; I will utter things which have been kept secret from the foundation of the world.

Like the similar text in verses 13–17, this passage underscores the illocutionary character of Jesus' performance. In saying what he says, Jesus is *doing* something. He is fulfilling what was said by the prophets. More than this, the agency of his discourse calls out the significance of other words and deeds, in the crowds and in the disciples. The request for an interpretation is also an illocutionary discourse, and the pair of interpretations which Jesus supplies (verses 18–23, 37–43) are themselves doing something with the words. The interpretations do not simply translate the parables into their "meanings," they supplement one set of illocutionary texts with other agenting verbal forms.

Thus far I have been treating this text as if it were transparent to itself—as if the events it records and the persons who appear in it are self-authorizing instruments. But in fact we know that most if not all of what Jesus is said to have done and said, here and throughout the gospels, has been supplied by the person (or sequence of persons) who put the text together from collections of received oral and written traditions. The events in chapter 13 are in various particular and definable ways *made* to be as they are by subsequent authorizers. This means that the Gospel of Matthew is itself an illocutionary discourse, a deed of words. As we make a distinction, in the dialogues, between Socrates and Plato, so here—and in even more complex ways—"Jesus" is to be distinguished from "Matthew"; the user of the work will have to distinguish as well many subsequent layers of authorization, all equally determinate and particular.

In pointing out that there are "authorial" and "editorial" agencies in a text, in addition to the "fictive" and "characterological" agencies, we indicate how close a relation exists between the so-called intrinsic and extrinsic dimensions of literary work. The "extrinsic" agencies operate largely through the productive (or documentary) Mastercode. In Matthew that permanent dimension surfaces *at the grammatological level* most clearly in the symbolical texts (like the visit of the Magi, the temptation in the desert, and the transfiguration), typological passages (the genealogy of Jesus, the flight to Egypt, the slaughter of the Innocents), and those passages where Jesus' words or deeds "prefigure" later events, either in his own life or in subsequent history. Such "events" plainly involve editorial interventions in the "historical" record. Similarly, a passage like the following in chapter 10 involves a kind of double exposure:

16. Behold, I sent you forth as sheep in the midst of wolves . . .

17. But beware of men: for they will deliver you up to the councils, and they will scourge you in their synagogues;

18. And ye shall be brought before governors and kings for my sake, for a testimony against them and the gentiles . . .

21. And the brother shall deliver up the brother to death, and the father the child; and the children shall rise up against their parents, and cause them to be put to death.

22. And ye shall be hated of all men for my name's sake: but he that endureth to the end shall be saved.

23. But when they persecute you in this city, flee ye unto another: for verily I say unto you, Ye shall not have gone over the cities of Israel, till the Son of man be come.

The Jesus of this text is in immediate contact with two audiences—the circle of the twelve original disciples and the audience of early Christians who had to struggle against the hostility of the established Jewish culture, as well as Roman authority and other Gentile communities. The Gospel of Matthew is here (and repeatedly) marked by an awareness of the social upheavals that led up to and followed upon the destruction of Jerusalem in 70 A.D. The early compilers of the gospel develop this illocutionary dimension of the text. For example, the phrase "their synagogues," in verse 17 above, calls attention to the *ex post facto* vantage here taken toward the original events in Jesus' life. That phrase—it recurs elsewhere—indicates what this text is being made to *do* at one of its most important levels.[3] In the same way the "character" Jesus, at the narrative level, is the vortex of that great sequence of illocutionary passages where Jesus is involved in controversy with the Jewish scribes and pharisees. In every instance we bear witness to (narrative) "characters" who are bearing witness themselves in their repeated disputations—who are, as we should now say, operating *engagé* texts. Equally apparent are the special interests of the various authors/compilers/editors/hermeneuts who, throughout the long composition and transmissive history of this work, perpetuate with ever new variations the illocutionary discourse which *is* the Matthew gospel.

That the Bible is characterized by performative discourse is perhaps not very surprising—at least to believers. But since the eighteenth century the Bible has been radically transformed by the new hermeneutics. Secularized and humanized, the Bible enters our horizon not as doxa but as literature; and since literature, in this view, is an aesthetic and nonperformative domain of language, we are urged to read the Bible like any other "poetical" work, as if it were an autonomous discourse system. I have been taking my examples, here and earlier, from the biblical texts because the tools which have, over the past two hundred years, served to illuminate so much about these texts, have introduced as well certain distorted views. In emphasizing the secularity of the Bible and the aesthesis of the poem, criticism often forgets the performative structure of literary texts.

Imaginative agency, poetic performativity, develops within the frameworks established by those interacting productive and grammatological Mastercodes. Nor do those Mastercodes cease to function when the texts seem to have slipped some of their original or apparent use-functions, as is certainly the case with Herodotus, for example, and with the Bible. The transformation of what was once a serious work of science and philosophy, Lucretius' *De rerum natura,* into a "literary work," is—like the analogous transformations of Herodotus and the Bible—an event in discourse which illuminates the performative functions of every imaginative text, whether ancient or modern. Thinking in narrowly functionalist terms, we sometimes treat imaginative works the way we treat the "literature" of the past: that is to say, as ornamental, luxurious, dispensable. The truth is that the poetic performs a critical function which is not found in other forms of discourse.

Unlike other language functions, however, the poetic also has certain representational functions. In this fact we may see a double significance. The poetic lays out its materials as representative things: it is an act of re-presenting. Furthermore, we are not to imagine that the poetic involves simple acts of imitation or "reference"—representations *of* a given reality or human world. Being an event of language, the poetic "makes representations," as one might say of persons that they "represent themselves" in certain ways. This quality of the poetic is important to keep in mind because it calls attention to poetry's mediated character—that in a crucial sense poetry's representations are self-representations. Finally, the poetic makes its representations *to* others, to its audience. This means, reciprocally, that the representations are not to be understood without taking account of the framework of their receptions. Hence the entire meaning-structure of the poetic is involved in the production of representations in all these interlocking relationships. The poetic thereby enables us to see (as it were) meaning as a function of a particular scene of language, where various figures are interacting with each other.

THESE INTERACTIONS may be critically displayed in a grammatological analysis, as I have tried to indicate in my remarks on the Matthew gospel. But that text shows quite clearly that the grammatological Mastercodes function in conjunction with the productive Mastercodes. And it is the analysis of the latter—of the composition, bibliography, and reception histories—which will define most clearly the performative horizon of the work.

Let us consider Matthew Arnold's "Sohrab and Rustum," which is the central document in a book through which Arnold would argue the transhistorical character of poetic discourse.[4] Normally the text before us would be either in an anthology of some sort or in one of the standard editions of Arnold. These represent finite textual options, and in any of the possible cases (other than one of the early editions) one would not be able to see the work very clearly in respect to its original documentary situation. What difference does that make, one might ask, so long as the words are accurately transmitted from the early editions? Well, the difference is in fact very great, for that initial documentary situation encodes important structures of meaning within which the later history of the poem's meanings is borne along. Furthermore, that initial documentary situation highlights, by its concrete and positive differentials, the fact that later texts are equally marked, at the level of production, by specific ideological interests.

Let me glance at just a few relevant matters. "Sohrab and Rustum" first appeared in Arnold's *Poems*, published 25 November 1853. The title page of the first edition says "Poems. A New Edition. by Matthew Arnold." This title addresses itself primarily to readers who already know something about Arnold's poetry, and to that extent it sets Arnold forth as a known quantity. Furthermore, those few simple words carry out a rather more dramatic self-presencing than one might suspect when reading them at a removed vantage like our own. In calling attention to Arnold's earlier editions, the title page recalls as well that Arnold's first two collections (published in 1849 and 1852, respectively) appeared anonymously: the title pages of each read merely "by A."[5] This fact is important because it operates as part of a network of similar details all of which were working to thrust Arnold forward in a posture of deliberate publicness—something he had not done before. This situation was explicitly noted by the early reviewers.[6]

The attempt to secure a wider audience and notoriety for his poetical work is an important aspect of both *Poems* (1853) as a whole and "Sohrab and Rustum" in particular. Arnold's anonymously published 1849 and 1852 volumes were issued under the imprint of B. Fellowes, a small London publisher who issued very few titles. Arnold first published with Fellowes because of a family connection: Fellowes was the publisher of many of Arnold's father's books.[7] The print runs for the 1849 and 1852 volumes were small—five hundred copies each—so the whole manner of proceeding was conceived on a very modest scale by all concerned.[8]

But it turned out that those two books received fairly wide notice in the reviews. Partly this was a consequence, once again, of Arnold's family connections. Though the books were published anonymously,

Arnold's authorship was not a secret. His authorial reserve, however, was deeply connected to his ideological stance as a writer. The early reviewers, for instance, while praising his work, consistently noted that it was written from a very specific and restricted vantage—that it was academic poetry, and even more that it was Oxford poetry. This was taken, generally, to be a serious limitation; it was taken as a limitation because these reviewers, like Arnold's friend Clough, assumed that literature ought to be addressing the important issues of the day. Books like the 1849 and 1852 volumes, for all their virtues, seemed fugitive and cloistered.[9]

The title page of the 1853 *Poems,* then, calls attention to this general situation. And the publisher's imprint at the foot of that page is also arresting. In place of "B. Fellowes" one now finds that Arnold is being published by the large and important house of Longmans. This is a significant change, and a little research shows that it was a decision deliberately made. In April 1853 Arnold wrote to his sister that he was planning to publish a collection of old and new poems, and in May he told his mother that he had "settled with Fellowes to publish ['Sohrab and Rustum'], and one or two more new ones, with the most popular of the old ones, next winter or spring, with a preface and my name."[10] Thus, since Arnold had originally contracted to publish his new book with Fellowes, the switch to Longmans must have been made deliberately and for imperative reasons. We do not know when or how the switch came about between June and November, but it was probably through Arnold's connection with John William Parker, Jr., the editor (between 1848–60) of *Fraser's Magazine,* which was published by Longmans and which had printed Arnold's "Memorial Verses" in June 1850.

However that may be, the switch to Longmans carried consequences which bore upon the book's discursive semiology. To publish "A New Edition" with Longmans instead of Fellowes meant that Arnold was deliberately seeking to extend the audience and circulation of his work. Equally important, Longmans gave a kind of institutional authority to the ideological position which Arnold took in his important preface written for the 1853 volume. Longmans had an extensive list, which appealed to the Victorians' interest in serious, practical, and topical matters. At the back of Arnold's 1853 *Poems* are thirty-one pages of publishers' advertisements for their new books. By far the largest group (sixty-six) is headed "Religious and Moral Works," and the second largest (sixty-one) is "Criticism, History, and Memoirs." The smallest (four) is "Fiction." Many new books of reference, science, mathematics, political economy, "Books of General Utility" and so forth made up a list for the earnest Victorian.

Finally, the decision to introduce the poems with the (now famous) Preface was a bold move which set an interpretive frame about the whole book as well as each poem within it. A number of Arnold's friends, and several of the reviewers, deplored his prose introduction as an intrusive piece of polemic, but the poems were being offered as part of an argument about the nature of poetry in general and about the function of poetic discourse at the present time. Furthermore, Arnold was taking the case of his own poetry as an exemplary event. Accused of producing precious and academic work, of writing on subjects which had little relevance to problems of moment and of writing for a small and elite coterie, Arnold responded on three fronts. First, he put his work before a wider public; second, he set out a prose argument for the relevance of what his critics had labeled precious and esoteric; and third, he placed his own verse in the foreground of his campaign for certain ideas about poetry. The ostentatious removal of "Empedocles on Etna" from the collection—a work even then widely regarded as his most impressive achievement—argued that Arnold was no mere "poet" but a writer with severe moral and cultural ideals. Indeed, it suggested that all his poetry was written within a critically self-conscious horizon, and that it therefore always displayed, at some level, precisely that horizon of critical values. And the move from Fellowes to Longmans argued that, far from expressing an elitist and coterie view, his work would prove its relevance and currency in the market.

A poem like "Sohrab and Rustum" has to be read in the context of this set of poetic structurations. *Poems* (1853) did not merely remove "Empedocles on Etna," it set "Sohrab and Rustum" in its stead as the centerpiece of the collection, the work which most fully illustrates and epitomizes the ideological polemic which the book as a whole raises up.

In fact, of course, the poem always *has* been read within that context. What I am trying to indicate is that poetic discourse, like all forms of discourse, uses a full range of communicative resources, grammatological and productive alike, in fashioning its particular eventuality. The poetic work is a nexus of reciprocating expectations and interactions between the various persons engaged over and within the poetic event. Criticism, therefore, has to explain the way those communicative resources operate. I also want to indicate, however, that attention to such matters highlights the ideological framework within which a poetic discourse will always be operating. We might be tempted to say of Arnold what Keats said of poets with a palpable design upon us. But if the ideological designs of Arnold are manifest and palpable, those of Keats and Rossetti, though less visible, are no less present and operative.

We may think otherwise because we may think something that Arnold's 1853 *Poems* wanted us to think—namely, that an aesthetic event is nonideological. But this is not the case, as Arnold's own work clearly shows. The apparent "argument" of Arnold's book is that poetry at its highest removes us from the anxieties of fractious and wearying contentions. It puts us in touch with models of fixed and foundational human ideas and values—ideas and values which transcend all that is local and disputatious, all that is in fact *ideological*. But the "argument" displayed in the productive Mastercode is that these "transcendent" values require an immediate polemic, that they are in fact subject to dispute, that they are not of all times and all places. Arnold's book says one thing *and* (not *but*) means another.

"Sohrab and Rustum" is conceived and produced as a poem about poetry. This is not a hidden or displaced subject, it is the poem's most explicit and forward topic. Furthermore, the poem approaches the topic from an ideological vantage which could not be more clearly presented. Because "the confusion of the present times is great,"[11] the example of classical cultures is peculiarly relevant to the modern situation. When contemporary English poets imitate Greek models, they offer their world images of "great actions" which reflect social stability and cultural wholeness. For in their poetry, as in their culture generally, "they regarded the whole"—whereas in Arnold's world "we regard the parts" only.[12] All of this represents, needless to say, a cultural differential which Arnold postulates—more particularly, which he judges to be a widespread contemporary sentiment and view. As he says in his advertisement to the 1854 edition: "I was speaking of actions as they presented themselves to us moderns."[13]

Arnold was pleased with "Sohrab and Rustum" because he felt that it had succeeded in translating his Greek idea (and Ideal) of wholeness into a contemporary English poem. The poem in fact does something rather different: it embodies, or illustrates, what kinds of tensions and contradictions are involved in a certain influential Victorian view of classical culture and its relation to the contemporary world. "Sohrab and Rustum" is not at all an Aristotelian "imitation" more or less successfully carried out; rather, it is an *idea* of such an imitation, an idea that has been socially and historically conditioned. "Sohrab and Rustum" is, in short, a Victorian—one must even say an "imperialist"—poem. Arnold of course wants it to be something else because he takes his model, Greek poetry, to be transhistorical, of no time and no place. In Greek art, Arnold says, "the date of an action . . . signifies nothing,"[14] and contemporary poetry should strive as well for that quality of timelessness. But when we read "Sohrab and Rustum" we are all the more forcibly reminded of the work's contemporaneity because of its effort to appear otherwise. And, ironically, we may well be equally reminded not of the timelessness, but of the historicality, of the classical models.

From its initial publication to the most recent commentators, the poem has been recurrently criticized for a pedantic adherence to a theoretical purpose. When Kenneth and Miriam Allott deplore Arnold's "polished Homeric similes and studied repetitions of words and phrases," they echo the earliest reviewers.[15] Such a critical line assumes that the best poetry, or even "real" poetry, should be spontaneous and unpremeditated. But this is a special view of the poetic, and to judge "Sohrab and Rustum" in its terms is to mistake the very character of Arnold's work, which is—as much as the poetry of Lucretius or Pope—a poetry of ideas. Equally, and reciprocally, to say that the poem is a good (or a bad) classical imitation is to mistake, slightly but crucially, what is happening in the verse. Each of these misconceptions will come more clearly into focus if we remind ourselves of certain facts about Arnold's exercise in poetic imitation.

That is to say, we have to remind ourselves about the actual terms of the imitation. Homer, of course, is a most prominent presence: the *Iliad* is specifically recalled and imitated on numerous occasions. But the poem is also clearly imitating classical tragedy. When Arnold subtitled his poem "An Episode," he recalled the *epeisodion* of Greek tragedy, or that part of the action which takes place between two choruses. And, as Warren Anderson has observed, "The famous closing description of the Oxus has reminded more than one commentator of a tragic chorus."[16] But then too, more than one commentator has observed numerous distinctively un-Greek elements in Arnold's pastiche. When J. D. Coleridge reviewed the poem in *The Christian Remembrancer,* he pointed out that lines 116–125 are "a very direct and very successful imitation of Milton's manner,"[17] and Arnold subsequently acknowledged the imitation. But Milton's manner, and Keats's through Milton, is evident throughout the poem—as more than one commentator has also pointed out. The similes in the poem gesture toward Homer and invoke specific passages from the *Iliad,* but Arnold's manner of proceeding with them is distinctively Miltonic and Keatsian.[18]

The more one attends to this imitative aspect of the poem, the more one sees how macaronic a text "Sohrab and Rustum" is. Contemporary and near-contemporary imitation and transliteration abound: most notably, perhaps, Arnold's translations from Mohl's French version of Firdausi's Persian epic the *Shah Nameh,* but also his echoes of Tennyson, Shelley, and Gray. Furthermore—and perhaps most paradoxically for such a supposedly Hellenic work—Arnold's deliberate effort to "orientalize" his imagery produces a recurrent echoing of the King James Bible.[19] At several points this stylistic imitation becomes a specific echo and allusion: lines 815–819, for example, reach back to invoke 2 Samuel 18:33, where David laments the death of his son Absalom.

In this context one observes a curious and important detail. The poem's anagnorisis hinges on the seal which Rustum gave to Sohrab's mother to mark the arm of his child. Rustum recognizes and acknowledges his son when he sees the seal, "so delicately prick'd . . . on Sohrab's arm, the sign of Rustum's seal":

> It was that griffin, which of old rear'd Zal,
> Rustum's great father, whom they left to die,
> A helpless babe, among the mountain-rocks;
> Him that kind creature found, and rear'd, and loved—
> And Rustum took it for his glorious sign.   (677–683)

Several things are striking about this passage. I pass by for the moment the allusion to the Oedipus story, which is certainly important, and note that neither the *Shah Nameh* nor Mohl's translation says anything about the particular image on the seal. The griffin is Arnold's invention. And it is clear that Arnold understands the significance of the choice. The Persian griffin, called a Senmurv, is a hoard-guarding beast, half lion and half eagle. In fact, Arnold partly has in mind the details set out in Milton's extended simile in *Paradise Lost* (II, 943–947), where we find an allusion to the story of the one-eyed Arimaspians' efforts to steal the gold hoarded by the griffins. The story ultimately goes back to Herodotus (book 3, section 116). "Sohrab and Rustum" invokes the entire complex in its repeated association of Rustum with hoard-guarding. The set of associations is established early in the poem when Gudurz provokes Rustum into combat by taunting him with this image:

> Take heed, lest men should say:
> *"Like some old miser, Rustum hoards his fame,*
> *And shuns to peril it with younger men."*   (246–248)

But in a poem which so emphasizes its literary progenitors, the image of the griffin carries as well Dantean associations as a figure of Christ. This is specifically reinforced in Arnold's poem at the death of Sohrab: his dying posture recalls nothing so much as the death of Jesus, whose blood flows out—the image is a central iconograph of Christian redemption—when his side is pierced with the centurion's spear.

In short, the griffin-figure appears in the poem in a double perspective: associated with Rustum it is the hoard-guarding Senmurv and an oriental or "pagan" image, but associated with Sohrab it is Dante's salvific beast and a western or "Christian" image. In the Oedipal context, it is a riddling figure whose meaning has to be solved if Rustum is to understand himself and his highest values. In the biblical context it is a kind of typological figure which places the oriental Senmurv in a "redemptive" western context.

I HAVE GONE into this kind of detail because it emphasizes the strange act of "imitation" which Arnold's poem has carried out. Clearly "Sohrab and Rustum" is *not* simply an imitation of Homer. It is instead a polyglottal text moaning round with many voices. Indeed, the true "model" for this work is neither Homer nor any other early authority, it is contemporary: "Sohrab and Rustum" is modeled on an *idea,* on the philological imagination of originary texts—literally, on the Higher Criticism. This is why the work is so "studied," so brainy. Arnold's poem is a "reconstructed text" built from certain theoretical and methodological principles of textual analysis which he learned studying the works of antiquity, both Hebraic and Hellenic.

Yet Arnold *meant* to imitate Homer—that is very clear.[20] But his principles of imitation, based as they are in the new philology, turned his poem into a network of contradictions and anachronisms. That is to say, once the poem's method encourages us to listen for echoes and imitations, we will not be checked by the predominance of the

Homeric ones. The poem is many-layered, the principal strata being composed of classical, biblical, and contemporary materials. The apparent deviations from Arnold's "intention" to carry out a Homeric imitation are not, however, faults in the poem, they are part of its structure of incommensurability. Echoes of Tennyson and Milton are pointed out to Arnold, and he is forced to acknowledge them either as deliberate or unconscious presences.[21] And when we hear Keats in the poem—as we certainly do hear him, for example in lines 857–864—we realize how complex this work is that we are dealing with.

> So on the bloody sand, Sohrab lay dead;
> And the great Rustum drew his horseman's cloak
> Down o'er his face, and sate by his dead son.
> As those black granite pillars, once high-rear'd
> By Jemshid in Persepolis, to bear
> His house, now 'mid their broken flights of steps
> Lie prone, enormous, down the mountain side—
> So in the sand lay Rustum by his son.

This is, among other things, Arnold's version of Keats's picture of the fallen Saturn in his two *Hyperions*. The allusion to Keats is remarkable here only because the whole thrust of Arnold's preface was to argue for a classical alternative of simplicity, clarity, and wholeness as against the contrary practice of Shakespeare and Keats. Yet "Sohrab and Rustum" is by no means simple and clear, it is replete with a "multitude of voices counseling different things,"[22] including those Romantic voices Arnold wished to silence.

But "Sohrab and Rustum" is not a Romantic work, despite the fact that many Romantic elements have been gathered within it. The poem's imagination is dominated by fundamental brainwork rather than by spontaneity and the play of fancy. To see this is by no means to derogate from the poem, which is a splendid instance of a certain kind of Victorian work.

Furthermore, the whole project which this poem embodies helps to clarify the relation between a work's ideological investments and its incommensurable details. More than many works, "Sohrab and Rustum" was explicitly produced in a programmatic framework. The poem entered an important contemporary, and continuing, argument about poetry and its relation to culture, and it took a definite position on a series of relevant issues in that debate. This is what I have called its ideological horizon—a frame of reference most clearly defined through an investigation of the work's productive Mastercode. In taking its ideological stance, however, "Sohrab and Rustum" proceeded along the representational lines which are specific to the poetic. As a consequence, although the work defines itself, ideologically, in relation to a particular point of view within a specific horizon of human interests, the representational structure of poetic discourse multiplies and complicates the communicative act. Poetic performativity overtakes and finally overcomes ideological performativity as the poetic strives to thicken and realize the entirety of the communicative field.

Unlike predicative and propositional discourse, poetry is obliged, as it were, to present all sides of a question. This includes bringing forth, *within a sympathetic structure,* those details and points of view which are by ordinary measures incommensurate with themselves and with each other. The fact of the incommensurable only appears, however, because the poem has adopted a specific ideological vantage which declares certain things to be true and others not. The consequence is a certain kind of nonnormative discourse: not a discourse *without* norms, but one in which we observe the collision of many different and even contradictory norms.

Most typically—and here Arnold's 1853 *Poems* is an especially useful case history—a poetical work will generate those contradictions out of its own imagined commitments to a set of normative ideas. What we observe in Arnold's volume could be displayed just as well for, say, the *Lyrical Ballads,* or for any other book of poetry. The importance of this example from Arnold lies in the fact that it has dramatized the question of poetry's relation to society's norms for what is to be considered the "good" and the "true." Thus we read Arnold correctly when we read his book as a polemical work, as a work with certain truth commitments, and as a work which argues a relation between poetry and truth. We also read him correctly when we observe his normative criteria for truth; and, finally, we are just to his work when we outline the means by which it undermines its own normative criteria.

Thus we are not to draw a distinction between poetic and nonpoetic discourse by assigning, say, "functionality" to the latter and "autonomy" or "disinterestedness" to the former. Imaginative discourse does not stand apart from norms, imperatives, and ideologies. Operating in modes of representation, the poetic acts to display truth as a function of lived realities rather than formal relations or empirical correlations.

For this reason one must say that, of all forms of communication, the poetic alone entails the *whole* of what is true; and this is the case because in the domain of the poetic—the domain of Imagination and Memory—all the details, and all the forms through which those details are known, remain conceptually free, remain open to their own discovery.

PART II 〰

Adverse Wheels: Literature and the Work of Knowing

While obstinately seeking to establish aesthetic truth, and trapping themselves thereby in an irresoluble dialectic, [works of art] stumble on the real truth . . . and so contribute to the destruction of art which is its salvation.

Theodor Adorno, *Minima Moralia*

5 ⌘

Beginning Again: Literary Studies and the Crisis of Legitimation

A second time? why? man of ill star,
Facing the sunless dead and this joyless region?

Ezra Pound, *Canto I*

SOMETHING IS WRONG with the disciplines of knowledge. Throughout the consciousness industries today we hear and read troubled commentaries from the brightest and most advanced scholars and students. Yet in a quotidian view the situation may seem far from dire: technology in the human and the natural sciences appears quite vigorous, and practical scholarly intercourse is maintained at a high and well-funded level. The problems, apparently more fundamental, are expressed in various skeptical formulas. The ground myths which have authorized our disciplines of knowledge—that the truth will set us free, that knowledge brings control over the inimical resistances of nature, the self, and society—fail to comfort or persuade. Knowledge increases, but people no longer feel in possession of its mastery, freedom, and security. On the contrary, in fact; one may well recall Byron's Manfred who—from the summit of his all but absolute knowledge—could only lament its ineffectualness: "The Tree of Knowledge is not that of Life" (*Manfred* I: 1: 12).

In a celebrated report to the government of Quebec, Jean-François Lyotard, following upon the work of Jürgen Habermas, described and studied the "crisis of legitimation" in the industries of knowledge in the late twentieth century.[1] Briefly, what Lyotard diagnosed was the increasing tendency of knowledge to seek out and render problematic the axia of its own procedures and discourses. A great many events in the consciousness industries during the past two centuries have contributed to the development of this crisis: most notably, perhaps, the revolutionary advances in non-Euclidean mathematics in the nineteenth century, the advent of relativity physics and quantum mechanics, and—probably most crucial of all—the startling growth of cybernetics, information theory, and communications in the twentieth century. We have come to see that all of the discourses of knowledge—even the discourses of the so-called "hard sciences"—are socially and historically determined; that the ideal of scientific "objectivity" and the quest for universal statements are at best a heuristic and enabling mechanism for a certain kind of knowledge-discourse and at worst an ideology—an illusion—of truth; that knowledge, in short, is a function of the particular lexicon, grammar, and usage in which it is pursued and framed. We have even recognized that an important part of the industries of knowledge is involved not in acquiring new information or extending the range of its discourse, but in maintaining and legitimating the discourse itself.

In the natural sciences and, to a certain extent, in the social sciences as well, this legitimation crisis has been mitigated by science's appeal to "performativity" as its criterion of legitimacy. The knowledge industries are *useful,* not merely in immediate and evidently practical ways (such as technology), but as long-range, self-correcting procedures for dealing with human problems. Of course, nearly everyone is now a good deal more skeptical of these scientific claims in a world where so much evil and danger has been created by the pursuit of science itself. Nonetheless, science justifies itself by its praxis. It gets things done.

I rehearse this too-well-known story because it helps to explain the much more serious legitimation crisis which the humanities, especially the practice of literature, have to confront. In the larger context of knowledge-production, where the performative criterion measures both relevance and achievement, literary studies today do not command much more than a marginal authority and importance. Other human sciences—history, the various social studies, even philosophy—have been able to maintain a certain legitimacy in relation to the performative criterion. By contrast, literature seems at best a kind of recreation—and a rather old-fashioned kind at that. That most hip of poets, Frank O'Hara, put it very well: "if [people] don't need poetry bully for them. I like the movies too. And after all, only Whitman and Crane and Williams, of the American poets, are better than the movies."[2]

O'Hara's urbanity is, nonetheless, a hipster's defense. In this respect, O'Hara's new apology for poetry calls attention to the devaluation of the two most important arguments for literary work. The first—that literary works memorialize and preserve past wisdom and greatness—is hardly even to be considered; no one of any literary consequence today marches to that drummer any longer.[3] Certain critics—like Wellek, Booth, Abrams, and Graff—recognize the danger involved in giving up this line of argument, but none of them can legitimate it except negatively.[4] The chief traditional defense of poetry now argues that it trains and expands the mind and the imagination. It is a demanding intellectual exercise to try to come to grips with *King Lear* or *Ulysses,* and to read *Tom Jones* or *Tristram Shandy* or *Don Juan* is an event which will expand one's awareness, one's experience—ultimately, one's imagination. "Writing is a labyrinth," Geoffrey Hartman tells us, "a topological puzzle and textual crossword" in which one may and should get lost in order to find, to make, one's resources of freedom.[5]

But outside the literary academy, in the world we are creating and discovering in this century, such arguments carry less and less conviction. In a smaller and slower world—if one lived in Amherst, Massachusetts, in the mid-nineteenth century—then one might well and truly say, "There is no frigate like a book." But now books can appear the least powerful media for expanding awareness, experience, imagination. And as for training the mind to deal with complex systems—for entering and decoding those "labyrinths" which Hartman cherishes—one can easily find any number of other complex systemic forms that will do as well, or perhaps even better. Anyone who has worked with the productive resources of cybernetic systems understands the creative and critical challenges, and opportunities, which they make available—in music, in art, in writing itself. What is so special about those *literary* labyrinths guarded so cunningly by the professors? Besides, if one wants to expand the mind and imagination by seeking to understand, manipulate, and even master these other mediating and artificial systems, one gains the added benefit of learning materials and structures which can be put to any number of practical uses. What possible use can a literary education serve, other than to train other literary persons?

This question poses an important problem for literary studies—indeed, I should say for the entire consciousness industry—today. Nor will the problem be solved until one is able to explain what cognitive function is served by writing and philology. If literature is simply "free play" and recreation, it faces a true crisis of its legitimacy. Criticism now may disclose a rich fund of hermeneutic skills, but unless it can first show that the literary works themselves are a crucial part of the institutions of knowledge, then such skills will increasingly be developed and exercised in and for other fields and disciplines—in psychology, law, informatics, anthropology, communications, advertising—even in history or philosophy. To adopt (and adapt) a distinction drawn by E. D. Hirsch, Jr., we may, by our present praxis, lend *significance* to the literary works of the past, but can we also say that they have, in themselves, any *meaning?*[6]

This is the context in which the current intramural debates about literature are taking place. The recent burgeoning of subdisciplinary literary work in theory and method is a reaction to the general legitimation crisis—is, specifically, a search for new terms on which the activities of literature can be grounded. The poststructural phase of this crisis has proved to be decisive in overthrowing the last strongholds of formalist, immanent, and objectivist conceptions of knowledge. As a consequence the original agenda, established in the late eighteenth century, of setting the disciplines of knowledge on a new historical and archaeological grounding, has been freed of those a priorist formalities which crippled so much of that early, revolutionary work. The demise of objective teleologies, whether humanist (for example, Marxian) or theological, has freed knowledge from its illusory quest after definitive finalities and totalizations. For literary studies as such, this freedom has meant that hermeneutics—though necessarily an ideological activity—need no longer be *subject to* ideology.

This book argues that literary studies can now be reconceived in ways that are both theoretically and operationally persuasive. That is to say, the reconception is assimilable both as a program of research and as a pedagogical (most immediately, a classroom) technique. Indeed, it is my view that the present so-called crisis is the context in which this reconception is being realized.

The second, related object of this book is to situate literary studies within the larger framework of knowledge and its different programs. My argument here is that, among the human sciences, literary studies are fundamental and primary—just as, within literary studies themselves, the study of texts is fundamental and primary. Both are primary because in all these fields we have to begin with texts of one sort or another—with records, deposits, compositions, and recompositions of all kinds. Knowledge here depends upon our ability to manipulate, decipher, and deploy the textual constitutions which make up that second nature we have called, at various times, culture, civilization, the human.

Because interpretation is generally assumed to be the ultimate task of literary criticism, the legitimation crisis has produced a widespread effort to reconstitute a hermeneutic model that would answer to the poststructural problematic of the destabilized text. Two influential projects—those developed by Paul de Man and Stanley Fish—provide useful examples for elucidating the current limits to our thinking about literary work.

De Man's work is interesting because, as a response to the legitimation crisis, it has been judged by more traditional literary critics simply to have exacerbated that crisis. De Man practices a kind of negative hermeneutics. Traditionally, the textual exegete strives to preserve and redeploy the received texts as part of a comprehensive interpretive order. The procedure is basically allegorical, and success is measured by the range of literary materials which the hermeneutic order is able to account for, both explicitly and implicitly. De Man's famous dialectic of blindness and insight is a critical exposure of the limits of any hermeneutic program. De Man shows that every hermeneutic move—whether a local interpretive act performed on a particular passage or a more general set of propositions defining the structure of a method or a theory—is fated, as it were, to replicate the dialectic of blindness and insight.[7] As the meanings are deployed and the orders set forth, a corresponding network of darknesses begins to grow as well: the fault lines and errors which are the correspondent breeze (or desert simoom) of all we believe to be stable and true. It is a process captured perfectly in Hardy's poem "The Convergence of the Twain":

> And as the smart ship grew
> In stature, grace, and hue,
> In shadowy silent distance grew the Iceberg too.   (stanza 8)

Of the various hermeneutic moves taken to neutralize this kind of deconstructive critique, Stanley Fish's model of "interpretive communities"—a late variant of what used to be called "critical plural-ism"—is probably the most comprehensive. Fish avoids the de-constructive problematic by declaring that interpretation is not a mat-ter of knowledge or truth, but of rhetoric and rewards. He sees the academy as a particular example of the Spectacularized capitalist market in which different interpretations and interpretive schemes compete with each other. Success is the standard by which herme-neusis is judged: if a certain critical move is able to make its way, it is, in virtue of that fact, "correct." Of course, because the competition is keen, one must always be prepared to shift and change. What is "right" now has no special permanence or privilege. No one can have a monopoly on the market, and the market displays, over time, a wide selection of new and attractive goods.[8]

The great virtue of Fish's scheme is that he has tried to historicize and socialize, in contemporary terms, the general approach known as critical pluralism. Like Fish, critical pluralists emphasize the need to encourage a free exchange of literary ideas. Unlike Fish, however, they draw a sharp distinction between the economic market and the "marketplace of ideas." Literature is an ontological and not a social field of work. Deeply influenced by the poststructural critique of the determinate text and the authoritative critic, Fish builds a new house of pluralism on the de Manian ruins. Fish's project is to declare that there is no legitimation crisis, that all is well, that literature is simply one of the games that certain people play, for certain specific rewards.

Fish's project has, of course, outraged some of the most cherished literary ideals of the academy—for example, that literary work is, in its essential character, involved with truth, freedom, and disinterest-edness. Nonetheless, the flexibility and empirical salience of his project have given it wide currency. His work has been "successful": that is to say, he has "persuaded" the community of his peers that what he is saying makes sense. Note, however, that in order for Fish to "be successful" it has not been necessary that he secure general agreement with his position. Fish is and has been "successful" not because he has secured general agreement, but because he has persuaded people that what he is saying should be taken seriously.

This is very different from de Man's position, which is still deeply involved in the ontological problematics of literary discourse. The function of literature, according to de Man, is the traditional one of enforcing and maintaining "the crucial distinction between an em-pirical and an ontological self."[9] De Man's skepticism is, therefore, brooding and troubled, whereas Fish's is played out as a kind of hermeneutical game. The very titles of his essays, and of his most recent book, testify to this fact about his work. And indeed it is a good question whether Fish's work in this area *should* be taken seriously. Such a question never arises in the case of de Man because he is still concerned about the rightness and wrongness of literary judgments. Fish, on the contrary, is concerned with the (institutional) success which such judgments can bring.

Nonetheless, for all the differences between them, de Man and Fish represent the obverse and reverse of a single hermeneutic circle. This fact comes clearly into view if one interrogates their work on the issue of the rightness or wrongness of literary judgments. In each case what one discovers is that the "text," or object of interpretation, is part of a self-replicating system. In this respect we can see that each is a direct descendant of New Critical progenitors. Whereas the New Critics saw "the poem itself" as the model of a self-subsisting system, de Man and Fish speak for a whole later generation when they declare that the model for such self-subsistence is to be found in the structure (de Man) or institution (Fish) of literary discourse. Ultimately, both men propose justifying explanations for the way critical discourse is being carried out.

Though de Man's work operates in a deconstructive mode, and though it has been denounced as "nihilistic," his project is not to undermine the authority of the literary institution or literary knowledge. On the contrary, the thrust of his work has been to try to cure literary studies of the diseases of what he calls "scientism" and "mysticism."[10] The latter is literary studies carried out in an unreflective mode of mere appreciation, while the former is literary studies conceived as a discipline which is capable of positive knowledge. De Man argues that literature conveys knowledge—that it is not "mystic"— but he goes on to argue that its knowledge is shifting and relative. The negative aspect of its knowledge is the void it reveals "in the nature of things." The positive aspect appears as the stability of the knowing process itself, and hence as the potential stability in the individual knowing subject, whose "errors" are redeemed in the hermeneutic process.[11]

As Stanley Corngold has shown, one will not understand de Man without understanding the distinction between "error" and "mistake," which is crucial in his work.[12] For de Man, "the skew of error implies a truth,"[13] and the relation of error is restructured, in the act of criticism, as the interplay of blindness and insight. Mistakes, on the other hand, occur only in the domain of objectivist knowledge and information: "within the restricted teleology of pragmatic acts or within the quasi-rigorous language of scientific description."[14] These are not the domains of literature, whether poetry or hermeneutics. As I have already noted, de Man insists that literature be read so as to preserve the "crucial distinction between an empirical and an ontological self."[15]

The fault line in de Man's work runs along these basic distinctions he draws between error and mistake, ontological self and empirical self, objective (scientific) knowing and literary (hermeneutic) knowing. Indeed, the fault line *is* the assumption that the world of mistakes, science, and the empirical is a world of "knowledge" rather than a world of "knowing." "Literature," de Man says, "is the only form of language free from the fallacy of unmediated expression."[16] Literature has this status because, unlike scientific or everyday language, it "knows and names itself as fiction" and hence "asserts its separation from empirical reality." In short, "a literary text is not a phenomenal event that can be granted any form of positive existence, whether as a fact of nature or as an act of the mind."[17]

The mistake here faces in two directions. In the first place, literature is by no means the only form of language conscious of its mediated and fictive status. Indeed, de Man's own fundamental views about the "oscillations" of subject and object trace their origins back to the work of Bohr and Heisenberg in the early history of quantum mechanics. The principles of complementarity and uncertainty went far beyond the perspectivism of earlier Romantic thought—Nietzsche's, for example, or the Blakean principle that "the eye altering alters all"—and de Man's work reflects (though it does not emphasize) that radical advance. These breakthroughs in theoretical physics now function as part of the standard operating procedures of various empirical and technological work in science.

This historical fact is important to see because it exposes the weakness of de Man's distinction between the empirical and the ontological. This distinction is an error (it is not a mistake, as in the first instance) which frees de Man to study literary texts in the mode that he does, that is, as self-reflexive discourse systems. A distinction between the empirical and the ontological can be *drawn,* of course, but it can also *not* be drawn. Outside of quantum mechanics a distinction is drawn between the subject and the object, but it is a distinction which is not and which cannot be drawn inside that field. The work done in quantum mechanics shows, therefore—to adapt de Man's terminology —that "positive knowledge" is possible even in cases where the phenomena to be studied are neither facts of nature nor acts of the mind. This turns out to be possible when the phenomena are *both* facts of nature *and* acts of the mind. De Man *mistakenly* believes that this situation cannot occupy, or be occupied with, "any form of positive existence." He then *erroneously* separates the worlds of hermeneutical and of positive knowledge in order to establish a pair of working premises: first, that hermeneutics deals with phenomena that are *both* facts of nature *and* acts of mind, and hence with phenomena that have no "positive existence"; and second, that science deals with matters of "positive existence," and hence with phenomena which are *either* facts of nature *or* acts of mind.

These distinctions, however, are heuristic and (to use a de Manian term) "rhetorical." They are drawn for certain purposes, at least some of which are plain enough: to situate literary studies as an autonomous activity whose aesthetic "mode of existence" does not occur in social space, and whose instituted structures and genealogies (individual and social) have no essential bearing on the hermeneutic operation; to define literary work as a faultless play of texts and hence to insulate it—both the originary and the secondary texts—from anything but insightful error (it cannot make mistakes and, most of all, it can do neither right nor wrong). These purposes, however, place such limits upon literary work that they themselves generate a counterurgency, a plea for other distinctions which will provide poetry and hermeneutics with self-conscious tools for dealing with ideology and deploying value. For the fact is that though we may bracket out such issues from literary discourse, they remain a presence which is not to be put by.

De Man himself felt the presence of that counterurgency as much as anyone. The last phase of his work—the material produced in the 1980s—sought to develop a rhetorical analysis which could accommodate the issues raised by ideology-critique and various kinds of "New Historical" criticism. But de Man's late work did not carry him out of those fundamental critical structures which he had developed earlier. The "rhetoric" and "performativity" of literary work which de Man was exploring remain wholly intertextual events because de Man was unable or unwilling to theorize literature as a concrete social institution. The limitation is very clear in *The Rhetoric of Romanticism* (1984) and *Allegories of Reading* (1979), but it extends as well to his very last works, such as the papers and lectures on Kant and Hegel. The "phenomenality and materiality in Kant" are elucidated in hermeneutic and ontological terms which bracket out attention to the way "Kant" performs, phenomenally and materially, in his sociohistorical field. Here de Man is still working within critical structures analogous to those he applied to Nietzsche and Rousseau. Similarly, "Sign and Symbol in Hegel's *Aesthetics*" repeats de Man's programmatic idea that literary works function primarily as symbols rather than as signs, and that when they do operate in structures of signification, what they signify is their own intertextuality ("allegories of reading").[18]

The great merit of de Man's criticism, from a social and ethical rather than a purely technical point of view, is the same as what we value in Derrida and the deconstructive movement generally: its ability to expose the contradictory status of the many myths of totalization and finality which our cultures have fostered. De Man usually concentrates on what he calls the myth of "unmediated knowledge." The weakness of the position is that it hems literary work within a very narrow and skeptical mode. For all its use of language, literature has little to say or do beyond itself. It is a system of language events; the poet is the programmer of the events, and the critic is their technician. Both are highly skilled, but neither deals with the events in terms of the larger field of which they are a part, with which they interact, and on which they exert their own influence.

We see this in de Man and the many critics he discusses when we reflect on what "interpretation" means in such work. In the first place, the production of interpretations is all but universally regarded as the function of criticism. This opinion about criticism, historically considered, represents a remarkable shift away from the critical modes which dominated well into the twentieth century. Only in the past fifty years or so have we witnessed this amazing revival of neo-Platonic (*not* Platonic) thought, in which criticism has decided that the originary texts either are, or represent themselves to be, the carriers of totalized meanings, and hence that the object of criticism is to reveal— or, finally to deconstruct—those meanings. Such an allegorical/symbolic conception of the poetic text is a tributary stream in the history of criticism until our immediate period. This historical fact is important to remember if literature is to reconceive its purposes and possibilities.

In the second place, as the "meanings" and "interpretations" which are seen to lie at the heart of literary works proliferate, the activities which generate them suffer the threat of trivialization (now called "the anxiety of influence" or "the burden of the past"). De Man's criticism, a model of deconstruction, typifies such work in its refusal to interrogate the grounds of an interpretive hermeneutics. Literary production, both original and critical, stands Beyond the Reflex Principle, an autonomous and self-validating activity where poetic meaning and the reflection of/on poetic meaning are purely intertextual events.

Numerous commentators have demurred at this separation of literature from "life" and "the world"—at the separation of *meaning* from its social ground and structure. The demurrals are justified, though I have not yet found in these commentators any detailed proposals for retheorizing literary meanings within their social ground. After the work of critics like de Man and Derrida, however, nothing less than a general reconception of "the mode of existence" of literary work will serve.

Because of the peculiar historical development of the concept of literary autonomy over the past two centuries, such a reconception, I believe, will have to begin with an investigation into the status of meaning in the particular work, the so-called "poem itself." A more general theory of literary meaning (along with the methodologies for deploying and studying such meanings) has to wait upon the presentation of a "special theory," as it were, because, *at this point in time,* the institutional assumption of the autonomy of art is grounded in the practice of what we call "close reading of the text" or, more generally, "interpretation."

The object of this kind of close reading and interpretation is to produce as complete an account as possible of the single and entire work in all its details. The "integrity" of the "work" is assumed, if not in empirical fact then at least in ontological idea. Also assumed is the idea that the purpose of hermeneutics is to reflect upon that poetic totalization, for one cannot come to grips with any of the work's particulars without understanding their function in the "organic" whole. These general goals of interpretation help to explain the dominant place which the individual work has assumed in twentieth-century critical activity: interpretive reflection discovers a practical model for its largest goals in the exercises with particular poems which were first systematically laid down in the New Criticism. These models have not been departed from by critics who found their voices in the world of structural and poststructural discourse.

Of course, we now understand that the goal of a totalized interpretation, even of a particular work, is an illusion, an impossible building as it were. What we do not understand is how interpretation is to proceed under such conditions. What is to be the "positive" or "objective" function of literary praxis? De Man himself understands that this problem cannot be finally evaded, that at some point the intertextual system will have to bear recognition as a positive entity, even a social entity. How is literature to declare and justify itself outside its own procedural and institutional structures?

De Man's response to this problem is extremely interesting. In the first place, he takes it for granted that literary work is a useful discipline of self-reflection. This is a traditional position, and de Man does not spend much effort or space in its explication. What draws his principal attention is what his critics have denominated as his "nihilism." In de Man's view, the repeated theme or moral which literature delivers up—under the pressure of interpretation—is the negative and "quasi-objective" knowledge that there is a void in (human) nature, "the unovercomable distance which must always prevail between the selves."[19] De Man calls this an "objective" or "positive" knowledge, we must assume, because it is socially dispersed, a general condition which is the shared possession, or experience, of all human beings; and it is "quasi" objective, presumably, either because it is knowledge of a negative or because it is not a knowledge which all people share in (conscious) *fact*.

The interesting aspect of de Man's critical work here is not that it shows a supposedly "nihilist" thematic ground, but that it has been driven to any thematic ground at all. Literature is not just an activity of knowing, a neutral subjectless and objectless process. It is a process within which neutralization is both operation and topic of concern. Traditional meanings, the old transactions of the author and the reader, yield to a new meaning: that author and reader are transacted by "the text." This new meaning, moreover, is very like the old meanings, that body of all the best that has been known and thought in the world. That is to say, the new meaning is transcendent and totalized, a "universal" meaning.

De Man is not wrong to think that his "nihilist" meanings carry general significance. The error lies in suggesting that the logical contraries and contradictories of such meanings may not or will not carry equally general significance. If literary work reveals "the unovercomable distance which must always prevail between the selves," it also reveals proximities and continuities; and sometimes it reveals nothing of these sorts at all, and sometimes it displays its revelations as occasional or random. Sometimes its conflicting displays are most apparent in different texts, sometimes in a single text; and sometimes these conflicts are wholly unapparent, or apparent but peripheral. The point is that any hermeneutic criticism is constrained to produce a thematized form of literary knowledge: a body of meanings or interpretations. Like all formalist hermeneuts, however, de Man does not see that the structure of such knowledge is fundamentally proverbial. We may wish to say, with Matthew Arnold (and de Man), that "we mortal millions live alone"; but we also wish to say, with Donne, that "no man is an island."

Both ideas, as ideas, are part of the best—and the worst—that has been known and thought in the world. Regarding them as literary ideas, however, Arnold was right; they are only part of the best. What is "best" about the literary form of knowledge is that it cannot deliver its knowledge in schematic or ideological forms without violating its own premises. This is the case because literary forms do not permit the archive of knowledge to be reduced to the abstractness of proverbs or the illusions of ideology. Literary forms deploy such abstractions and illusions all the time, but they dispel these ghostly shapes by transforming them into recognizable human forms: by incarnating them in worlds that are detailed, specific, and circumstantial. A thematizing hermeneutics which does not emphasize the sociohistorical particularities of the literary ideas and knowledge which it deploys runs a grave risk, therefore, of reproducing ideology rather than literature.

The work of de Man, and of deconstruction generally, provides an extremely useful instance of critical activity. Its critique of earlier formalist and thematizing hermeneutics has been a wholly positive—if also wholly technical—achievement.[20] Its critique, however, is a revision, a modification which has preserved the distance between literature and its sociohistorical ground. As a consequence, we will not find in that work any practical changes in the following crucial areas: first, the status of the "isolated" work of art and its place in the practice of literary criticism; second, the function of ideas and ideology in literary work; and third, the precise relation of literary work to the larger human world in which it is carried on and with which it interacts.

Thus the de Manian deconstruction of criticism is finally a benevolent and conserving set of operations for both the critic and the received literary works. Critics typically set out to "explain" or even to "demystify" their poetical texts, but de Man argues that neither object is possible. Every "explanation" intervenes with the object to be explained and thereby places it perpetually beyond the grasp of the explanatory operation. As for "demystifying" the hermeneutic object, this too remains impossible because such texts are self-consciously "fictive" and hence are "demystified from the start."[21] Literature remains, then, untouched by the razors of criticism—as Matthew Arnold once said it should: "Others abide our queston. Thou art free . . ." What happens in literary studies, therefore, is the deconstruction of the reader: "When modern critics think they are demystifying literature, they are in fact being demystified by it; but since this necessarily occurs in the form of a crisis, they are blind to what takes place within themselves."[22] This necessary blindness in the hermeneut is what drives de Man "to write critically about critics,"[23] which is one of his most characteristic modes. Writing about criticism is, for de Man, the most advanced form of critical discourse, since criticism of criticism is the "way to reflect upon the paradoxical effectiveness of a blinded vision that has to be rectified by means of insights that it unwittingly provides."[24] The salutary, if painful, effect of literary studies is, then, the secondary "insight" that succeeds upon the initial interpretive event where blindness and insight operate together in the reading of originary texts. This secondary insight is basically a Socratic one, the self-knowledge of a particular person— a particular literary person, a reader of texts—who comes to understand that he or she shares the fate of all readers: the inability "to report correctly what [has been] perceived in the course of [the interpretive] journey."[25]

One might think that de Man's oscillating ratios of blindness would lead him to a skepticism about his own conclusions. The "logic" of his logic might be read skeptically, so that the final "insight" into the character of critical activity would be judged an unstable truth. De Man does not read his own texts as self-deconstructing, however, but argues that they are exercises in self-knowledge which lead to "quasi-objective" truth. "Literature [is] a primary source of knowledge," he argues, because it is able "to give rational integrity to a process that exists independently of the self."[26]

If we turn to the work of Stanley Fish, we observe a similar intention to preserve and justify the known world of literary criticism. Like de Man, Fish has a reputation for being a severe controversialist—a critic of critics. And indeed he does often engage in arguments with other critics. Once again, however, his message is entirely benevolent and conservative. Critical disputes are a function of "interpretive communities" which provide specific readers with hermeneutic codes for "interpreting texts." Once again we are dealing with a fluid but internally self-replicating system. In such a world—as in de Man's—there is no room for radically antithetical moves. The absence of any Lucretian swerve turns hermeneusis into various mirroring operations. Persistences and changes are functions of codes that have been pre-established.

In a superficial view Fish may appear to be simply another adherent to the idea of the unstable text because he insists that interpretation is the art of making rather than the art of construing. But in fact Fish is little concerned with whether the "text" is (in fact, in itself) "unstable" or with whether the act of interpreting is (or is not) a display of the free imagination. These are unanswerable—even uninteresting—questions to him. What he wants to show is the commonality of the interpretive process. Indeed, what most engages Fish is the desire to legitimate and justify the current institution of literary studies. Far from attacking or undermining that institution—he has been accused of both—Fish insists that his "message . . . is finally not challenging, but consoling—not to worry."[27] We are afraid of an illusion if we are troubled by the idea that "interpreters do not decode poems; they make them."[28] In Fish's hands this idea does not carry any bad consequences for the practice of literary studies—on the contrary, in fact: "One can respond with a cheerful yes to the question 'Do readers make meanings?' and commit oneself to very little because it would be equally true to say that meanings, in the form of culturally derived interpretive categories, make readers."[29] The "consequence" of Fish's theoretical arguments will make no difference in the practice of criticism. The institution will go on doing what it is doing—whatever it is doing. Indeed, Fish will go on to argue that no theoretical argument has or can have consequences for interpretive practice. Theory is just another type of literary activity, and the system is accommodating. Not to worry.

But in fact Fish's arguments do have consequences,[30] and the most important of these is the uncritical validation of all literary practice within a self-legitimating system of *de facto* practices. What legitimates literary practice, as all of Fish's central metaphors indicate, is the specific material rewards which can be reaped by those who operate successfully in the system. Poetry and philology are conceived as types of social praxis, but the conceptual scheme is at all points defined in entrepreneurial and capitalist terms. When Fish says that the practice of theory carries no consequences, he might just as well have said that the practice of literature carries no consequences. For what he means is that they carry no cognitive or critical consequences. They do carry consequences, however: their praxis brings various material rewards. In addition, literary studies conceived or carried out in a Fishian mode have the not inconsequential result of reifying a capitalistic definition of literary studies.

As different as Fish and de Man can be, then, they share several crucial ideas about literary practice. De Man's nihilism is entirely correspondent to Fish's inconsequence because neither can see that such practice has any transpersonal functions. To de Man literature still has a critical function, but this is relegated to personal self-reflection. Literature has no "positive existence," self-reflection no necessary social relation. To Fish, on the other hand, literature has no critical function—it is "inconsequential"; and while it is seen as a form of social praxis, that praxis is limited to personal acquirements and gratifications.

Both men also agree that criticism is fundamentally a hermeneutic activity. When Fish says that "thematizing remains the primary mode of literary criticism,"[31] he iterates one of the deepest commonplaces of current literary thinking. For his part, when de Man states that "neither reading nor writing resemble action; both tend to fuse in their common deviation from referential models, whether they be things, acts, or feelings,"[32] he underwrites another critical commonplace of our period. This is de Man's version of Fish's inconsequence.

I have concentrated on these two critics because their work defines with particular clarity the premises of most literary-critical work currently operating, at least in the United States. Their respective projects, moreover, are explicitly developed in response to the legitimation crisis as it appears in literature. And while both formulate apologies for literary work, it should be obvious that neither has cleared away the judgments or attitudes which underlie the delegitimation of literary studies. This inadequacy results from their continued adherence to an intertextual model of literary production, on one hand, and a hermeneutic model of literary reproduction on the other. Under such a view both the cognitive and the ideological functions of literary work are undermined in the commitment to the idea of the work's autonomy. As a consequence literature loses what Paul Ricoeur has called its "critical instance"[33]—loses it, on the de Manian side, in self-reflection and social disengagement, and, on the Fishian side, in self-promotion and social reification.

Ricoeur's analysis of the debate between hermeneutics and critical theory—and specifically between Gadamer and Habermas—has elucidated very well why hermeneutics has been unable, even if it is not unwilling, to institute a critique of ideology.[34] I began this chapter by sketching the legitimation crisis as it is reflected in current literary practice because, like Ricoeur, I accept Habermas's representation of that crisis. Because modern states—capitalist and socialist alike—are more committed "to eliminating the disfunctions of the industrial system" than to representing the interests of a dominant class, the principal feature of these systems "is the productivity of rationality itself, incorporated into self-regulating systems; what is to be legitimated, therefore, is the maintenance and growth of the system itself."[35] As Baudrillard and many others have shown, systematization is now global, having completely appropriated the "critical instance" once represented by international socialism.[36] And as for the (polarized) interpretive procedures of de Man (reflective) and Fish (productive), neither develops a "critical instance" because both practice a system-regulating hermeneutics. These two cases are important to understand because, as antithetical as their exegetical practices can seem, they are, from a Habermasian or critical perspective, cooperative ventures. They therefore typify, together, the programs and possibilities of a hermeneutics which is committed merely to interpretive action: to borrow a school metaphor, merely to reading and writing. They will serve.

What I have been saying to this point about the problematic in contemporary hermeneutics is offered not as an argument but as a corroborative sketch of what, I assume, is already recognized to be the case. The sketch has two functions: first, to suggest that a comprehensive argument against our current literary commonplaces is unnecessary—because that argument is, in fact, already in place and functioning as the legitimation crisis; and second, to indicate the conditions under which one must abandon forensics in favor of an alternative model.

Such a model may be found by exploring in detail the institutional function of literary work: the production and reproduction of ideology. In our current epoch this activity reflects and reproduces social values like system-regulation and marketing (the ideal of consumption). Whatever the historically specific character of its ideologies, however, authentic literary work, both productive and reproductive, has always mediated the contradictions which ideology necessarily both represses and, in virtue of that fact, sustains. This truth about literature explains why conservative and reactionary work—or even work which may simply appear past and irrelevant—is able to maintain a "critical instance." Whether seen from a mimetic or a mediative position, poetry carries—and carries out—social contradictions. Similarly, since the pursuit of knowledge takes place in terms of (the conficts of) human interests, and since this is as true of the pursuit of literary knowledge (philology) as of any other kind, hermeneutics is equally marked by the conflicts it suppresses or promotes.

In an adequate critical practice, therefore, literary texts are to be seen and treated as communicative actions—the deeds of those who operate in one part of the field of ideology production. As elsewhere, then, I distinguish the term "text" from the term "work" when speaking of the literary object because I would emphasize that literature is always something that is *done,* is always a function of active agencies. In this assumption I am seeking to accommodate a Habermasian perspective to literary work. Similarly, I take for granted the Bakhtinian insight that both text and work are heteroglot—indeed, that heteroglossia in literature locates the patterns of domination and resistance which make up all conflicts of human interests.[37]

In terms of the recent history of criticism and hermeneutics, therefore, I would argue the need to appropriate critically four influential modes of discourse: historicism, formalism (structuralism), deconstruction, and Marxism. Through these modes of discourse we save and reimagine the past and the works it delivers into our hands. These modes dominate our current thinking, but they operate in relation to each other in a variety of uneasy half-connections, accommodations, and antitheses. The global reality of our literary work tells us that we cannot do without any of these modes of discourse, but it also tells us that we have not been able to imagine their mutual dynamics. That imagining should not proceed from or conclude in a structure of ideas. The aim is rather to incorporate these four great modes in a series of functional operations where the limits of each can be tested, and their deficiencies, we hope, supplied.

From historicism we draw an appreciation of the concrete forms of a particular sociohistory and an awareness of the facticity of independent worlds; from formalism, models of synchronic order for diachronic randomness; from deconstruction, procedures for destabilizing the self-conceptions of a discourse; and from Marxism, an activist theory of human society and history, with corresponding demands for commitment to the promotion of fundamental social change. Each of these critical forms has its peculiar powers and limitations which the other forms work to expose.

The first three are fundamentally technologies for gathering, organizing, and reorganizing specific bodies of knowledge and forms of thought. As such, they function, among themselves, to modify their respective intramural procedures and ideas.[38] Their critical relation to each other operates, however, within the horizon of literary work conceived as an autonomous activity. (This is why we must speak of them as "technologies.") Consequently, although each performs, in relation to the other two, imperative critical functions—positively, to widen the experiential field, and negatively, to emancipate the mind from its self-constructed limits—all three lie open, in a Marxist perspective, to the danger of inconsequence.

The Marxist vantage is in this sense (as Sartre pointed out some time ago) the most comprehensive of these critical forms.[39] Yet the scope of its pretensions can easily weaken its pragmatic grip upon what is local and immediate, both at the level of theory and at the level of fact. This is as true for literary as for social studies. The other three modes of discourse are all more effective in dealing with texts and literary work at their micro-levels. On the other hand, only the Marxist perspective preserves the idea of social change as a *concrete* imperative—as a demand laid upon individuals in their particular social and institutional conditions. Literary work is implicated in that demand because such work is at the heart of what we call "ideology," that is, the forms and ways "in which meaning (signification) serves to sustain relations of domination."[40] The Marxist critique, therefore, holds all the others open to their largest responsibilities.

To deploy these four modes of critical discourse in a fruitful series of antithetical exchanges is the procedural object of criticism—or rather, should be its object. One speaks here for criticism as it is

practiced in the theater of the Euro-American cultural empire. Similarly, the principal substantive interest of such criticism lies in what
has been called "the uses of the past," that is to say, in the functional
relation which our inherited cultural materials, whether traditional
or marginal, have for the present.

Why are we committed to these things? The brief answer is: because
they represent, and themselves enact, programmatic goals which simultaneously display their own insufficiencies, alienations, self-con-
tradictions. Only imaginative work does this: *et tout le reste est idéologie.*

The ideal of a critical act is to explicate these agencies of imagination. If we do not wish to be enslaved by our insularities (which
mask themselves as hegemonies), to have our practices of knowledge
reified, we shall have to imagine what we know. For literary work—
imaginative and critical alike—locates what is complex and heterological in our sociohistories; it shows that all of these histories are,
to adapt Marshall Sahlins's trenchant formulation, no more than
"islands of history."[41] As interpreters of texts, including the (alienated)
texts of our own past, we are in the position of Captain Cook ap-
proaching the Hawaiian Islands: islanded ourselves and confronted—
all unknowing—with the illusions of our knowledge and the realities
of what we do not know. Nor is blindness here a sentimental drama
of the interpreting mind—that is only one of our last interpretive
illusions. Blindness here is a social failure, the collapse of one's ability
not merely to read symbols, but to understand their social reality, to
understand how those symbols simultaneously function as signs *precisely in and through their symbolical status.* Writing and reading are
social acts with public and transpersonal agencies and consequences.
The question is whether, as citizens of an imperial world, as "imperial
intellects," we have yet any desire, or capacity, to discover our insularities.[42]

6 ⟨∞⟩

The Scandal of Referentiality

> We feel as if we had to penetrate phenomena: our investiga-
> tion, however, is directed not toward phenomena, but, as
> one might say, the "possibility" of phenomena.
>
> Ludwig Wittgenstein, *Philosophical Investigations*

MY TITLE HERE is taken from a passing reference Geoffrey Hartman once made in a lecture. He was reflecting on the development of the immanent critical traditions of the twentieth century, along with their authorizing premise: that literary works are self-enclosed objects, or looped intertextual fields of autonomous signifiers and signifieds. This view, initially applied exclusively to the literary text—that is, to the *objects* of literary criticism—helped to supply the New Criticism and its stepchildren, structuralism and intertextual studies, with their basic frames of reference. Later, however, it underwrote as well the programs of reader-response and deconstructive criticism, where the focus of attention shifted from the literary work to the critical eye which sought to gain knowledge of the work.

Each of these cases represents an effort to break away from the philological and historicist programs of study which dominated the theory of texts from the late eighteenth to the early twentieth century. From the point of view of the later, immanentist programs, these earlier programs all fell into what Umberto Eco has called "the Referential Fallacy"—that is, "the belief that an actual state of the world must underwrite the functioning of every semiotic entity."[1] This Referential Fallacy is merely the most comprehensive formulation of a host of other "fallacies" turned up by twentieth-century minds. The Affective Fallacy, the Fallacy of Imitative Form, the Intentional Fallacy: all were deep pits awaiting those who went forth unarmed with the new literary technologies.

It is to Hartman's credit that he spoke, in his characteristically ironical mode, of the *scandal* of referentiality. For while he could not see any theoretical way around the presence of the literary referent, he was at the same time quite aware that the contemporary theologies of immanentism have not banished it altogether from our attention—indeed, that they must not and cannot do so.

Of this state of affairs two things may be initially said. First, referentiality appears as "a problem" in formalist and text-centered studies precisely by its absence. Though everyone knows and agrees that literary works have sociohistorical dimensions, theories and practices generated in text-centered critical traditions bracket out these matters from consideration, particularly at the level of theory.[2] Second, referentiality appears as a problem in historically grounded criticism because such criticism has thus far been unable to revise its theoretical bases so as to take account of the criticisms which were brought against it in this century, in particular the criticisms developed out of the theory of literary mediations. Involved here is the view, pressed strongly on various fronts in the past fifty years, that language and language structures (including, perforce, literary works) are modeling rather than mirroring forms. They do not point to a prior, authorizing reality (whether "realist" or "idealist"), they themselves *constitute*—in both senses—what must be taken as reality (both "in fact" and "in ideals"). To the extent that traditional forms of historical criticism have not been able to assimilate or refute such ideas, to that extent those historicist traditions have been moved to the periphery of literary studies.

In recent years, however, textual and intertextual approaches have begun to yield up their own theoretical problems, and literary studies have witnessed a renewed interest in various kinds of sociohistorical critical work. Marxist and Marxist-influenced criticism has been especially important in this event, largely, I think, because the questions it poses are founded in a powerful and dynamically coherent tradition of critical inquiry. Feminist studies have also done much to expose the sociohistorical dimensions of literary work. Because both of these critical approaches necessarily practice a hermeneutics of a repressed or invisibilized content, both have found no difficulty in assimilating the basic poststructural programmatic. At the same time, the traditional methods of historicist philology have also begun to reappear in interpretive studies. Bibliography, manuscript studies of various kinds, analyses of the forms, methods, and materials of literary production: these materialist and empirical branches of learning have begun to renew their theoretical ground. Hermeneutical studies are increasingly realizing that the symbolic discourse which is literature operates with and through many forms of mediation besides "language," narrowly conceived. The price of a book, its place of publication, even its physical form and the institutional structures by which it is distributed and received, all bear upon the production of literary meaning, and hence all must be critically analyzed and explained.

When we speak of the referential dimensions of literary work, therefore, we have in mind several different things. In the first place, literary work can be practiced, can constitute itself, only in and through various institutional forms which are not themselves "literary" at all, though they are meaning-constitutive. The most important of these institutions, for the past 150 years anyway, are the commercial publishing network in all its complex parts and the academy. The church and the court have, in the past, also served crucial mediating functions for writers. Literary works are produced *with reference to* these mediational structures, are in fact embodied in such structures, and criticism is therefore obliged to explain and reconstitute such structures in relation to the literary work. As we now realize more clearly than ever before, criticism must factor itself and its own mediations into its explanations. In the final accounting, "the work" and its mediations are as inseparable as are "the (original) work" and its (subsequent) critical explanations.

HISTORICALLY, the problem of referentiality first appeared not as a fault line in empirically based critical studies, but much earlier, in the Kantian response to the philosophic grounds of empiricism. Derrida's influential account of the textual dynamic ("the joyous affirmation of the play of the world and of the innocence of becoming, the affirmation of a world of signs without fault, without truth, without origin, offered to an active interpretation")[3] recalls nothing so much as the opening of Kant's *Critique of Judgment,* in which the radical subjectivity of the aesthetic event is founded—indeed, is founded via an explication of the judging subject rather than the "work of art." Coleridge's important variation on this Kantian move was to emphasize even more clearly the "ideal" content which the poetic text constitutes. Poetical works do not "copy" the phenomena of the external world, they "imitate" the ideal forms which we know through the operations of the human mind.[4] As a good recent critic of Coleridge has put the matter: "The 'reality' that poems 'imitate' is not the objective world as such, but . . . the consciousness of the poet himself *in his encounters with* the objective world . . . The poet's only genuine subject matter is himself, and the only ideas he presents will be ideas about the activity of consciousness in the world around him."[5] Coleridge's critique of the insistently referential aspects of Wordsworth's poetry—what he calls its "accidentiality" and its "matter-of-factness"—is the critical reflex of his positive position: that "poetry as poetry is essentially *ideal,* [and] avoids and excludes all *accident* [and] apparent individualities."[6]

Coleridge is himself an impressive historicist critic, as his commentaries on the biblical tradition show. Nevertheless, his theoretical ground would eventually be appropriated by those idealist and subjectivist forms of criticism which emerged out of twentieth-century linguistics and semiology. If "poetry as poetry" has reference only to a field of subjectivity, then the criticism and interpretation of poetry which pursue the accidentalities and matters-of-fact of philology will itself be misguided.

Coleridge's view is recapitulated, in a variety of ways, by all twentieth-century practitioners of purely immanent critical methods. C. S. Lewis's remarks on "The Personal Heresy" in 1934, and Cleanth Brooks's in *The Well Wrought Urn* in 1947, typify the New Critical position on the matter of poetry's relation to sociohistorical actualities.[7] That is to say, while the New Criticism was a vigorously antihistorical movement, and consciously in reaction to the traditions of philological and historicist methods which had come to preeminence in literary studies during the eighteenth and nineteenth centuries, it always made practical provision for certain "extrinsic" materials in the poetic product. Their position is epitomized in Wellek and Warren's widely used handbook *Theory of Literature* (1949), in which the concepts of "intrinsic" and "extrinsic" interpretation are enshrined. Equally characteristic are formulations like the following by Cleanth Brooks, who means to have an organic-intrinsic idea of the poem, but cannot altogether evade the informational-extrinsic dimensions of the text: "If we see that any item in a poem is to be judged only in terms of the total effect of the poem, we shall readily grant the importance for criticism of the work of the linguist and the literary historian."[8]

In short, the intrinsic and text-centered approaches of the early and middle twentieth century made certain tactical accommodations and compromises in their critical programs and arguments. Indeed, it was precisely this compromised status of their theory which brought them to ruin at the hands of their ungrateful children, the deconstructionists. For the latter had no difficulty in showing that New Critical strategies were based upon an illusory and mystified form of the very empiricism which those strategies were consciously designed to displace. The idea of "the poem itself," of the stable (if paradoxical) object of critical attention, was swept away in the aftermath of structuralism. "De-ferral," "de-stabilization," "de-centering," "de-construction": the history of the emergence of these ideas during the 1970s is well known and needs no rehearsing again here. Nor will it be necessary to point out what is equally well known, that the deconstructionist movement was (and of course is) a form of immanent criticism's twentieth-century wilderness.

Two important aspects of these late forms of immanent criticism do need to be attended to, however. The first is the extremity of their antihistorical position. None of the earlier twentieth-century text-centered critics ever spoke, as Hillis Miller has spoken in one of his most celebrated essays, of "the fiction of the referential, the illusion that the terms of the poem refer literally to something that exists."[9] This bold pronouncement offers a final solution to the problem of the social actuality of poetical work, and it is quite typical of at least the American deconstructive establishment. The repudiation of referentiality is made, as Miller says, "according to the logic of a theory of language which bases meaning on the solid referentiality of literal names for visible physical objects."[10] Here Miller intends to dispose once and for all of that Great Satan of so many humanists, "empiricism," by dismissing at last the supposed "theory of language" on which it rests.

In making his attack, however, Miller unwittingly exposes another important aspect of his critical position. That is to say, he reveals his assent to a particular concept of referentiality. A "solid" correspondence of "literal names for visible physical objects" is certainly *an* idea of referentiality, but it is manifestly an impoverished concept.

This idea of how language "refers" to the actual world where those language forms called poems operate may reflect the view which someone (besides Miller) has held at some time or other. It is not, in any case, characteristic of the thought of the great traditional philological and historical critics. When Miller dismisses this concept of referentiality, then, he is merely trying to cast out a phantom. His dismissal confirms his own critical practice on the ground of an irreality.

Of course one can, with some searching, find other critics who have subscribed to excessively simple concepts of referentiality. When Daniel Aaron, for example, says that "the historian who writes about the past might be likened to a naturalist as he observes and analyzes specimens in a museum or perhaps animals caged in a zoo,"[11] his words betray a concept of referentiality that is comparable to Miller's. One merely wants to say that this is not a persuasive idea, and that it runs counter to the lines of historical thought which have dominated criticism for almost three centuries. But one might better do more, and quote, for example, Vico's stronger thought, that "human history differs from natural history in this, that we have made the former, but not the latter."[12] Indeed, it is Miller's sympathy with Vico's thought which has helped to set him, along with so many other recent literary critics, in opposition to what he calls "referentiality."

What is necessary at this juncture, therefore, is not to bracket the referential dimensions of poetry out of critical consideration on the basis of an improverished theory of language and literary reference. Rather, we should be trying to recover and reformulate the idea of referentiality which underlies the thought of the great historical critics of the recent past. Only in this way will the full significance of Miller's excellent critical work—and the work of many other immanentist critics—be revealed. The American line of Derridean thought in particular would do well to recall the following passage from Derrida himself: "A deconstructive practice which would not bear upon 'institutional apparatuses and historical processes' . . . , which would remain content to operate upon philosophemes or conceptual signified[s], or discourses, etc., would not be deconstructive; whatever its originality, it would but reproduce the gesture of self criticism in philosophy in its internal tradition."[13] When Miller, in his essay "The Critic as Host," speaks of "deconstructive strategy" as "going with a given text as far as it will go, to its limits," he echoes Derrida, as he does when he goes on to add that all criticism, including deconstructive criticism, "contains, necessarily, its enemy within itself."[14] But the fact is that American deconstructionism does not go to those limits and does not expose its internal fault lines. On the contrary, it hides and obscures them at every turn. The enemy which deconstructive critics like Miller will not face is history, and the fault line of such criticism appears as its elision of the sociohistorical dimensions of literary work.

AT THE BEGINNING of his first book, *L'Épithète traditionnelle dans Homère* (1928), Milman Parry consciously set his work in the line of the great tradition of modern historical scholarship. "The literature of every country and of every time is understood as it ought to be only by the author and his contemporaries . . . The task, therefore of one who lives in another age and wants to appreciate that work correctly, consists precisely in rediscovering the varied information and complexes of ideas which the author assumed to be the natural property of his audience."[15] Parry is quick to observe that this scholarly project of "reconstructing that [original] community of thought through which the poet made himself understood" is a task "so complex as to be impossible of realization in an entirely satisfactory manner."[16] Nevertheless, the project must be pursued if we are to hope to have any reliable understanding of the culture of the past.

The twentieth-century attack upon the historical method in criticism, initially focused on the so-called intentional fallacy, soon became a broad-based critique of genetic studies in general. John M. Ellis's *The Theory of Literary Criticism: A Logical Analysis* (1974) summarized and completed this line of critique. His argument is not merely that genetic studies cannot recover the "original context," but that the human meaning of literary works does not lie in that context. Rather, it lies in the context of immediate use: "If we insist on relating the text primarily to the context of its composition and to the life and social context of its author, we are cutting it off from that relation to life which is the relevant one."[17] In addition, genetic criticism limits and shrinks the dynamic potential of literary products by reducing their meanings to "static" forms and by suggesting that certain "information" can supply "the key to the text" and its meaning.[18] Poststructural critics like Miller would take this (ultimately Nietzschean) line of thought to a more extreme position. Genetic criticism is the epitome of all critical forms which seek after the "univocal reading" of a text.[19] For deconstructionists it does not matter whether the finished reading stands as an "originary" form to which criticism seeks to return or an accomplished form which criticism makes in its own rhetorical praxis. All are unstable and operating under the sign of *differance*. Thus Miller: "Nihilism is an inalienable alien presence within Occidental metaphysics, both in poems and in the criticism of poems."[20]

Ellis's view that criticism justifies itself in its social praxis is an important one that I shall reconsider shortly. Before taking up that matter, however, I want to inquire into the idea that genetic criticism offers static and univocal meanings for literary works. In fact, all the great historicist critics were well aware that their method could not do this. The ideal of reconstructing the originary material and ideological context, even if fully achieved, would provide the later reader only with what "the author assumed to be the natural property of his audience." The method does not offer static and univocal readings, it attempts to specify the concrete and particular forms in which certain human events constituted themselves. The "meanings" of those events, whether for the original persons involved or for any subsequent persons, are themselves specifically constituted events which can and will be reconstituted in the subsequent historical passage of the poem. The "reading" and the "criticism" of poems and the human events they represent set what Blake called a "bounding line" to human action. In this sense criticism—and historical criticism paradigmatically—does not establish the "meanings" of poems, it tries to re-present them to us in "minute particulars," in forms that recover (as it were) their *physique* in as complete detail as possible. Thus Parry says of the historical reconstruction which his criticism brings about: "I make for myself a picture of great detail,"[21] *not* "I translate for myself and my world the meaning of the ancient texts." The originary "meanings" (Parry's "complexes of ideas which the author assumed") are themselves concrete particulars, not concrete universals, and their complexity involves diverse and often contradictory lines of relations. Historical criticism's great critical advance lay in its ability to reconstruct, in methodical ways, the differential and contradictory patterns within which poetical works constitute themselves and are constituted.

Parry and those like him understood very well that texts and the criticism of texts labored under various destablizing forces.

If I say that Grote's account of democracy at Athens is more revealing of the mind of an English Liberal of the nineteenth century after Christ, than it recalls what actually took place in Athens in the fifth century before Christ, and then go on to admit that the opinion which I have just expressed about Grote may in turn reveal even more my own state of mind than it does that of Grote (indeed, I know that I am expressing this thought here because I came across it about two weeks ago in one of the essays submitted for the Bowdoin prize essay contest and it struck me)—even in that case I am still doing no more than to try to attain a more perfect method for the historical approach to the thought of the past.[22]

This is Parry's version of "the critic as host," and it explains why he will state the following basic paradox of historical method: that by it "we learn to keep ourselves out of the past, or rather we learn to go into it."[23] Historical method in criticism clarifies and defines the differentials in concrete ways for the originary and the continuing past, as well as for the immediate present (and the as yet unconstructed future).

These passages are taken from Parry's great essay "The Historical Method in Literary Criticism" (1936), where he also expresses "a certain feeling of fear" that this method will "destroy itself."[24] His fear recalls Nietzsche's critique of philological studies expressed in *On the Advantage and the Disadvantage of History for Life,* and anticipates the antihistorical arguments of the immanentist critical methods which, in the early 1930s, were just beginning to gain force and prominence. "I have seen myself, only too often and too clearly, how, because those who teach and study Greek and Latin literature have lost the sense of its importance for humanity, the study of those literatures has declined."[25] What Parry proposes is that scholars "create their heroic legend" of the importance of historicity—of the historicity of truth, on the one hand, and of the search for truth, on the other: "Otherwise they will be choosing a future in which they must see themselves confined not by choice, but by compulsion, to be forever ineffective, if they would not be untruthful."[26]

In fact, however, historical criticism—at least as it was practiced in the western academy—did not go on to fulfill what Parry called for. This failure occurred, I believe, because historicist criticism always tended to conceive its terms in a recollective frame. Thus "referentiality," in this program, tended to be construed as bearing upon persons and events which lay behind us, in a completed form of pastness. Language "refers to" particular actualities. No historical critic of any standing ever understood this referential connection in the simple empiricist terms laid down by Miller, but—on the other hand—neither did they explore the full theoretical implications of some of the most important historicist principles.

"I make for myself a picture of great detail." This is the heart of the historicist program. But the traditional historicists—even late figures like Parry—tended to "read" this picture with their gaze turned backward. Parry knew perfectly well that the picture he made for himself contained historical layers (himself, Grote, fifth-century Greece, as well as many intervenient distances), but when he actually *made* the picture for his audience, the layers and intervenient distances tended to disappear into the outlines of the originary picture. This blurring of the palimpsest seems clearest to us, now, in the picture's avoidance of its projected future details. These we now call, in general, the "prejudice" (after Gadamer) or "ideology" (after the Marxist tradition) of the critical account.

Present deployments of historical criticism will have to renovate the original program along such lines. The picture which the historical critic makes is one which includes a future as well as a present and a past, which includes, perhaps, several pasts, presents, and possible futures. Historical criticism can no longer make any part of that sweeping picture in an unself-conscious way. The problem with Parry's brief anecdote about fifth-century Greece, Grote, and himself is that he was unable to incorporate the shrewd insight of this anecdote into his explicit programmatic scheme. As a result, the anecdote stands apart, an ancillary sketch which would not find its way into a single picture of great detail.

IN THIS CONTEXT we can begin to reconstitute the idea of "referentiality" and even sketch the outlines of a renovated historical criticism. We begin with what Parry called the "detail." For a properly historical criticism—which is to say, in my view, a dialectical criticism—those much maligned matters-of-fact are the postulates of a critical discourse. The historical particularity of a poem by Wordsworth or a novel by Austen have to be clearly specified in the act of criticism if that act is to proceed dialectically, that is, if that act is not simply to project upon "the work" its own conceptual interests.

Such elementary particulars establish the ground for a whole system of critical differentials that stretch across the continuing social life of a literary work from its point of origin to its current operations.

These matters ought to be clear enough. What also needs to be said, however, is that the "referent" of any discourse—whether the "original" creative discourse, the intervening discourses of the work's reception, or the immediate discourses of current criticism—cannot by simply conceived as an empirical datum. The matters-of-fact which poems and criticism embody (or constitute) are not—to borrow Coleridge's phraseology—"objects as objects"; rather they are objects-as-subjects, objects which have been (and continue to be) a focus of important human interests.[27] The poems themselves, because they are "social texts" and events, are also objects-as-subjects, but the poems acquire this character because they "have reference to" the larger (human) world of social interactions. Literary works represent, and are representative of, that larger world.

All this does not mean, however, that the task of criticism is a historicist reconstruction or glossing of a particular work's originary referential field. The critical ideal must be a totalizing one, for literary "works" *continue* to live and move and have their being.[28] The referential field of Byron's *Don Juan* is by no means limited to the period 1789-1824, though that is the explicit frame of the poem's narrativization. *Don Juan* "has reference to" a larger share of the past than the period of its immediate focus. Indeed, that focusing period, as reconstituted through *Don Juan,* is revealed to be itself a vehicle (or system of mediations) by which history is rendered up for human use. In the end, what we must see is that works like *Don Juan* have reference to—make use of and assume an interest in—some more or less comprehensive aspects of the past, the present, and the future as well. Because critical activity shares in that work, it too operates with its own various, and more or less explicit, sociohistorical interests.

This historical multiplication of an originary work is most easily grasped, and graphed, along the (often conflicting) lines of its various textualizations, on the one hand, and its reception history on the other. The printing history of any work implicitly narrates the stories of its polyglottal existence. "Meaning" in literary works is a function of the uses to which persons and social organizations put those works. The use variances reflect the changes in social circumstances which emerge over time. One has merely to reflect upon Blake's discussion of Milton and the biblical tradition in *The Marriage of Heaven and Hell* to recollect this fundamental aspect of all literary work.

But the Babel of human voices—this secular struggle against the god who would place all things human under a single authority (as Blake lamented, "One King, One God, One Law")—this secular struggle is carried on as well even in those apparently singular moments epitomized in specific textual events. Bakhtin was the first to enunciate clearly the idea that every particular text locates and expresses a heteroglossial event. Byron's *Don Juan,* for example, is clearly shot through with the most contradictory sort of attitudes, ideas, images. One of the reasons this work, more than any other of that period, amounts to an epic of its age is because it comprehends such a diversity of heteronomous materials and projects. This heteronomy is reflected, once again, in the original set of critical responses to the poem—a wildly varying group of reviewers' texts which offer the most diverse set of readings and interpretations.

To establish an appropriate concept of referentiality for literary works, then, we have to reconceive "the mode of existence of a literary work of art." In the first place, the idea that poems are simply verbal structures has to be emphatically discarded. Poems are materialized in far more complex structures than merely verbal ones. The entire institution of discourse-production operates within any work of poetry, both in options taken and in options refused, and in the circumstantial networks which set out the options that were possible in the first place.

These material particulars which make up all texts embody the basic "facts" within which critical reflection will operate. But we begin with these concrete details by reminding ourselves that such "facts" are not mere data, objects, or monads, they are heuristic isolates which bring into focus some more or less complex network of human events and relations. As such, "facts" always have to be reconstituted if those networks are to be clarified and redeployed. One of the special graces of poetic works—probably their chief social value—is that they are conceptual forms which operate at a high level of generality, on the one hand, and at an equally high level of particularity on the other. The particulars, the "matters-of-fact," are subjected to a general organizing structure which precisely *does not* reduce those particulars to conceptual finishedness, but instead preserves them in a state of (as it were) freedom. The particulars are grains of sand in which the world may be seen—may be seen again and again, in new sets of relations and differentials.

In this respect it may be useful to recall again the more traditional theory of literary imitation. Sidney's *Defence of Poesie,* the finest English re-presentation of the Aristotelian doctrine of mimesis, concerns itself principally with what he calls "right poets," that is, those poets who in their art of imitation "borrow nothing of what is, hath been, or shall be; but range . . . into the divine consideration of what may be and should be."[29] When Coleridge, in the *Biographia Literaria* and his related essay "On Poesy or Art," distinguishes between what he calls "imitation" and "mere copying," he is recollecting the Aristotelian tradition.[30] In this view, what the poet imitates is not simply matters-of-fact or accidentalities or minute particulars; the poet imitates the essential qualities of his subject, human beings or individual persons in their generic distinctiveness. As a consequence, since human life—in contrast to the natural world—is distinguished by its spiritual or moral dimensions, the object of poetic imitation will have to be a re-presentation, via a judicious selection of phenomenal details, of noumenal realities.

The authority of this theory of imitation, along with its related concept of referentiality, began to be undermined with the development of eighteenth-century empiricism and modern historical thought. The rise of the novel is connected to the emergence of what we now call "realism," in which accidentalities and matters-of-fact are crucial to the deployment of a new type of poetic imitation. Among poets, Wordsworth has the distinction of being the first—in the "Preface" to the *Lyrical Ballads*—to intimate the relevance of these new ideas. Minute particulars of time, place, and circumstance gain in importance (for artists as well as for people in general) when the character of human morals is seen to be a function of social and political processes. Erstwhile "noumenal" realities are *functionally* related both to the determinations of given phenomenal circumstances, on the one hand, and to the manipulations of current human perspectives and engagements, on the other. Briefly, it came to be believed that if one wanted to understand "human nature" in general, one had to proceed along two dialectically related paths: along the path of a thorough sociohistorical set of observations and along the path of the, now so-called, sciences of the artificial.[31] For "human nature" was not (is not) "made" by God, it was (and continues to be) artfully, artificially, constructed by human beings, within certain given limits, in the course of their social development.

What art "imitates," then, what it "has reference to," is this totality of human changes in all its diverse manifestations. Since the totality neither is nor ever can be *conceptually* completed, however, art works intersect with it at a differential. That is to say, art establishes its referential systems—including its reference to the totality—in the forms of dynamic particulars which at once gesture toward the place of these particulars in the ceaseless process of totalization, and also assert their freedom within the process. Such freedom is relational, and it illustrates a key element in the maintenance of the process of dynamic totalization: that the particulars which are to count in art, the particular acts, events, circumstances, details, and so forth, along with the textualizations through which they are constituted, are those which in fact *make (and/or have made) a difference*—particulars which will be seen to have been (and to be still) positively engaged in processes of change. Whether these processes offer themselves as progressive or conservative does not in itself matter; in either case the reader's attention will be drawn via such details to the socially located tensions and contradictions, as well as the responses to such things, which poetry imitates and participates in. In art and poetry these particulars appear as *incommensurates:* details, persons, events which the work's own (reflected) conceptual formulas and ideologies must admit, but which they cannot wholly account for.

One may see here the emergence of a new theory of representation that has modified the traditional Aristotelian theory. Modern idealist and deconstructive attacks on literary referentiality, and hence on any criticism which presupposes such a concept, assume—as the traditional theory had assumed—that no natural relation exists between "what is, hath been, or shall be" and "what may be or should be." (In traditional theory, the relation between the two is supernatural, whereas in the poststructural model the relation is at best arbitrary and at worst illusory.) Sociohistorical criticism, however, argues that "what may be or should be" is always a direct function of "what is, hath been, or shall be," and its theory of representation holds that art imitates not merely the "fact" and the "ideal," but also the dynamic relation which operates between the two.

In addition, sociohistorical criticism both assumes and seeks to display the *determinate* character of this dynamic relation. This emphasis upon the determinate is fundamental if "what is" is to stand in a *natural* or scientific relation to "what should be." But because knowledge is a project rather than a possession, it falls short of a complete grasp of its objects. The determinate relation between "what is" and "what should be" is what Shelley had in mind when he spoke of "something longed for, never seen." The determinate is—in the alternative sense of that word—what exists by acts of determination. Knowledge as a project is knowledge grounded in a platonic *Eros,* which is in the end both determined and determinative, in every sense of those two terms. Kant's "categorical imperative" is an analogous concept, though it seems to me that subsequent readers of Kant have misleadingly emphasized the categorical rather than the imperative salient in his thought.

This is the context in which we are to understand the idea of the "incommensurate" in poetry and art—the "irrelevant detail," the "accidentalities," all those arresting particulars of fact, language, text, and event which seem to escape both the ideologies of the works themselves as well as the ideologies of criticism. Poetry aims to establish a holistic and totalizing act of representation, but this project or purpose can be achieved only in the dynamic condition of the work itself—which is to say that it must look to have, like the human life it reflects, an *actual* rather than a conceptual fulfillment, a completion in the continuous deed and event which is the poetic work. Accidentalities and incommensurates in art localize this permanent discontinuity between "the consciousness" of the poetical work and its complete if unrealized self-understanding. The deep truths that poetry knows are, as Shelley observed, "imageless" even in the poems themselves; and that tension in the unrealized desire of the images points toward the absent totalization. The process was captured, and perhaps never so cunningly iterated, by Pope when he spoke of poetry as "what oft was thought, but ne'er so well expressed."

In sum, poetical work epitomizes the referentiality of communicative action. Criticism moves in constant pursuit of the text's lost and unrealized points of reference—all the verbal and eventual matters-of-fact which constitute the work's complex symbolic networks, and without which criticism cannot hope to *re*constitute those networks. That reconstituion is not achieved, however, as some factive historicist reconstruction of the "original context" of the work. Poetry operates a form of finishedness, but that form cannot be finished in conceptual fact. On the other hand, when immanent criticism condescends to the historicist and philological effort to reestablish an image of some originary form of a poetical work, it has missed the point of why criticism pursues referential particularity and concreteness. The project of historicist work, its insistence upon matters-of-fact and accidentalities, is a critical reflection (and redeployment) of poetry's incommensurable procedures. Far from closing off poetic meaning, factive reconstructions operate such an array of overdetermined particulars that they tend to widen the abyss which is the communicative potential of every poem. It is as if, reading Wolf on Homer, or Driver on Genesis, one were able to glimpse, however briefly, the deep and totalizing truth in and toward which literary works are always moving, and to feel as well how and why their images have preserved an imageless and referential import.

SUCH A CRITICAL PROJECT requires, I believe, a resort to an operational rather than a mirroring concept of mimesis. Theodor Adorno's "subversive" concept of imitation seems to me an especially fruitful one to follow.[32] For Adorno mimesis is properly conceived as "reaction to the Other" rather than as "imitation of the Other."[33] As a consequence, "all works of art . . . are *a priori* polemical".[34] This position does not mean that poems have always to be explicitly *engagé;* what Adorno means is that poems must embody the tensions of their human purposes and interests. They always carry the moral imperative "Es soll anders sein"—"even in the most sublimated work of art," Adorno says, "there is concealed an 'It ought to be different.' "[35]

This critical project will succeed only if it is founded upon a careful and thorough materialist criticism. Immanent hermeneutics from New Criticism through deconstruction have looked upon nineteenth-century philology as a critical desert, dryasdust terrain. Yet now, in the wasteland we have watched emerging from the First World War to the Age of Reagan, dryasdust seem those texts which continue to pursue uncritical and intramural pointlessness. Habermas, Lyotard, and others have exposed and resisted the legitimation crisis in the discourse of the humanities. There is no question that this crisis is deeply connected with the authorizing premise of so much of today's literary work—that discourse is an intertextual dance. The texts produced out of such a view, both creative and scholarly, reflect—have reference to—the epoch which they have done much to fashion. They respond to that epoch, both positively and negatively. They are its characteristic forms of expression.

As such, hermeneutical texts of these kinds operate in an expressive and demonstrative, but not in a critical, mode. They reflect, often brilliantly, the legitimation crisis in current literary work. The issue of referentiality, however, not only brings this crisis into clear view, it suggests as well the avenues which must be explored if the crisis is to be—however provisionally—met. Essential to this task is a critical turn upon the hermeneutical operations which immanent criticism at present deploys. If we cannot clarify the meanings of our own meanings without setting our work in a reflexive relation with itself and its history, we cannot know that history outside its documentary and otherwise material forms. This is why historical criticism must also be material and sociological. It will be, finally, dialectical, when the pasts reconstituted by present literary studies are established for *critical* purposes: to expose to itself the mind of the present in order that it may be better able to execute its human interests and projects for the future.

7 ❧

Some Forms of Critical Discourse

What are those golden builders doing?
William Blake, *Jerusalem*

CONTEMPORARY AMERICAN POETRY, especially that produced from the academy and the dominant New York publishing houses, has recently taken a turn in the direction of narrative. In itself an important event, this trend mirrors the recent scholarly interest in narrative and narrativity, and the ways in which "the real" is instituted through narrativizing procedures. Michel de Certeau, an acute observer of such forms of discourse, has interrogated historiographical narratives in order to elucidate the "dogmatizing tendency" which is often deployed in such narratives: "the 'real' as represented by historiography does not correspond to the 'real' that determines its production. It hides[,] behind a picture of the past[,] the present that produces and organizes it. Expressed bluntly, the problem is as follows: a *mise en scène* of a (past) actuality . . . occults the technical apparatus of the professional institution that produces it."[1] This occultation process need not be confined to narrativized historical texts. If the text is narrativized, however, one ideological matter that will be represented is continuity: eventuality as a "development" or "process" that is released from anything but peripheral discontinuities and "digressions."

If one is interested in *critical* knowledge, one has to be wary of this impulse to generate continuities—either in the texts we produce or in the social structures which those texts, as de Certeau has shown, replicate. In the discourses of criticism, and most typically in philosophy and literary discourse, narrativized forms are so common that their narrativity is often not even noticed. Even more remarkable, however, is that critical discourse has available to it certain traditional forms which offer special opportunities—particularly in our period—for resisting the tendency to generate knowledge in forms of continuity. Such forms typically serve to maintain an idea of the "real" which avoids forms of change and discontinuity that cannot be appropriated to a processive or developmental model.

I would like to explore here two particular types of critical discourse which are not narrative: the array and the dialectic. They are important for at least two reasons. In the first place, the array is almost never recognized as an integral form of critical discourse. Secondly, both of these forms offer special opportunities for those interested in exploiting the critical strategies available to writers. Narrativized discourse can be used critically, of course; one thinks of a host of instances, for example, *The Eighteenth Brumaire*. In our day, however, when narrativity dominates the form of writing, it is not characteristically deployed in an antithetical mode. Indeed, its formal commitment to the maintenance of continuity can throw up obstacles to its critical use. In this respect the forms of array and dialectic are particularly important, not merely as alternative critical modes, but as forms which cast an important critical light on the structure of narrativized discourse.

I SHALL BEGIN with a brief consideration of Hayden White's important essay on narrativizing discourse, "The Value of Narrativity in the Representation of Reality."[2] I take this as my point of departure because this essay, in point of fact, initially set my mind to work on the topic of the forms of discourse.

In his essay White helps to define his view of narrativized history by asking, "What would a non-narrative representation of historical reality look like?"[3] The question generates White's discussion of the form of annals and chronicles as examples of nonnarrative historical texts. The choice of these examples has a crucial bearing on the development of White's complete argument, which is fundamentally processive and even Hegelian in its view of historical texts. That is to say, annals yield to chronicles, which in turn yield to narrativized histories, which in their turn yield to the "fourth" and most self-conscious mode of historical writing, metahistory. The presence of this Hegelian argument becomes more apparent if we pose White's question again and look for different kinds of nonnarrative historical texts—that is to say, kinds which will not submit to the Hegelian convenience of historical obsolescence, as annals and chronicles seem to do. The most obvious are those sets of historical writings which arose out of the antiquarian tradition: catalogs, digests, almanacs, and compilations of various types. These things remain a fundamental part of history as it is a project of human knowledge. The elementary forms of such works have succeeded, in our own day, to some of the most advanced and sophisticated works of historical analysis, not least of all in the field of quantitative history. Out of the antiquarian tradition emerged, directly, a variety of historical texts which have facilitated the accessing and organized study of large bodies of information; and, indirectly, those (preeminently) quantitative texts which promote an analytic grasp of the historical field.[4]

When we turn from historical works to literary criticism, we may observe a number of interesting symmetries and asymmetries. Consider, for example, the following directions for producing a critical paper in literary studies, as set forth in a standard introductory text for graduate students. Should a person wish to propose a "new interpretation" of a passage or work,

> let him set down, in orderly fashion, all the arguments in favor of his interpretation, and then, with equal or greater scrupulousness, all those against. Let him study the evidence, giving full value to every argument; for it may very well happen that a single bit of contra evidence will make the piling up of pro arguments like the adding together of zeros . . . Having assured himself that he has a case, let the student then present his hypothesis . . . as a tentative suggestion for the consideration of those who may be able to bring further evidence to bear on the matter.[5]

The passage gives directions for producing a type of critical work whose model has been appropriated from natural science. Here the study of a literary work begins under the auspices of previous investigators, whose views are the hypotheses which bring order and direction to the study of the phenomena. The critic's own reading of the work measures both itself and the work against the received, enabling hypotheses. Finally, the working critic judges how adequate the hypotheses are to the work and in the process either proposes a wholly new hypothesis (for example, Cleanth Brooks's chapter on Keats's "Ode on a Grecian Urn") or revises, supplements, or otherwise alters—without overthrowing—the received views.[6] At that point— and this is crucial—the entire critical process is translated into a verbal form as a lecture or, more normatively, as an essay or a monograph. The various acts of analysis and reading are re-presented in a narrative form.

I shall return to consider the character of these narrative forms shortly, since they are the forms of critical discourse by which we tend to define the very essence of literary criticism today. In fact, however, they constitute a special type of criticism and do not by any means define the field. The kinds of critical representation which are available to the historian, and which are not taken up in White's historiography, have their counterparts in the field of literary studies. An index of the manuscripts of *Piers Plowman,* a record of the provenance of the engraved works of William Blake, a bibliographical account of Tennyson's works or of a single poem of W. H. Auden (say, "September 1, 1939")—these are all massive acts of critical analysis whose significance for the aesthetic engagement with poems (whether by scholar or by lay reader) is not easily calculated. Such works do not merely provide us with "facts" that may elucidate certain words or passages; they characteristically define those vast and regulating structures which alone give meaning to the poetic semiosis. Through such critical works we begin to unravel the inception and reception histories of literary products and thereby the textual structures which re-present those histories in iconic forms.

So far as I can see, literary interpretation in the past forty years gradually lost the ability to speak or read the languages of such nonnarrative criticism, and in the past twenty-five years or so the academy seems to have abetted the process in an active way. Few scholars who speak the various languages of hermeneutics have any fluency in textual and "bibliocritical" discourse, though in fact the two forms of criticism will not be restored until we understand more clearly the kinds of discourse which criticism is capable of, along with the limits and the powers of those various kinds. White's discussion of narrativity in historical criticism is an important development precisely because it forces us to think about the possible forms which criticism may assume.

THUS FAR I have sketched the differential which antiquarian and quantitative historiography represent for narrativized historical texts and have suggested a parallel differential in literary critical discourse (between textual and bibliocritical forms, on the one hand, and hermeneutical narrative, on the other). I want to proceed along this line of inquiry in order to attempt a description of certain possible modes of critical discourse. I will shift the investigation to include not only White's historiography but the fields of literary criticism and philosophy as well. This move forces the analysis to account for a wider variety of critical formats and permits it to operate at a more general level of description.

Criticism as array. A bibliographical description of some particular literary work or a set of graphs describing population trends in the Middle Ages does not display a narrative form. We commonly assume that such texts require some sort of narrative explanation before they can be said to have a meaning for the historian or the literary critic. This assumption is wrong and merely indicates the terms under which a form of narrative discourse can incorporate texts of these kinds. Indeed, to explain the discursive meaning of such texts in my present context is extremely difficult precisely because I am now working in a narrative mode. Nevertheless, we can glimpse the critical force which such texts inherently possess if we reflect upon the referential contexts which such works assume. Take a bibliographical description like the following, for example.

BYRON (GEORGE GORDON NOEL, BARON BYRON).—Don Juan. / *"Difficile est proprie communia dicere."* / Hor. Epist. ad Pison. / London: / Printed by Thomas Davison, Whitefriars. / 1819.

Collation: Demy quarto, pp. iv + 227; consisting of Half-title (with blank reverse) pp. i–ii; Title-page, as above (with blank reverse) pp. iii–iv; Fly-title to *Canto I* (with blank reverse) pp.1–2; Text of *Canto I* with *Notes* pp. 3–116; Fly-title to *Canto II* (with blank reverse) pp. 117–118; and Text of *Canto II* pp. 119–227. Upon the reverse of page 227 is the following imprint, *"London: /Printed by Thomas Davison, Whitefriars."* The head-line is *Don Juan* throughout, upon both sides of the page. Each page has also at its head the number of the particular

Canto occupying it. The signatures are A (2 leaves), B to U (19 sheets, each 4 leaves), X to Z (3 sheets, each 4 leaves), AA to FF (6 sheets, each 4 leaves), and GG (2 leaves).

The *First Edition*. Uncut in the original blue-gray paper boards, with white paper back-label lettered "*Don Juan. / £1 11s. 6d.*", and preserved in a dark blue folding case by Riviere. The leaves measure 11½ × 8⅞ inches. Inserted at the commencement of the volume is a much-corrected fragment, one page folio, of the original holograph Manuscript.

In the same year, 1819, a second edition was published in demy octavo size to range with the succeeding cantos. The title-page reads—

Don Juan. / "Difficile est proprie communia dicere." / Hor. Epist. ad Pison / A New Edition. / London: / Printed by Thomas Davison, White-friars. / 1819.

The collation is pp. ii + 227. The book was issued in drab paper boards, with white paper back label.

Of the first edition of the first two Cantos of *Don Juan* fifteen hundred copies were printed. But of these 150 copies were 'wasted'. This means that after the book had been reprinted in octavo no further copies in quarto were required, and that the 150 still in the hands of the binders, no doubt in the form of unbound sheets, were sold as waste-paper. For the copyright of the two cantos Byron received the sum of £1525.[7]

The most important (and most apparent) quality of this type of discourse is its lack of narrativized completion. The material in the text may be definitive enough (for example, the number of copies printed of *Don Juan* cantos 1–2 in its first edition), but the text format does not organize the material in terms of a finished structure, nor even in terms of the *idea* of a finished structure. How the various facts are implicated in each other is not determined by this text.

Furthermore, the format as a whole declares that the particular information here is susceptible to formal and abstract description and, hence, that if this work and its several physical forms are unique, the work is also—in its physical forms—typical of literary works, and typical in several important respects that bear upon its publication and reception histories. Indeed, the structuring of the particular information affirms (by assuming in the structure itself) several fundamental matters for literary criticism: for example, that literary works are by nature social products and social structures, that their social dimensions are reflected in their physical constitutions, and that the semiotic character of literary works is not to be located merely at the linguistic or verbal level. The particular details of this bibliographical entry intend to (and actually do) elucidate the specific work in question, but the meaning of those details can be grasped only if we understand the grammer underlying the critical form represented in the entry.

For example, I might draw attention to several interesting matters brought up in this text: the fact that the original edition was priced at £1 11s. 6d., that the title page did not show the names of either the author or the publisher, and that 1,500 copies were printed in a quarto format. One could expand upon the meaning of these details in a subsidiary interpretive text, but that recourse would be taken only if one judged that readers either did not know of or did not understand how to read the bibliographical entry. For the fact is that the entry, in its arrayed form, offers these (and other) materials in a discourse that is already full of significance. Arrayed forms organize their materials in certain preestablished patterns and grammars. In a bibliography, for example, the size of a book, the contents of the title page, the print run, the price—all these are standard subjects to be detailed in the entry. Their standardized treatment implicitly declares that these matters are prima facie significant for anyone studying or interpreting works of literature, as does the standardized format. The standardized format also declares that, for each specific bibliographical entry, one cannot decide in advance how and in what way these matters will be significant.

One further thing: an arrayed form like a bibliography demands that people master its grammar and usage if they are to read it. One does not read a bibliography as one reads a novel or a discursive essay. For example, this *Don Juan* entry contains a great deal of information which will come to view only when it is read in a larger bibliographical context—in the context of the *Don Juan* bibliography, of course, but also of the Byron bibliography in general. The significance of the quarto format and the 1,500 copies printed begins to emerge only when one also knows something about the early printing history of Byron's works. This entry presupposes the reader's familiarity with the larger context, and the fact of such a familiarity will perforce throw these and other details into dramatic prominence.

The entry gains significance from its context, then, but not at all in the way that a narrativized unit gains its contextualized meaning. We must read each entry in the larger bibliographical context not because that larger context establishes the "story" or the "plot" which gives order to the details but because it sets (as it were) the gestalt in terms of which all the details can find their possible lines of interconnection. We need to know all that is in the bibliography rather than the whole of which the bibliography is constituted. We are not interested in how the parts go to make up a (probable/Aristotelian or organic/Romantic) whole; rather, we want to know where and in what way the necessary connections of the parts will establish their unforeseen, particular relations, where the possibilities (which are theoretically legion) have become, in fact, actual.

Such a discourse form can be usefully approached only if one understands that its text does not have a beginning-middle-end structure, a finished or finishing form. That fact is plain enough. We should also see, however, that an arrayed form like a bibliography establishes its referential connections beyond the text, in the world of social space and referential event. The absence of the author's and publisher's names from their expected places on the title page of *Don Juan* cantos 1–2 is a fact whose full presence is delivered in the bibliographical entry but whose full significance resides in the actual history of the book's production and subsequent reproduction.

The schematic form is a function of the large amount of particular information which is being processed—not merely large numbers of special, so-called facts but facts whose referential existence assumes the simultaneous presence of certain frames of reference, as well as the fact that those frames of reference operate in complex, intersecting networks. A narrative form could generate the critical analysis incorporated in such a schema, but it could not do so with anything that would approximate the economy and precision of a good bibliographical entry. Such a text, in other words, speaks in a form that is critically appropriate to the needs of its audience; if its meaning is obscure, the obscurity may not be a function of the text.

The intention of such a form of literary analysis is to be exhaustive with respect to its subject matter and open with respect to its audience. This characteristic of such critical forms explains why one can speak of a "definitive" bibliography: such a work is theoretically possible and even practically achievable within certain specific limits. The same cannot be said of any narrative form of criticism, whose respective intentions toward subject matter and audience are precisely the contrary of the bibliography's. This theoretical ideal, incidentally, betrays the weakness of the particular Byron entry I have been discussing. The problem with this text is that it does not give us nearly enough of the information about the book that we ought to have under the circumstances. The author (T. J. Wise) does not tell us, for example, how large the print run was for the second edition or when precisely the two editions were published; he does not even give us the descriptive particulars for the two editions. We are glad to have the information he supplies, but we know as well that the author has sold us short, especially for so crucial a book as the first two cantos of *Don Juan*.

Criticism as narrative. A bibliographical entry is a good example of criticism in the form of an array, of which there seem to be a great many types, ranging from elementary catalogs to various kinds of indexes with complex networks of cross-references; from fundamental orderings like the periodic table to elaborate systems of related graphs and lists. Having sketched some of the positive qualities of arrays, I shall now try to illuminate by contrast the critical form of narrative. White explores a type of critical narrative which he calls the "narrativized" text, where the writer builds into the discourse an illusion of completion and moral "finishedness," indeed, an illusion which suggests that completion is inherent to the historical events rather than to the narrative of those events. No such moral illusion is solicited in a critical array.

The narrative form dominates literary criticism, and it produces fictions of moral completion which are entirely analogous to those indicated by White. We glimpse this narrativity in the structures of prosopopeia which operate in literary critical writings. Whether the scholar thinks of the literary work as a "poem" or a "text" or a "discourse structure," from Erich Auerbach to J. Hillis Miller, the same tropes recur in literary criticism.

> The Homeric poems . . . are yet comparatively simple in their picture of human beings . . . Delight in physical existence is everything to them, and their highest aim is to make that delight perceptible to us . . .
>
> It is all very different in the Biblical stories. Their aim is not to bewitch the senses, and if nevertheless they produce lively sensory effects, it is only because the moral, religious, and psychological phenomena which are their sole concern are made concrete in the sensible matter of life.

> The novel itself performs a large-scale act of interpretation . . . It frees
> itself from the guilt of this only by giving the reader, not least in its
> inconsistencies, the evidence necessary to see that it *is* an interpretation.[8]

This resort to prosopopeia is the sure sign, in Stanley Fish's view,
that matters and meanings are being ascribed to "the text," put in
"the text," by the interpreting reader. His view is very close to White's:
"Intention is no more embodied 'in' the text than are formal units;
rather an intention, like a formal unit, is made when perceptual or
interpretive closure is hazarded."[9]

Let me offer two examples of how narrativization operates in contemporary criticism—that is to say, in scholarly discourse which has
been influenced by the power of scientific methods of induction: Auerbach's famous essay "Odysseus' Scar," which is the opening chapter
of *Mimesis,* and Harold Bloom's equally famous, not to say notorious,
Anxiety of Influence. The two essays are alike in that each marshals
evidence by the appearance of inductive procedures we feel familiar
with—though perhaps one should call them, following David Hackett
Fischer, "adductive" procedures.[10] Arguments from authority are sup-
pressed or structurally sublimated, and a series of examples is paraded
before the reader to illustrate the critics' "hypotheses." The "adduction" of these examples accumulates to a "proof" or a persuasion,
by force of numbers, on the one hand, and by force of the structural
relations which the examples exhibit among themselves, on the other.

Unlike Bloom, however, Auerbach promotes the view that he is
arguing for an objective state of affairs—for what he calls a "style"
in Homeric and Biblical narrative. The essay opens by recounting (by
renarrating) the key events in book 19 of the *Odyssey,* and this opening critical move dominates the essay. Auerbach's narrative defers to
the priority of the *Odyssey* and argues, by its narrativization, what
the rest of the essay will repeat and confirm: that certain qualities
and patterns inhere in the Homeric work (as other patterns and qualities inhere in the Bible), which critical method can uncover and represent.

Bloom's book works very differently, as we see from its opening
sentences:

> This short book offers a theory of poetry by way of a description of
> poetic influence, or the story of intra-poetic relationships. One aim of
> this theory is corrective: to de-idealize our accepted accounts of how

one poet helps to form another. Another aim, also corrective, is to try to provide a poetics that will foster a more adequate practical criticism.

Poetic history, in this book's argument, is held to be indistinguishable from poetic influence, since strong poets make that history by misreading one another, so as to clear imaginative space for themselves.

My concern is only with strong poets, major figures with the persistence to wrestle with their strong precursors, even to the death. Weaker talents idealize; figures of capable imagination appropriate for themselves.[11]

Here Bloom sets forth his hypotheses, as it were, and in this gesture one glimpses his deference to the discourse of scientific induction. But Bloom's hypotheses are presented in the most aggressive and authoritative way, and this procedure is maintained throughout the book. We note its presence in the brevity of the first two paragraphs, the second being no paragraph at all, except rhetorically. Or observe the authoritative tone of the fourth sentence ("since strong poets" and so forth) and the pattern of naked assertion which proceeds into the fifth and sixth sentences. These passages are not put forward in a hypothetical style but in a definitive one, and they exemplify that breathtaking quality so evident in all of Bloom's work. Like Jesus, he always "speaks as one having authority"—indeed, as one having an authority vouchsafed to no other person. Bloom begins by calling his work a theory, but he initiates it in terms of an assertive rhetoric which offers the reader certain "facts" that are not merely unsupported (how could they be supported?) but that are represented as unarguable and manifest. Bloom later tries shore up these assertions by an adduction of examples, but this adduction offers no more than an apparition of hypothetical procedures. No structure of falsification ever enters Bloom's critical discourse, which is authoritative and definitive throughout.

Related to these matters is a second important aspect of his style exemplified in the passage: the slightly cryptic quality of the assertions. The effect is paradoxical, for Bloom's narrative style seems four square and is such at one level; but the direct syntax (think how different is the syntax of a sentence by Geoffrey Hartman) clashes with a slightly unfamiliar lexicon and set of assertions (What does the concept of clearing imaginative space *mean*?). The sharp contrast of this prose with Auerbach's appears unmistakably in a passage like the following, where Bloom narrates a story we knew (or thought we knew).

The greatest poet in our language is excluded from the argument of this book for several reasons. One is necessarily historical; Shakespeare belongs to the giant age before the flood, before the anxiety of influence became central to poetic consciousness. Another has to do with the contrast between dramatic and lyric form. As poetry has become more subjective, the shadow cast by the precursors has become more dominant. The main cause, though, is that Shakespeare's prime precursor was Marlowe, a poet very much smaller than his inheritor. Milton, with all his strength, yet had to struggle, subtly and crucially, with a major precursor in Spenser . . . Coleridge, ephebe of Milton and later of Wordsworth, would have been glad to find his Marlowe in Cowper . . . , but influence cannot be willed. Shakespeare is the largest instance in the language of a phenomenon that stands outside the concern of this book: the absolute absorption of the precursor.[12]

Here the familiar becomes strange, and the narrative suggests that a history known to every literary academic is not what we always understood it to be. The reason this passage skirts so close to nonsense—it may in fact *be* nonsense—is that it represents as critical fact what is patently narrative mythology. The narrative style is, once again, extremely paradoxical. Bloom adopts a standard mode of literary-historical discourse, wherein we expect to encounter "matters of fact," and he fills it with metaphors and myth. The shock of the style comes from its foursquare manner: not only does Bloom not apologize for his paradoxical moves, he assumes a posture which suggests that what he is saying and doing is not paradoxical at all. It only appears paradoxical to a mind accustomed to think that the discourse of literary criticism is scientific and objective and, hence, fundamentally unlike the discourse of imagination, which is poetic and subjective. Bloom explicitly rejects such a distinction. Consequently, where Auerbach's narrative suggests that authority is objective and residual in the work, Bloom's fosters another illusion: that authority is subjective and residual in the "strong" imagination of a poetic reader like himself. Bloom's "historical" narrative is, in short, a psychic form projected into what scholars normally call "literary history."

As different as the literary narratives of Auerbach and Bloom are, however, each moves in the hermeneutic circle, each employs the narrative form to generate an illusion of completion and moral finishedness for the critical treatment. Their narrativity closes their discourse to the processes of disconfirmation and falsification which all *critical* discourse, by its methodology, can and must seek after. These literary texts are holistic, not hypothetical, accounts; one of their principal accomplishments is to suggest that a single person can gain by his study (Auerbach) or give by his imagination (Bloom) a complete account of an artistic experience. (The ethical implication of such a suggestion is that every individual is at least theoretically capable of giving a complete account of *any* human experience.)

Of course, although such narratives work to foreclose disconfirmation, they cannot succeed in this aim. We willingly suspend our disbelief in their illusions of completion only for a time, and only provisionally. In the end we will recall what they have left out of their account or how they have avoided certain problems. Auerbach's essay, for example, seems to us now much less compelling and definitive than it once seemed to many. We question, for example, his general hermeneutic procedures: the bold use of single texts and short passages to support the most sweeping literary-historical generalizations. Similarly we are troubled by the basis on which his whole discussion of "mixed styles" is founded, and we wonder why he did not at least discuss obvious distinctions such as the styles of the *Iliad* and the *Odyssey* or the differences between the E, J, and P narratives in the Old Testament.

The causes seem to lie in the imperatives of narrativization itself rather than in some critical lapse by the individual critic. When critical discourse assumes a narrative format, the analysis generates a structure of self-confirmation. Narrativity entails order and completion, so any details which would stand outside the (ideological) order cannot enter the discourse. Thus, the "arguments" developed by Auerbach and Bloom present only those counterexamples which can be overcome (and thus incorporated) by the narrative. For Bloom, Shakespeare is brought into the account by an imperial act of exclusion: Shakespeare is outside Bloom's "history," an antedeluvian figure whose presence in Bloom's narrative is useful for defining the nature and shape of Bloom's conception of "poetic history." The entire presentation will seem merely arbitrary, even fantastic, when observed from a critical vantage which places itself outside the narrativity of Bloom's supreme fiction.

Every scholar's work, whether narrativized or not, operates in a field which it cannot comprehend within itself. Narrativity is used by the critic to struggle against the apparently arbitrary limits of that referential field. Whatever authority a particular discourse may gain at any particular place or time—and even then it cannot achieve completion—will be modified in subsequent and alternate scholarly usage. Particular works have their limits defined for them in the endless discourse whose text can never be established (since it is always being modified and extended). The narratives of literary criticism, then, will have their limits exposed, necessarily, by other critical views and scholarly narratives. Nevertheless, this exposure offers no criticism of the form of narrativity itself or of the apparitions of order and completeness which that form insists upon.

Criticism as dialectic. Narrative is the most synthetic of all the forms of nonpoetic discourse. Consequently, its limits will be defined only if its orderly ideal is studied and read in terms of other, non-narrative forms of critical discourse. An arrayed format can break the spell cast by a narrativized discourse, but only if the specific arrayed materials are not merely consumed by the narrativization. Leon Trotsky's *History of the Russian Revolution,* volume 1, chapter 3, offers a splendid example of such a consumption in its famous table of political strikes for the years 1903-1917. This is a simple case, of course, but it epitomizes how narrativization can subjugate the authority of statistics and quantification.

Although G. E. Bentley, Jr.'s *Blake Records* (Oxford, 1969) is neither so great nor so well known a work as Trotsky's, it illustrates very well how an arrayed form of discourse can maintain its own integrity within a narrativized field. This book collects all the known contemporary records which relate to the life of Blake and arranges them in a loose chronological string. The arrangement is necessarily loose because the original "records" are exceedingly diverse. Bentley's "narrative" connects the records in such a way that a coherent story of Blake's life emerges through the narrative. But each of the records has its own integrity which Bentley's narrative normally does not invade. As a result, the book offers the reader a peculiar freedom, an unusual array of diverse points of view. Bentley's narrative holds the various parts together but not under the determinate authority of its narrativization; the story Bentley tells is continually subjected to a critique from other materials, including other narratives which he has collected in his book. The array of records which Bentley has gathered is the mine from which he has drawn his narrative of Blake's life, but it is equally—*within this book's own self-defined terms*—the differential which measures and judges the limits of Bentley's own narrative.

The eclipse of antiquarian scholarship has endangered this important hybrid species of critical discourse. Most scholars and critics who wish to bring their own narrativization under an immediate critical inspection do not resort to it and may not even be aware of it as an option. More common is the choice of dialectic. The renascence of this critical format in our own day should probably be credited to Ludwig Wittgenstein and particularly to the example he set in the *Philosophical Investigations*. The influence of this trenchant, even obsessive, exercise in rigorous self-critical discourse is evident throughout the modern academy. Wittgenstein's most prominent American inheritor, Stanley Cavell, has recently produced an all but explicit pastiche of the dialectical format in part 4 of *The Claim of Reason*. This is a 170-page dialectical meditation carried out under the topic "Skepticism and the Problem of Others." The work is arranged under forty-six separate headings or subheadings, each of which constitutes what Cavell sees as a (loose) integral unit; and of course each of the units, because they are strung together so closely, can be read into other, confederated units. These units, however the reader may define their particular limits in individual cases, are narrativized forms which develop their own structures of completion and finishedness. Nevertheless, the governing structure of "Skepticism and the Problem of Others" is, like that of the *Philosophical Investigations*, dialectical rather than narrativized. The situation is nicely described by Cavell himself when he sets forth, in his book's table of contents, a brief description of how part 4 is arranged. We should note that this description is not formally conceived; rather, it presents itself in an operational mode, as a set of directions for reading.

> [Few of the following entries are meant as headings, as if each extends over the tracts of material to follow until another entry stops it, say like signs for city limits. They are better regarded as road signs; shifting numbers of them may simultaneously extend over one or more segments of the whole. Accordingly, these entries only accidentally coincide with the occasional large breaks left in the text between paragraphs. These breaks register convenient resting places, to let the mind clear, or a thought complete itself—matters which may or may not coincide with the introducing or the dropping of a theme.][13]

Cavell's dialectic works to illuminate skeptically his own discourse on skepticism, and in this way it operates in an antithetical relation to the narratives which are collected under the discourse. The discourse is dialectical in the way that *Philosophical Investigations* is dialectical but not, of course, in the manner of Platonic dialectic, where the aim is rhetorical. In an important early essay on Wittgenstein, Cavell calls the discourse "confessional" because the space of the dialectic is interior. It is what Arnold called "the dialogue of the mind with itself."

The classic type of the internalized dialectic which descends to us is the Montaigne essay; the perfected form of that essay—the text which fully reveals Montaigne's method—first appears in the unique book known as the Bordeaux copy of the *Essais* (that is, Montaigne's own copy of the 1588 edition with his autograph additions, which comprise approximately one-quarter of the *Essais* as a whole). Readers today encounter that text in those contemporary editions which exhibit the famous "layering" process whereby Montaigne gradually built up his essays with a series of additions and interpolations.

Sometimes these additions represent an (as it were) organic development of what is already implicit in the earlier form of the essay. The additions to "That Intention Is Judge of Our Actions" are of this kind.[14] Montaigne supplements the pre-1588 essay with a series of reflections which, on the one side, expand the initial anecdote with some general philosophical meditations and, on the other side, focus the essay to a final, pointed, and highly personal conclusion: "If I can, I shall keep my death from saying anything that my life has not already said"(20). The procedure appears frequently in Montaigne's revisions, sometimes in local ways, as when he is developing some single part of an essay, sometimes more generally. This type of revisionary procedure shows the mind in a dialogue with itself, but it is a dialogue that moves in a hermeneutic circle. The return made upon the original text is carried out in a mode we associate today with Martin Heidegger, a rhetoric of self-revelation.

Montaigne's essays develop another type of internal dialogue, however. In this the revisionary move strikes back at the originary text in a more radical way, so that although the ideas and forms of thought of the initial text are not canceled or taken back, they are forced to bear either contradiction or digression. In either case they are departed from, and the new form of the essay reveals the presence of a dialectic which is not organic but critical. Two excellent examples of this type of discourse are "That Our Happiness Must Not Be Judged until after Our Death" and "Of the Power of the Imagination." In the former, the pre-1588 essay undergoes a major shift in the 1588 printing. The first (pre-1588) text develops in a typical Montaigne pattern: from anecdote through some general reflections to a striking personal conclusion: "But in the last scene, between death and ourselves, there is no more pretending . . . That is why all the other actions of our life must be tried and tested by this last act. It is the master day, the day that is judge of all the others . . . We shall see then whether my reasonings come from my mouth or from my heart" (55). This aggressive conclusion, this confidence born of an implacable and courageous skepticism, is entirely contradicted in the 1588 additions, where the tone abandons its imperious and armed vision for a modesty that passes a fundamental judgment upon what has gone before. The difference is plain if we compare the original conclusion (above) with the conclusion of 1588. "In judging the life of another, I always observe how it ended; and one of my principal concerns about my own end is that it shall go well, that is to say quietly and insensibly" (55). Perhaps, on that master day, we shall *not* see anything finally or definitively or be certain about the integrity of our words and deeds; perhaps, on that master day, we shall give over the passion to establish a rational measure for such an integrity and look only, in the end, to die in peace.

"Of the Power of the Imagination" does not turn upon itself in such an arresting fashion; for contradiction it substitutes digression. Yet the formal result is analogous and quite unlike what we observed in "That Intention Is Judge of Our Actions." In the latter the discourse mode is dialogic without also being dialectical. "Of the Power of the Imagination" secures dialectic by veering into a final set of digressions that have only the most arbitrary relation to the original body of text. I have in mind specifically the post-1588 revisions with which the essay concludes, where Montaigne unexpectedly turns from his topic ("the power of imagination") to certain related but unprepared subjects (the reliability of his facts and his lack of concern for their historical accuracy). The digression does not cancel or overthrow what has gone before, nor does it subject the original text to any direct critique. The digressive move simply dramatizes the limited and arbitrary nature of every discourse and, not least of all, that discourse which presents itself as an ordered unit. For its very unity and orderedness develop a set of invisible constraints which dialectic alone—whether as critique or as digression—can break through.

Montaigne chooses the way of digression, and in this particular instance he explicates his own procedure through a digression within his final digression. In the midst of his discussion of historical accuracy and the value of fact, Montaigne remarks that "some urge me to write the events of my time" because they believe him peculiarly qualified to do so, being by nature dispassionate and by circumstances widely connected (76). Montaigne's refusal is striking because it is not directed at the project of writing on contemporary events but at an implication of such a project. Montaigne refuses by digressing into an unexpected, yet obviously pertinent, subject: the nature of connected and ordered discourse itself. "What they forget is that even for all the glory of Sallust, I would not take the trouble, being a sworn enemy of obligation, assiduity, perseverance; and that there is nothing so contrary to my style as an extended narration . . . If I took a subject that would lead me along, I might not be able to measure up to it; and with my freedom being so very free, I might publish judgments which, even according to my own opinion and to reason, would be illegitimate and punishable" (76). Montaigne does not trust himself to use the mode of "extended narration" because it would exert such pressure upon his digressive style that his discourse would be in danger of total collapse. Critique itself is a limited intellectual operation whose demons are not the illusions and bad faith of narrativity but anarchy and perversion.

ALTHOUGH THESE THREE TYPES of critical discourse (array, narrative, dialectic) exhibit the *form* of criticism, that form is no guarantee that the discourse will in fact be critical. True criticism entails a self-conscious response to certain social and historical factors; it is a function of an objective state of affairs rather than a set of verbal configurations. Thus, because a narrativized discourse is most easily assimilated to acts of interpretation rather than to acts of criticism, the presence of narrativity in discourse may appear to weaken the critical content. Similarly, because dialectic is a discourse which we always associate with critique, its presence may be taken to indicate the de facto operation of a critical discourse.

Neither of these assumptions seems to me justified. Take, for instance, the case of narrativized discourse. Within the general domain of critical thought, such models function best when they introduce the idea of order—the power of such an idea—into a situation which suffers from a deficiency of ideas or a lack of theoretical self-consciousness. Auerbach's work as a literary critic gained its prominence from the power of its critical narrative, which seemed to bring order, purpose, and comprehensiveness to the activity of literary scholarship. Behind Auerbach lies what was perceived to be the immediate wasteland of scholarship, a widespread dryasdust pedantry which was no longer inspired by the comprehensive vision that brought it to birth at the end of the eighteenth century. The holistic view of Auerbach's work is a judgment upon the absence of such a view in the more commonplace scholarship of his day. Furthermore, the date and compositional circumstances of *Mimesis*—written in exile at Istanbul between 1942 and 1945—emphasize the general social significance which his book necessarily had for the west. In these respects his work represents one of the most advanced and innovative works of our midcentury.

The critical status of ideological discourse, in other words, can be assessed only in terms of its specific historical frame of reference. Consider, for instance, the widespread recent appearance of internally dialogic texts, from the essays of Heidegger to the many current forms of deconstructive study. An excellent example of this phenomenon of modern scholarship can be seen in Hartman's essay "The Interpreter: A Self-Analysis." The title suggests that the work will turn back upon itself, and Hartman explicitly declares later in the essay, as he is finishing his presentation, that there is a program for interpretation which is "beyond interpretation": "Even as interpreters," he declares, "we must set interpretation *against* hermeneutics."[15] This is Hartman's formulation of what we now generally call "deconstruction." What is crucial to see about this dialogic form, however, is that it is formally narrativized, that its end is in its beginning, that the revisionary move is not made against the discourse which Hartman is actually writing but merely against the tradition of that discourse (as it were), against the idea of his text. The subject "against" which "we" must move is "the interpreter" or the sublimed and abstract form of Geoffrey Hartman: not the actual, historically and socially located critic but the metacritic, the person with the magical or Platonic—not the human or the social—name.[16]

The importance of Hartman's or Bloom's or Auerbach's work is functionally related to the disciplinary problems which they have called up and proposed (successfully or unsuccessfully) to solve. How much genuine self-criticism does a scholar's or an ideologue's work seek after and encourage? This is a fundamental question which criticism must always put to every form of ideological discourse. Here I have been concentrating on the nonnarrative types because they seem to possess a singular advantage in our current scholarly climate. Where narrativity dominates the exploration of ideas, nonnarrative forms may provide unique critical opportunities. This we can see in the great example of eighteenth-century antiquarian criticism, whose arrayed critical forms cut across received ideas about the nature of history and historical research and prepared the way for the reconstitution of historiography, a movement which is clearly still taking place.

It appears that nonnarrative discourse is once again emerging as a force in criticism, probably because such discourse offers for our use critical forms (like the array and the dialectic) which can invade the strongholds of contemporary ideological narratives and force them to face their meanings and their limits. Not without reason does contemporary scholarship give such honor to Wittgenstein, Nietzsche, and Adorno, and not without reason has Cavell, an honest dialectician, produced a book on *Walden*. Few works in the tradition of American letters can match Henry David Thoreau's for the severity of its dialectics, its genius for generating and then undermining not merely its overall narrative discourse but each of the smaller, preliminary narrative units of which it is composed. In such a climate we may perhaps speculate on the possibility that a critical edition or even a bibliography is now being assembled somewhere which will induce a major shift in scholarly understanding. It has happened before and, strange as it may seem, I suspect that it is happening, or will soon happen, once again.

8 ⌒

The Idea of an Indeterminate Text:
Blake's Bible of Hell
and Dr. Alexander Geddes

A complete history of the Hebrew text would enumerate . . .
all the essential and accidental changes, whether for good or
for evil . . . The basic variations . . . have awakened in us the
spirit of inquiry and have led us to discoveries.

J. G. Eichhorn, *Introduction to the Old Testament*

IN BLAKE SCHOLARSHIP, one of the most vexing problems involves
the variant textual states of several of his works. Among the illuminated books, different copies of the *Songs of Innocence and of Experience, The [First] Book of Urizen, Milton,* and *Jerusalem* contain
different plate sequences which markedly affect the way we will read
those works. All such differences are of great interest to Blake scholars,
but the most important of them all—because the most problematic—
are the variances to be found in and between the texts of *Urizen*.[1]

In this particular case, moreover, what appears at first as a local
problem for students of Blake, on further investigation begins to reveal
connections with more broadly dispersed issues—issues that bear upon
fundamental areas of Romantic and post-Romantic artistic practice,
as well as the ideological context within which those practices emerged
and developed. To be specific: Blake's *Urizen* is the first English poem
whose structure was developed in conscious response to the new
developments in textual studies which we associate with eighteenth-
century German scholarship—with classicists like C. G. Heyne and
F. A. Wolf, and biblical scholars like J. G. Eichhorn and J. P. Gabler.
In this respect *Urizen* stands at the head of a line of works which
would include "The Rime of the Ancient Mariner," *The Giaour,*
"Sohrab and Rustum," several of Morris's best poems, and—the

culminant text—Pound's *Cantos*. Furthermore, a great many of our most important Romantic and post-Romantic works deploy layering structures which are clearly in debt to this textual tradition: one thinks immediately of Keats's two "Hyperions," a number of Browning's poems, *The Waste Land,* and the works of David Jones.

That *Urizen* is a parody of the Book of Genesis is well and widely known. Indeed, many scholars now take it for granted that *Urizen* is, in the words of G. E. Bentley, Jr., "the first book of 'The Bible of Hell' with which Blake threatened the world in the *Marriage* (?1790–3) pl. 24."[2] Much evidence supports that view. The fact that Blake drafted a title page for his Bible of Hell in the mid-1790s shows that his declaration in the *Marriage* was not simply a satiric gesture.[3] *Urizen* was initially titled "The *First* Book of Urizen" in order to emphasize the biblical connection: Genesis is traditionally called "the first book of Moses" or "the first book of the Pentateuch" (the latter, by convention, attributed to Moses's authorship). Furthermore, Blake engraved and printed two more books for his parodic Pentateuch, *The Book of Ahania* (1795) and *The Book of Los* (1795). Of all Blake's engraved works, only three are printed in double columns with divisions into chapters and verses as well. The physical appearance of these three works, that is to say, was intended to recall the typical format of those Bibles of Heaven owned and read by everyone.[4]

The parodic relation of these three works to the Bible led Northrop Frye to the following remarks in 1947: "*The Book of Ahania* is a sequel to *The Book of Urizen,* and *The Book of Los* intersects *The Book of Urizen* at its fourth chapter, somewhat as the J and E narratives intertwine in Genesis."[5] That general view of the matter remains in force to this day. More particularly, Frye's description of the relation between *Los* and *Urizen,* advanced in a metaphor drawn from modern biblical exegesis, has recently been picked up by Leslie Tannenbaum in his *Biblical Tradition in Blake's Early Prophecies.* Tannenbaum argues quite straightforwardly that "From these distinctions [between the J and the E strands in Genesis] Blake derives his conception of Urizen and Los."[6] And later: "Blake's most immediate source" for "the story of the division of the Elohim and Jehovah . . . and . . . the triumph of justice [Elohim/Urizen] over mercy [Jehovah/Los] . . . would be, of course, the debate between the Father and the Son in Book III of *Paradise Lost*."[7]

Most critics now would agree with Tannenbaum's thematic conception of the relation between Los and Urizen. What is problematic in his argument is the suggestion, first, that Blake's "most immediate source" for the distinction between an Elohist and a Jahwist version of Genesis is to be found in Milton, and, second, that Blake's work could have any actual relation to the textual tradition in biblical studies which produced the distinction between J and E strands in the first place. Quite simply, Milton as a source for an Elohist versus Jahwist version of Genesis is impossible, and equally impossible—on the face of it any rate—is the idea that Blake could have had any direct knowledge about J and E strands in the biblical texts. For the idea of "strands" in the biblical texts—that is to say, the now-famous "documentary hypothesis" about the biblical texts—was first formulated between 1779 and 1783 by J. G. Eichhorn in two seminal works written in German. They were not translated, and Blake did not know German.

All this may seem a mere tempest in the teapot of Blake scholarship, but in fact the problems located here bear upon important and widely dispersed literary issues, as I have already suggested. This is why we must be even more particular about Blake's biblical parody in *Urizen*. And we can be. We can say, for example, that Blake's critical parody of the Bible is specifically mounted from the vantage of the late Enlightenment revolution in textual studies of the biblical deposits. We can say that Blake probably knew Eichhorn's documentary hypothesis, and we can say further that he did *not* use it as a model when he fashioned any of the three books of the Bible of Hell. We can go further still and say that Blake's Bible of Hell, and *Urizen* in particular, has modeled its formal procedures on a theory of the biblical texts which was the chief rival, in Blake's period, to Eichhorn's now more celebrated documentary hypothesis. Indeed, the more one studies the textual problems of *Urizen* in this larger textual context, the more one realizes that *Urizen* (as well as its two associated "biblical" texts, *Ahania* and *Los*) reflects the influence of the new biblical scholarship precisely in those bibliographical aspects of its text which have caused so much trouble for readers of Blake. We can even be reasonably confident in identifying the chief conduit for Blake's knowledge of the new biblical scholarship. It was the radical scholar and Roman Catholic priest, Dr. Alexander Geddes. Geddes was one of the two biblical critics of the period who developed—as an alternative to

Eichhorn's documentary hypothesis—the theory of biblical texts known as the "fragment hypothesis."[8]

WE BEGIN TO UNRAVEL this complex of issues by recapitulating the problems in the texts of *Urizen*. This matter is best approached, initially, by comparing *Urizen* with Blake's other illuminated writings. Except for the various copies of the *Songs*—a work which is, in any case, an anthology or collection of pieces, and hence without narrative aspirations as such—Blake's other illuminated books rarely exhibit the extreme variances in ordering that we find in *Urizen*. Comparisons with those works most closely associated with it, *The Book of Ahania* and *The Book of Los,* are not useful since the latter works survive only in unique copies. *The Marriage of Heaven and Hell,* on the other hand, a tangentially related work, does exhibit variant orderings, but these have not seemed problematic to Blake's scholars and critics. Finally, though *Milton* and *Jerusalem* show certain alterations in the plate sequencing, these variances—particularly in works of such length and narrative complexity—are less consequential than are the variances in *Urizen.* Indeed, disorder both within and between the various copies of the latter seems almost the rule which Blake followed when he put the work together. Or rather, disorder is a permanent presence with which the work's conventional narrative inertia seems always to be engaged.[9]

The ordering problem in *Urizen* is basically twofold. First, certain plates which appear in some copies are absent from others. In some cases the missing plates contain only illustrative material, but in several others they contain important verbal material as well. A variant of this problem involves plates 7–8, which are absent in one copy (C). These plates seem to contain redundant material—that is, an "extra" passage headed by Blake "Chap. IV." Thus, in this case the six copies containing plates 7–8 have two chapters four, as if Blake had neglected to choose between the two and thus left most of the copies of *Urizen* with an unnecessary accretion. Later editions of Blake produced by scholars, by refusing to delete either of the two chapters four, have established the problem on a permanent basis. Other missing plates include plate 4 (not in copies D–G), plates 9 and 24 (not in copy E), and plate 16 (not in C–F).

The second problem involves the ordering of the plates in the individual copies. In this case the anomaly is itself of two kinds. On the one hand, none of the plate orderings in any of the copies of *Urizen* provides a narrative continuity which scholars have found acceptable. Each copy has certain plate sequencing problems which disturb the internal consistency of the material. Furthermore, no two copies ever agree on any one sequence. We see this immediately in Bentley's tabular description of the binding order[10] of the seven copies:

Copy	Binding order
A	1–2, 22, 24, 3–4, 12, 5–7, 17, 8, 10–11, 14, 13, 18, 21, 19, 15–16, 20, 9, 23, 26, 25, 28, 27
B	1–4, 14, 5–7, 10, 12, 8, 11, 22, 13, 9, 15–16, 18, 17, 19, 24, 20–1, 23, 25–8
C	1, 2, 3–4, 12, 5–6, 9–11, 13, 22, 15, 14, 18, 17, 19, 21, 20, 23, 27, 24–6, 28
D	1–3, 5–15, 17–28
E	1, 3, 5, 12, 2, 6, 14, 7, 10, 8, 11, 22, 13, 15, 18, 17, 19, 25, 20–1, 23, 26–8
F	1–3, 5, 12, 6–7, 14, 10, 8–9, 11, 13, 22, 15, 18, 17, 19–21, 23–8
G	1–3, 9, 5, 12, 6, 14, 7–8, 22, 10–11, 16, 13, 15, 17–21, 23, 27, 24–6, 28
H–I	Loose

As Bentley observes, "The problem of arranging the plates is confusing, for each of the seven copies is bound quite differently from the others, and three of these orders [i.e., copies B, D, G] are justified by Blake's foliation."[11]

Like other scholars, however, Bentley thinks that "if we separate the plates bearing text from those consisting only of designs, the patterns become clearer."[12] This is certainly true, but equally certain is that serious ordering problems remain. In plates 1–11, for example, the extant copies offer four distinct sequences for the verbal text: 1–4, 5–7, 8, 10–11 (copy A); 1–4, 5–7, 10, 8, 11 (copy B); 1–3, 5–7, 10, 8, 11 (copies E, F); 1–3, 5–7, 8, 10, 11 (copies D, G). And of course copy C has its own special sequence (1–4, 5–6, 10–11) because plates 7–8 are absent. Notable here is that in Blake's own foliated copies two different sequences are provided. Only slightly less troubling is that copy A has the following sequence later in the poem for the verbal text (13, 18, 19, 15, 20) where all the other copies have 13, 15, 18–20.

In face of these kinds of textual problems Blake's best editors have striven to find an authoritative order. Bentley says that "despite the extraordinary inconsistency of the orders in which copies are numbered and bound, the proper arrangement of the text is fairly plain": 1–4, 12, 5–11, 13–28. This is, he notes, an "eclectic" text which corresponds "most closely to the numbered copy D" but which is in fact "chiefly based upon narrative consistency, foliation, binding, and the relationship of design to text."[13] Erdman's approach and general view are the same: "There is only one possible arrangement of the text, since it is organized into numbered chapters—except that Plate 8, duplicating the numbers of Plate 10, was probably meant to replace it. Yet Plate 2 is out of order in copy E, 15 follows 18 in copy A, and 8 follows rather than precedes 10 in copies B, E, and F."[14] Erdman's "one possible arrangement" for the verbal text is the same as Bentley's.

Now there is no question but that, *from the point of view of narrative consistency,* Bentley and Erdman are correct to think that their ordering preference is the most reasonable. Yet neither editor is willing to pursue their quest for narrative consistency so far as to remove one or another of the duplicate chapters 4. Furthermore, all later editions enshrine the problem of this unstable text in that curious title—so difficult to read aloud—with the bracketed word: *The [First] Book of Urizen.* Scholars can neither wholly give up nor entirely accept that problematic word, preserved in most copies of the work but erased by Blake in others.[15] Thus a residue of the text's "extraordinary inconsistency" always remains a dramatic presence in our received and scholarly editions. In the various facsimile editions the textual irregularities are especially prominent.

Of course, many readers of Blake would regard these kinds of scholarly preoccupations with the "correct" order as profoundly anti-Blakean operations—a kind of quest for, as it were, a textual "solid without fluctuation" (plate 4: 10). All readers of Blake are aware that his is a prolific and not a devouring art—an art whose chief aim is to "rouze the faculties to act."[16] Reasonable orders are not imaginative orders. Erdman's awareness of this general truth about Blake's work, for example, leads him to the following conclusion about the *Songs of Innocence and of Experience.* Since the arrangement of the poems in this work differs markedly among the twenty-one surviving copies, Erdman suggests "that the reader experiment, as Blake did, to find what different tensions and resonances are produced by different juxtapositions."[17] That suggestion has subsequently been taken by many critics as a guiding principle for reading all of Blake's works.

Urizen will yield to such a principle very nicely. What I want to suggest here, however, is that *Urizen*'s unstable text is of a determinate type, and that it owes its imaginative conception to Blake's discovery, in the early 1790s, of the new scholarly investigations into the state of the biblical texts.

BIBLICAL SCHOLARS from antiquity have been aware of various textual anomalies in both the Old and the New Testaments. Not until the eighteenth-century, however, were systematic methods found for clarifying (if not unraveling) the many problems of those texts. This came about largely as a consequence of the application to biblical studies of the recent advances made in the elucidation of similar problems relating to classical texts. The single most important figure among the classicists was Heyne, for it was Heyne who led directly to Eichhorn, and from Eichhorn came Gabler. With Gabler's revised edition of Eichhorn's *Urgeschichte, Ein Versuch*, originally published in 1779, but reissued in 1790–1793 in Gabler's enormously augmented work, the new biblical scholarship was established on a firm and clear foundation.

Blake, of course, did not read any of this German work directly. What he would have read was the work of Geddes, one of Joseph Johnson's authors and a man who moved in the same circles with Blake in the early 1790s. Geddes was the chief conduit in England for the ideas being pursued and elaborated by the new German scholars of the Bible. In addition, Blake seems to have been familiar with the many discussions of the new biblical criticism which appeared in the most important periodical associated with Johnson's circle, the *Analytical Review*. Indeed, between 1788 and 1791 Geddes was Johnson's principal reviewer of this material, which included all of the leading works being produced in Germany by scholars like J. D. Michaelis and Eichhorn.[18]

So far as the structural problems associated with Blake's Bible of Hell are concerned, Geddes is important because he provided Blake with crucial insights into the character of the biblical texts. Geddes's textual ideas developed out of his original encounter with the new biblical studies being pursued in Germany. This scholarship, which effected a revolution in biblical studies, was neither well nor widely received in England at the time. Insofar as it was known at all, it was viewed with suspicion, and Geddes was consequently the object of sharp attack as one whose work was undermining the basis of England's ideological order.

This field of dispute is the context within which I will pursue the textual problems in the Bible of Hell. Before considering the specific instabilities we have already observed in Blake's works, however, I shall have to make an excursus into the question of Blake's ideas about myth. This move is necessary for two reasons. First, Geddes, like his counterparts in Germany, developed his ideas about the biblical texts via a set of critical reflections in comparative mythography. Consequently, Geddes's textual ideas with respect to the Bible are not easily separated from his ideas about myth, and the same is true of Blake. Second, received scholarly opinion on Blake's ideas about myth is seriously deficient in several crucial areas, and this deficiency needs to be rectified.

Geddes first became involved in translating the Bible in connection with the project of his patron, the Roman Catholic Lord Petre, who wanted to provide English Catholics with a revision of the Douai and Challoner bibles. When this plan was preempted by the Catholic bishops, who were wary that the work of the young priest might prove too liberal, Geddes decided to undertake his translation as an independent scholarly task. He first announced the method and goal of this work in his *Prospectus of a New Translation of the Holy Bible* (1786). This work argued that the received biblical texts were corrupt because they all derived from unreliable base texts—indeed, that the problems arose because of a failure to understand the historical character of the base texts. Geddes maintained that the foundational Hebrew text, the Masoretic Bible, was a heteroglot work and hence did not reflect some original and pure inspiration. The other early texts, the Greek Septuagint and the Latin Vulgate, were obviously secondary and equally in need of critical examination. A "new translation" could only be produced, then, by returning to the original Hebrew documents, which would have to be critically examined and purified. In Geddes's view this meant, so far as the Pentateuch was concerned, returning to the Samaritan Pentateuch as "a far more faithful representative of the prototype than any masoretic copy at this day extant."[19]

Geddes's *Prospectus* was noticed principally by scholars, who took exception to his work in several ways. But the larger ideological issues concealed in the technical disputes did not pass without comment, so Geddes was induced to bring out three more pamphlets—in 1787, 1788, and 1790—responding to the criticisms which were raised against his plans. These criticisms came both from establishment Protestant quarters—which looked warily on any suggestion that the received Bible might be textually unreliable—and from Geddes's own Roman Catholics, who were institutionally committed to the authority of the Latin Vulgate.

When the first volume of Geddes's Bible finally appeared in June 1792, it was variously hailed and denounced.[20] The Roman Catholic bishop of London condemned the work and suspended Geddes from the exercise of his priestly functions. The notices in the more liberal press, like the *Critical Review* and the *Monthly Review*, were favorable, but the conservative (and Protestant) *British Critic* followed the bishop of London in condemning the work as "dangerous" and "insidious." Geddes responded to his critics in two further pamphlets published in 1793 and 1794. In 1797 the second volume of Geddes's Bible finally appeared, and the third volume—containing his *Critical Remarks* on the first two volumes of his translation—was issued in 1800. Geddes died in 1801.

GEDDES WAS a highly visible advocate of the most liberal ideas of the period. His Bible was a work of the English Left and was recognized as such at the time. This is important to remember when we reflect upon Geddes's influence upon Blake's *Urizen* and the whole project of a Bible of Hell. Such a project all but declared its association with the advanced Enlightenment traditions of biblical scholarship, which were seen at the time in conservative quarters as destructive of the foundations of religion. But neither Geddes nor Blake saw his own work in this way—on the contrary, in fact. Both thought their work would set Christianity on a deeper, firmer footing.

Two lines of Geddes's thinking on biblical matters were important for Blake, both in general and in relation to his Bible of Hell particularly. The first of these I have already touched upon. That is to say, Blake's ideas about myth coincide with, and in certain respects even derive from, the new classical and biblical hermeneutics. Since Blake did not have direct access to the works of the new German scholarship, his connection to this material requires explanation.

The point of intersection between Blake's early work and Geddes's research—the reason why Blake would have been initially drawn to Geddes's biblical studies—lies in each man's ideas about mythology. Both were syncretic mythographers. That is to say, they both believed that ancient texts (like Homer, the Bible, and early national scriptures such as the Icelandic Eddas) employed comparable modes of discourse:

> For the syncretists, [all] gods and fables . . . were variants of an archetypal pattern of history and/or religion. In the hands of orthodox theologians like [Jacob] Bryant . . . such syncretism could demonstrate that myths were derivative of certain primary Christian myths and hence the truths of Christianity were affirmed; while on the other hand such skeptics as Drummond and Dupuis could syncretize all myths and assert that Christian ones had no more priority to truth than pagan ones since both proceeded from naturalistic archetypal symbols in primitive thought and imagination.[21]

Blake scholars still follow Ruthven Todd's view that Blake's ideas about myth coincide fairly closely with those of Bryant. And while there is no reason to question the pertinence of Bryant's work to Blake's, the connection is not nearly so central as Todd thought.

The key Blakean idea in the 1790s[22]—that "all Bibles or sacred codes" (*The Marriage of Heaven and Hell,* plate 4: 1) contain ideologically skewed poetic materials, or "forms of worship" fashioned out of "poetic tales" (*Marriage,* plate 11)—is not derivable from mythographers like Bryant. To such readers the Bible was a special case and in no way comparable to the ancient pagan mythological texts. Bryant, for example, made the biblical "history" into a set of factual truths which were then obscurely reflected in, and corroborated by, various coincident pagan texts. But Blake's idea, first fully elaborated in the *Marriage* (especially in plates 11-13), was that all the ancient texts, biblical and pagan alike, contained what Blake's contemporaries called "mythologues"—"poetic tales" which encoded various culturally specific ideas and attitudes. Blake read the Bible in the same way that he read any other ancient text. In this respect his method of reading recalls Enlightenment figures like Bayle, Dupuis, and even Paine. Nicholas Bonneville's *De l'Esprit des Religions* (1792) is a work very much in that line of "skeptical" mythography.[23] It was reviewed in Johnson's *Analytical Review,* and the phrasing of this notice distinctly recalls Blake's *Marriage* plates 11–13: "Every thing of old became animated in the opinion of a people, who consulted nothing but their *senses* . . . they accordingly not only imagined, that men like themselves, and the animals that surrounded them, were thinking creatures, but also that the sun, the moon, the rivers, and the plants were so also. The style became dramatic, and the stars and the flowers were described as men."[24] Blake read the primitive parts of the Bible in the light of a similar anthropomorphic theory. So far as he was concerned, what distinguished the Bible from the ancient pagan texts was the New Testament, which provided the reader of the Old Testament (and of the equivalent ancient pagan texts) with a deconstructive key for elucidating received scripture.

This way of reading the texts of Holy Scriptures, and especially the Old Testament texts, came to Blake through the work of men like Bishop Lowth, whose *Lectures* were first translated into English in 1787. But the approach as it is employed by Blake—particularly between 1790 and 1798—carries a *critical* edge which one does not find in Lowth and which one associates with the "skeptical" and Enlightenment tradition of mythography. The *Marriage* and the whole project of a Bible of Hell, after all, assume a fundamentally satiric and critical posture. In this context the new German textual scholarship, as that was mediated for Blake by Geddes, would have supplied the poet with a point of view which coincided, in many respects, with his own.

So far as the status of fable and myth is concerned, an alternative can be marked out between the orthodox position (Bryant) and the skeptical (Bayle, Bonneville, Dupuis). Both Blake and Geddes occupied that position in slightly different ways.[25] Unlike Bryant, Blake did not see the biblical texts as more privileged than other comparably primitive documents from different cultures. Throughout the 1790s, Blake's position does not vary from what we find in the *Marriage* and, earlier, in *All Religions are One*:

> Principle 5. The Religeons of all Nations are derived from each Nation's different reception of the Poetic Genius which is every where call'd the Spirit of Prophecy.

> Principle 6 The Jewish & Christian Testaments are An original derivation from the Poetic Genius. this is necessary from the confined nature of bodily sensation

> Principle 7th As all men are alike (tho' infinitely various) So all Religions & as all similars have one source.
>   The true Man is the source he being the Poetic Genius.[26]

Blake's position here is a gnostic one, and it conforms to certain Neo-Platonic structures of thought, as Kathleen Raine has shown. Todd's remark that in Blake we find "the nitric acid of Boehme applied to the copper plate of Bryant" is a peculiarly apt formulation.[27]

What Todd and Raine do not see, however, is that Blake's view of "all Bibles or sacred codes" put him in a position that would be especially sympathetic to the new biblical scholarship as set out for English audiences in the work of Geddes and the *Analytical Review*. Though a Romantic in many cultural respects, Blake was, like most of the Romantics, deeply marked by certain Enlightenment modes of thought. Thus his frequent attacks upon priestcraft are entirely coincident with the most radical lines of Enlightenment thinking. The idea that "forms of worship" were fashioned from "poetic tales" by tyrannizing moralists differs not at all from what Volney wrote in chapters 22–23 of his *Les Ruines*, a work reviewed in the *Analytical* in 1792.

Similarly, though critical of Paine in certain respects, Blake stood with him against Bishop Watson on the matter of how one should read the Bible. In this case the relevance to Geddes is quite interesting. To Blake, "Paine has not attacked Christianity. Watson has defended Antichrist."[28] Watson's attack on Paine's critique of the Bible is "wicked & blasphemous" in Blake's eyes in two principal respects: first, Watson denies both that conscience is the ultimate standard of judgment and that "honest indignation" is the mark of Poetic Genius; and second, Watson defends every word and deed in the Bible as a record of divine providence. But to Blake, "Conscience . . . is unequivocal, it is the voice of God."[29] Paine, therefore, is an oracle of conscience, one of those "who give themselves to their Energetic Genius" rather than one of those, like Watson, who "pretend to be a modest Enquirer" into the Bible but who are in fact hypocrites and defenders of state religion.[30]

Similarly, Blake dismisses Watson's traditional ideas about the status of the biblical record:

> To me who believe the Bible & profess myself a Christian a defence of the Wickedness of the Israelites in murdering so many thousands under pretence of a command from God is altogether Abominable & Blasphemous Was not Christ murderd because he taught that God loved all Men & was their father & forbad all contention for Worldly prosperity in opposition to the Jewish Scriptures which are only an Example

of the wickedness & deceit of the Jews . . . Christ died an Unbeliever.
& . . . the Holy Ghost . . . in Paine strives with Christendom as in Christ
he strove with the Jews.[31]

To Blake, if the Bible is not read out of "Conscience or the Word of
God Universal"[32] it will be read out of a narrow ideology, or what
he calls "state religion." The Bible must be read critically and not in
terms of its own self-conceptions, moral codes, or forms of worship.
This is why he says, once again echoing his earlier thought in the
Marriage: "That the Jews assumed a right <exclusively> to the benefits
of God. will be a lasting witness against them. & the same will it be
against Christians."[33]

This way of reading the text of Holy Scripture, especially the Old
Testament texts, sets Blake alongside Geddes's more scholarly procedures. Blake's unswerving view that "the Holy Bible & the Gospel
of Jesus are not allegory"[34] and must not be read allegorically recalls
Geddes's own firm conviction that any allegorical elements in the
biblical texts are not a part of their originary character but have been
interpolated and insinuated by later editors and commentators. Geddes's
quest for what he calls "the bare literal meaning"[35] is entirely equivalent to Blake's project, set out in the *Marriage,* of revealing the infinite
that is hidden beneath the obscured surfaces of all texts.[36] Similarly,
Blake would have been impressed with all of Geddes's writings, as
he was impressed with Paine, because they exhibited a candid and
total adherence to intellectual honesty. Thus, Geddes's response to
his critics in his 1793 pamphlet is entirely characteristic. "I am," he
states, "a sworn enemy to implicit faith, as well as to implicit obe-
dience [and] have ever been accustomed to think for myself . . .
and . . . will speak and write as I think."[37]

These coincidences between Blake and Geddes should not be particularly surprising since the two men moved in the same radical
circles. To this point, however, only one critic has noticed a specific
connection between Geddes and a text by Blake, and in this instance
no general conclusions are suggested. Against the background I have
been sketching, however, we may further distinguish the two points
of contact which throw significant new light on Blake's work.

F. B. Curtis found in *Urizen* an echo of Geddes's preface to his
translation of the Bible, and several other local points of intersection
might be reasonably argued.[38] The correlations are especially noticeable, however, in Blake's and Geddes's ideas about myth. Previous

critics have seen in these ideas the influence of Bryant's deluvian thesis, and while a connection to Bryant must not be dismissed, we should see that Blake's thought runs on a longer and far more significant parallel with Geddes's.

For example, Blake's notion that the natural world of the earth is the creation of a fallen deity, and that it is all a "watry shore" and a "starry floor," distinctly recalls Geddes's ideas about the condition of the world before the events described in Genesis. The first five plates of *Urizen* do not correspond to anything in Genesis; rather, they depict the state of affairs just before the events recorded at the beginning of Genesis—which is to say a psychopolitical, or ideological state of affairs that stand as the background for the subsequent acts of "creation" carried out, in Blake's translation of these events, by Urizen and then by Los.

The Genesis account, for Blake, does not give us a true picture of a divinely created world (that is to say, an Original Existence); rather, its record preserves only a broken set of images. The beginning of *Urizen*, then, depicts a Urizenic view of existence, and Blake seems to have found his model for this scene in Geddes's Bible. According to Geddes, before the "creation" began in Genesis 1:3, the stellar universe was already in place, and the earth was "*formed out of water and by means of water.*"[39] This is the equivalent of the state of existence conjured in the fearful and deranged imagination of Urizen as he is separating himself from Eternity. It is what Blake will later see as the world of Ulro. Geddes describes it this way: "Could there, indeed, be conceived a more desolate and dismal situation than that in which our little planet was then plunged? A mass of unformed matter, totally immersed in water, and surrounded with a dense, dark, tempestuous air!—Well, what must be done? This dark mass of earth and water must be enlightened."[40] At this point the Genesis account takes over with the creation of light in the form of the sun. "The sun, could not . . . illuminate more than half the earth at once . . . and this is fitly called *separating the light from the darkness*; namely, by that ever-flitting boundary called by us the *horizon*."[41] Geddes's footnote to this passage and to the word *horizon* is as close as we are likely to come to the point of origin of his own [*First*] *Book of Urizen*: "From a Greek word . . . which signifies to *bound* or *terminate*." Most Blake scholars now agree that the name Urizen derives from the Greek word which Geddes noted, but no one has suggested what may have stimulated Blake to his play upon the Greek.

That it was Geddes who provided Blake with the local habitation and the name for his own parodic book of Genesis is not important simply as a philological fact. Its significance lies in the total context of relationships which the Geddes-Blake connection opens up for us. In the present instance, Blake's *Urizen* follows Geddes's idea, which he shared with the leading contemporary German scholars, that Genesis represents an edited collection of mythological narratives which have their basis in the cultural history of the ancient Hebrews. The whole account of the Fall, Geddes later remarks in the preface to his Bible, is actually "an excellent *mythologue*" reflecting the ideas of primitive Judaism.[42] His discussion of "the Mosaic divinity"—the figure Blake will name Urizen, recollecting Geddes,—is particularly apposite in relation to Blake's various accounts of this being. Although the Mosaic God has "various positive and absolute attributes," Geddes observes, these are always

> clothed in colours that inspire rather fear than love: the empire of this latter was, long after, to be established, by a greater lawgiver than Moses. The God of Moses is a *jealous God, who punisheth the iniquity of the fathers in their children, unto the third or fourth generation*; an irascible and avenging God, who *consumeth like a devouring fire; who maketh his arrows drunk with the blood of his enemies, and his sword satiated with their flesh*. He is even said to *harden*, sometimes, *the hearts* of wicked men, that he may take more flagrant vengeance of them. Indeed, the whole tenor of the Pentateuch convinces me, that the more ancient Hebrews were real anthropomorphites. At any rate, all such expressions must be considered as metaphorical imagery, adapted to the ideas of a stupid, carnal people.[43]

This god is the being Blake names Urizen, the god of boundaries and moral codes. He is to be distinguished from Los, the god of sex and pity, the god who creates the body of Urizen and who is also associated with the creation of Adam and Eve (rather than the creation of the "World") and with the Los(s) of paradise.

These two gods represent different (mythologized) perspectives, and as such they epitomize the idea that everything is as it is ideologically perceived. Ahania, Orc, Fuzon, and all of Blake's odd assortment of mythic figures locate special points of vision. Geddes was not especially important in helping Blake clarify his own views on these matters. But Geddes's mythological conception of the ancient Hebrew texts operated with another set of ideas about those texts which did have a profound effect on Blake's management of the structure of *Urizen* and the entire Bible of Hell project. This second set of ideas in the Geddes Bible is at least as important as Geddes's Enlightenment theory of myth. That is to say, Geddes was Blake's chief source for his knowledge of the state of the biblical texts. So far as our understanding of *The [First] Book of Urizen* is concerned, these textual insights are extremely important, and, once again, they have hitherto gone completely unnoticed.

READING GEDDES, Blake would have discovered that the biblical texts did not comprise a seamless narrative marked by occasional ruptures and mistakes. Of course, the hiatuses, corruptions, oddly repeated passages, and stories had been well known to scholarship for centuries. Spinoza's disparaging comments on the state of the biblical texts dramatize the problem which the scriptural scholar had to face:

> If anyone pays attention to the way in which all the histories and precepts in [the Pentateuch] are set down promiscuously and without order, with no regard for dates; and further, how the same story is often repeated, sometimes in a different version, he will easily, I say, discern that all the materials were promiscuously collected and heaped together, in order that they might at some subsequent time be more readily examined and reduced to order. Not only these five books, but also the narratives contained in the remaining seven, going down to the destruction of the city, are compiled in the same way.[44]

Spinoza set forth, in his *Theologico-Political Treatise,* a set of rational procedures for negotiating this difficult territory. But he lacked the philological tools—both ethnographic and textual—which would be developed later in the Higher Criticism. What the new German scholarship of Eichhorn and Gabler provided was a coherent and totalized theory for explaining these problems. Geddes developed his own special version of that theory which later became known as "the fragment hypothesis."

In his preface to the first volume of his Bible translation, Geddes, like his German counterparts, operated on two related principles: that the texts of Holy Writ had to be examined in the light of human reason since they were, fundamentally, human documents; and second, that the texts had to be studied in the sociohistorical context of their institution, both original and transmissive. In adopting this approach, these scholars were essentially following the track first cleared by Spinoza. Thus when Geddes notes that the division of the Bible into chapters and verses is often done arbitrarily, and just as often obscures the actual makeup of the book, he appeals to facts which scholars like Spinoza had already called attention to many times. Similarly, Spinoza pointed out the numerous contradictions between different texts in the Bible and the just as frequent repetitions of various stories and passages. For Spinoza, however, clarification of these problems in the "contents of Scripture, must be sought from Scripture alone."[45] Furthermore, he took it for granted that the Bible, being under divine authority, "teaches true moral doctrines": that is, "true" by the standards which reason can apply.[46]

The new element in Geddes's Enlightenment scholarship is the argument that the text before us now can be understood only if we step outside the text and examine it in the light of the historical, linguistic, and ethnographic frameworks within which it defines its special, even unique, character. The Bible is a particular example of a general case that can and must be applied to all textual deposits which descend to us over long periods of time. The Bible is the product of a long history, and the application of a scientific method can elucidate the layers and stages of that history as they are reflected in the received texts. Spinoza's promiscuous heap was not achieved in one place or time; it is the product of a complex, continuous, and often arbitrary set of historical interactions.

In the preface to his translation of the Bible Geddes outlines Eichhorn's so-called documentary theory of the biblical texts as originally set forth in both the *Urgeschichte* (1779) and the *Einleitung ins Alte Testament* (1780–1783). This theory is the now widely accepted one which holds—in the case of Genesis, for example—that in its most primitive state it comprised two separate written documents (the so-called J and E strands) which were redacted together. A third document (the P strand), according to Eichhorn, was then interpolated at various points into this redaction. Genesis is, then, in this view, a layered text made up of at least three different textual strands that correspond to two original and relatively coherent documents along with a third whose character was less precisely determinable. The philological, cultural, and historical differences between these strands are the original source of the Bible's textual problems. Sometimes the different documents have not been woven together very well, sometimes they offer different versions of the same material, and sometimes the editors of the original texts were unable to understand the documents they had to deal with.

The Pentateuch, for example, traditionally ascribed to Moses, is in fact something else altogether—a compiled text put together at different times and which

> has not come down to us in its full integrity, nor without alterations: but what work of antiquity has not had a similar fate? . . . Two rival peoples, the Jews and the Samaritans, have preserved separate exemplars of it, in different characters. It was excellently translated into Greek, at a period when the copies must have been much less imperfect than they afterwards became: this translation we have entire, though not uncorrupted. We have also fragments of three other Greek versions, all prior to the commencement of the third century. We have a Chaldee version, and a Chaldee paraphrase, of uncertain date. We have a Syriac translation . . . In the fourth century we have a Latin version by St. Jerom[e].[47]

Geddes's argument is that the biblical compilation is not so uniformly layered as the Eichhorn theory suggested. According to Geddes's fragment hypothesis, the Bible comprised a heterogeneous collection of materials gathered together at different times by different redactors. As for the Pentateuch, it was not written or compiled by Moses but was "reduced to its present form in the reign of Solomon." It was a compilation "from ancient documents, some of which were coeval with Moses, and some even anterior to Moses. Whether all these were written records, or many of them only oral traditions, it would be rash to determine. It is my opinion that the Hebrews had no written documents before the days of Moses . . . Oral testimony was transmitted, from generation to generation, in simple narratives, or rustic songs."[48] Like his contemporary J. S. Vater, who also subscribed to a fragment theory,[49] Geddes saw in the book a great many fragments of different ancient texts of varying length, origin, date, and textual integrity. According to the fragment hypothesis, the Bible is a more disorderly text than the work hypothesized by scholars like Eichhorn, and a far more disorderly text than most ordinary readers would have been able to imagine.

Among scholars of the period, Geddes's work was taken seriously and widely discussed. Eichhorn and Geddes engaged in a long correspondence in which they each compared and tested their views on these questions. To Eichhorn, Geddes's biblical project was an im-

portant event in the new investigation of the ancient texts. But in
England, among a population—including the learned community—
which remained committed to most traditional types of biblical study,
the situation was very different. To produce a Bible on the hermeneutic
premises of Geddes's work (mythic material, fragmentary texts), particularly in the volatile period of the 1790s, was a "dangerous" and
"impious" exercise, and Geddes felt the full force of reaction to his
work. It was, both politically and theologically, a veritable "Bible of
Hell."

HAVING LAID OUT the context within which Blake's *Urizen* was
produced, we are now prepared to consider directly the problem of
its textual disorderliness. The influence of Geddes's fragment hypothesis on Blake's *Urizen* is most dramatically evident in the poem's
two most important textual cruces: that is to say, in relation to the
problem of plate 4, which is missing from four copies, including two
of the three which Blake foliated himself, and in relation to plates 7-
8, which are present in six of the seven copies, but which contain the
redundant chapter 4.

Recently Robert Essick has developed an explanation for the absence of plate 4 from Copy G, the latest of the seven copies.[50] His
argument rests upon an unexamined piece of documentary material—
a loose copy of plate 4 which was probably printed for Copy G and
which shows an improperly aligned plate image. Essick's argument is
that the misalignment of the plate during printing resulted in a bad
copy. He further hypothesizes that Blake must not have been able to
print another copy, for reasons unknown to us, and that he may not
have been able to correct the misalignment because he had already
decided on the trim-size of Copy G.

Essick's is an interesting argument which bears upon Blake's work
in an important general way. Even if his hypothesis about Copy G is
correct, however, it does not explain the state of the copies of *Urizen*
produced in the 1790s, when the influence of Geddes's work would
have been strongest. Nor does it explain the problem of the redundant
chapter 4 on plates 7–8, still present in Copy G. But when we reflect
that *Urizen* was conceived as the "First" book in Blake's projected
Bible of Hell, and that the textual problems of plates 4 and 7–8 recall
the same sort of problem which men like Geddes were laboring to
clarify for the Bible (of Heaven), the true significance of Blake's dis-

orderly texts begins to emerge. These passages do not locate authorial lapses or unresolved incoherences, they represent deliberate acts on Blake's part, textualizations which make *Urizen* a parody of Genesis carried out along lines opened up by the new biblical criticism and by the radical priest Alexander Geddes in particular. That Blake's ideas about myth—initially developed in the *Marriage,* but carried forward in *Urizen* and his later works as well—also correspond to Geddes's thinking is surely no mere coincidence. Add to this the fact that Blake and Geddes moved in the same circles, that they were both devoted students of the Bible and committed to latitudinarian—if not radical—principles in religion and politics, and the correspondences between *Urizen* and Geddes's ideas become impossible to set aside.

Copies of *Urizen* which lack plate 4 do not have a chapter 3 in their text, whereas the copies which have plates 7–8 have an extra chapter 4. Furthermore, three different orderings of the textual materials in plates 13–20 are extant in the different copies, as we have already seen, and the different copies exhibit all kinds of other, less dramatic discontinuities. Geddes's work showed Blake, however, not only that many texts of the Bible of Heaven existed, but also that those texts exhibited lacunae and redundancies within and between themselves. Geddes's investigations licensed Blake to deal with his own works quite freely, and they gave him a model for making a parody Bible which would expose and explain the deceptive transparencies and stabilities of the received Bible of Heaven.

Blake eventually abandoned his projected Bible of Hell, but not before he had engraved two further books for it. That *The Book of Ahania* and *The Book of Los* were both originally conceived as part of Blake's Bible of Hell is strongly suggested by the textual format of these works, as we have already seen. But the two later works also follow *Urizen* by reflecting in their textual procedures the influence of the new biblical criticism. This correspondence among the three works, in the context of Geddes's biblical criticism, may not be noticeable at first, because we do not observe in the two later works the same sort of incongruities as are apparent in *Urizen.* This lack of immediate similarity is partly a consequence of the fact that the two later works survive only in unique copies.

Nevertheless, that Blake is still parodying the Bible along the Geddes line in *The Book of Ahania* and *The Book of Los* is clear. *The Book of Los* repeats much of the narrative of *Urizen,* but from a slightly different point of view. Furthermore, both *Ahania* and *Los* report details which contradict equivalent texts in *Urizen*.[51] None of this represents carelessness on Blake's part or an uncertainty about how to deploy his mythic materials, although these two conclusions could easily be drawn from the textual circumstances. On the contrary, the textual anomalies are structural; they are part of an effort to critique the received Bible and its traditional exegetes from the point of view of the latest research findings of the new historical philology.

Urizen and its two companion works are formally related to the fictional reconstructions carried out by Macpherson and Chatterton. The models for the Ossian and Rowley poems are taken from the antiquarian tradition, however, whereas Blake's poems would not have been possible without the historical scholarship of men like Griesbach, Eichhorn, and Geddes. Such men, along with their contemporary counterparts in classical philology, laid the groundwork for a whole new hermeneutics. These scholarly advances had the most profound impact upon the poetry and fiction of the nineteenth century, especially in the imaginative treatment of historical and legendary materials. They are the equivalent, in literary studies, of the archaeological and anthropological research carried out by men like Winckelmann and Sir William Jones, and sponsored by organizations like the Society of the Dilettanti. In Blake and the other writers of the early nineteenth century, these new scholarly models served as tools for revealing—in the words of Armytage, Wordsworth's local antiquarian—"things which you cannot see." To read *The [First] Book of Urizen* is to discover a Bible one had never known before; it is to learn to read the traditional Bible in an entirely new way.

9

Ulysses as a Postmodern Work

> Sundering truth from falsehood is the goal of the materialist
> method, not its point of departure. In other words, its point
> of departure is the object riddled with error . . . and it can-
> not present this object as mixed or uncritical enough. If it
> claimed to approach the object the way it is "in truth," it
> would only greatly reduce its chances. These chances are . . .
> considerably augmented if the materialist method . . . aban-
> dons such a claim, thus preparing for the insight that "the
> matter in itself" is not "in truth."
>
> Walter Benjamin,
> *The Paris of the Second Empire in Baudelaire*

IN ALL FIELDS of knowledge, certain scholarly works appear and
immediately establish themselves as epochal events. Modern textual
studies orient themselves in relation to a few seminal works. Initially
these were investigations into the texts of antiquity: Wolf's *Prolegomena ad Homerum* (1795), Eichhorn's *Einleitung ins Alte Testament* (1780–1783), Lachmann's edition of Lucretius (1850). Students
of modern national scriptures, toward the end of the nineteenth and
at the beginning of the twentieth century, gradually began to realize
the importance of the textual disciplines developed by classical and
biblical scholars. Once again the name of Lachmann is crucial—
specifically for his work on the *Niebelungenlied*.[1] In vernacular literatures, systematic textual studies began with medieval texts and
culminated in Joseph Bédier's work on the *Lai de L'Ombre*.[2]

For modern English studies the point of departure has been the
work on the Elizabethan texts begun in the early part of this century.
Here the central document has been a small but powerful essay by
W. W. Greg, the famous "Rationale of Copy-Text."[3] All critical editing of vernacular English texts must at some point come to grips
with Greg's discussion. The work of Fredson Bowers and those other
distinguished scholars who followed him has been a studied meditation upon the meaning, in practical editorial terms, of Greg's essay.

Two later events in English textual studies must be mentioned before I turn to Gabler's new edition of Joyce's *Ulysses*.[4] First is the editorial work by Kane and Donaldson on the texts of Langland's *Piers Plowman,* and the second is the revolution in Shakespearean textual studies which has been slowly taking place for the past ten or fifteen years.[5] In each of these cases a serious theoretical challenge has been raised against certain prevailing editorial and textual views. More than any other, this work on Langland and Shakespeare has brought the problems of traditional textual methods into sharp and critical focus.

Gabler's edition of *Ulysses,* then, appears at a moment when the theory and practice of English textual studies are in a highly volatile state. This circumstance calls attention to the (so to speak) climatic importance of the edition. Equally significant are three other factors. In the first place, the edition has taken full advantage of the most recent developments—themselves revolutionary for literary studies— in computer-based text processing. Second, Gabler is editing a specifically *modern* work—indeed, a text which is arguably the most important literary work in English of this century. Third, the recent publication of the *James Joyce Archive,* as well as the facsimile of the Rosenbach manuscript, has made it possible for any student anywhere in the world to follow Gabler's work in the most minute and exacting detail.[6]

Even if it were a bad edition, then, this work would be prima facie important. It will require close studies of its methodology, its execution, and its archival basis before we know how well and carefully Gabler has carried out his work.[7] These three volumes ought therefore to be a required object of study for every scholar working in English literature. Nor do I have in mind here only textual scholars or editors. More clearly and practically than any of the recent spate of theoretical work in criticism and hermeneutics, this edition raises all the central questions that have brought such a fruitful crisis to literary work in the postmodern period. My own purpose in the present essay is restricted to an exploration of the general methodological significance of the edition in its immediate historical context.

Prominent scholars were quick to review the edition in prominent literary organs with broad general circulation, such as the *New York Review of Books,* the *Times Literary Supplement,* and so forth. Understandably, praise was lavish. Even the general reader had known that the hitherto received texts of *Ulysses*—the ones available in bookstores and for use in classes—were corrupt or unreliable in a number of ways. Consequently, Gabler's *Ulysses* might have been taken to represent a carefully prepared corrected edition of the work we had long known. But this is not precisely the case. Gabler's edition is not a text of Joyce's *Ulysses* presented now for the first time with all the errors and corruptions removed. Gabler himself says that he has not tried to produce "a corrected edition of the work's hitherto received text" ("Afterword," p. 1895). On the contrary, Gabler's *Ulysses* is what he calls (variously) an "ideal" text and a "critical" text.

In setting up the general framework for understanding his new edition he observes: "The composition of *Ulysses* was directed toward publication. It advanced from notes and drafts via final draft, fair copy, typescript and extensive revisions on the typescripts and multiple proofs to its culmination in the first edition of February 1922. The first edition comes closest to what Joyce aimed for as the public text of *Ulysses*. Yet it does not present the text of the work as he wrote it" (1891). Gabler's intention is not the usual editor's goal: to give what "Joyce aimed for as the public text of *Ulysses*." Rather, he is after "the text of the work as he wrote it." For this reason, "the innovative feature of this edition," according to Gabler, is "the emended continuous manuscript text . . . displayed synoptically by a system of diacritics to analyse its layers of growth" (1901). That is to say, Gabler offers a text of *Ulysses* in which we can follow, in a seriatim reading process, the work of *Ulysses* as Joyce actually produced it in a continuous act of writing and rewriting.

Gabler's volumes are arranged with the synoptic continuous manuscript text running consecutively on the verso pages and with a "reading text" running opposite on the rectos. The reading text Gabler calls "the emended continuous manuscript text at its ultimate level of compositional development" (p. 1903). Each volume is headed with an annotated list of the symbols used throughout the edition, and the third volume concludes with thirty-four pages of textual notes in which various cruces are discussed; ninety-nine pages of historical collation; and a fifty-two-page "Afterword" where the aims and procedures of the edition are laid out in considerable detail.

The character of the edition is epitomized in the historical collations, which in this case supply a "record of the departures from the new reading text in a selection of previous texts of *Ulysses* in print" (1904). This selection of previous texts means to include all the important editions of *Ulysses* from the first edition of 1922 to the Random House text of 1961. Particularly notable is the inclusion of the

1922 (first edition) variants in the historical collation rather than in the synoptic text or an *apparatus criticus*. This placement tells us that for Gabler the text of the first edition is prima facie a part of the "full record of corruption" (1905) of the text rather than an authoritative text of high, if not culminant, importance. As Gabler puts it, "divergences between the text of this [Gabler's] edition and the hitherto received text are defined as departures of the first and subsequent editions from the work's text as now critically established, and they are thus properly documented in the historical collation list" (1898).

Ultimately, what has guided the production of this edition is a certain theory of copytext, on the one hand, and a particular decision about the "compositional development" (1894) of *Ulysses* on the other. Since the latter is a simpler matter, I shall take it up first.

Gabler breaks the compositional development of *Ulysses* into two parts. The first part, which includes all the autograph manuscript documents, traces the history of the text from its earliest drafts to its latest autograph copies. Included here are hypothetically reconstructed "lost" documents, particularly the "final working drafts" for episodes 4–9, 11, and 13–14. For Gabler the lost final working drafts sometimes represent, in these instances, a later stage of compositional development of the text than the Rosenbach manuscripts, which contain Joyce's fair copies. He arrives at this conclusion by a critical analysis of the relations between the Rosenbach manuscripts and various subsequent (nonautograph) documents.

The latter documents, taken together, constitute what Gabler sees as the second part of the compositional development. Included at this stage are the typescripts (some lost, and none typed by Joyce), the various proof texts, and finally—the "ultimate stage of compositional development" (1894)—the first edition. Other materials are obviously important in establishing the text—the *Little Review* and *Egoist* printings, the errata lists and corrections made subsequent to the book's publication, and so forth. For Gabler, however, these materials fall outside the main line of the work's compositional development and hence exercise only a secondary influence upon the process of critical editing. Of course, numerous readings are incorporated into Gabler's established text from these sources, but this fact does not affect their status in the work's "compositional development."

One further distinction is important for Gabler: that between documents of composition and documents of transmission. In the former, "the text is held to possess full authority, unless it can be shown to be faulty"; in the latter, "the text is held to be potentially faulty, unless it can be proved to possess authority" (1892). In making this distinction Gabler argues that Joyce himself must be seen as the producer of both kinds of documents—that not every piece of autograph manuscript should be regarded as part of the line of "compositional development." Joyce is sometimes merely his own scribe, a textual transmitter and not a textual maker.

Gabler seeks, then, to "define a continuous manuscript text for *Ulysses*," to assemble that text in a synoptic act of critical editing, and finally to declare the assembled text to be his "copytext." That is to say, a continuous manuscript text is assembled toward which all editorial decisions gravitate as to their text of presumptive and highest authority. This text represents the ultimate state of the work's composition (not of its transmission). Because Gabler wants to assemble a text of the work's compositional development, therefore, and because he regards the act of composition as an entirely isolated and personal affair, he always sets a privilege on autograph manuscript texts. The typescripts, the proofs, and the first edition involve the intervention of other, purely *transmissive* authorities, and hence they fall outside the process of compositional development. Exceptions are made for certain passages of "compositional overlay" in the typescripts and proofs.

This entire procedure operates with a theory or concept of "copytext" which needs to be clearly understood, since it departs in certain crucial ways from the usual understanding of the term. In the post-Greg context, the term signifies what an editor chooses to take as the text of highest presumptive authority in the preparation of an eclectic, or critical, edition. That is to say, after examining the surviving documents in which the text is transmitted forward, the editor chooses one of these—or sometimes a combination—as his copytext. The copytext serves as the basis of the critical edition that is to be produced. The theory is that the readings of the copytext will be taken over into the critical edition unless other readings—either readings taken from other documents or original readings produced by the editor through a process of critical inference—are positively shown to carry a higher authority. In this theory, copytext is practically equivalent to some document or set of documents.

In Gabler's *Ulysses*, what is called the copytext is not a document or set of documents at all; rather, it is "the ideal state of [the text's] development as it was achieved through the traceable processes of composition and revision at the time of the book's publication" (1892). Gabler's copytext is what he calls "the continuous manuscript text." Before this edition its existence was ideal, or perhaps hypothetical. Indeed, it is possible, even probable, that this manuscript text never existed at all in the form that Gabler's edition has hypothesized. The copytext comes into existence with the publication of this edition. It is the basis for the genetic text produced on the verso pages as "the continuous manuscript text."

This then serves as the basis for the "reading" text on the rectos; as such, it might be called the "copytext" for Gabler's reading edition of *Ulysses*. Gabler does not call it that, and indeed the term is not strictly applicable. Nevertheless, scholars should be aware of these various textual relationships if they are to understand what Gabler has done in his edition.

One hears it said that Gabler's work proceeded without resort to the use of copytext, as traditionally understood. But this is not the case. A careful scrutiny of his procedures shows that his edition is based on a series of copytexts for each of the eighteen episodes.[8] Sometimes the copytext is a single document. The various manuscripts assembled together and now called the Rosenbach manuscript are the copytexts for most of the episodes. But for episodes 4-9, 11, and 13-14 the copytexts are the surviving typescripts, which Gabler argues were prepared not from the Rosenbach fair copies but collaterally with those fair copies from a set of (now lost) working drafts. Gabler's argument is that after the preparation of the Rosenbach fair copies from the lost working drafts, Joyce incorporated new material into those working drafts . The typescripts, he argues, descend from these later revised and augmented working drafts. As such, they carry a text which most closely resembles the revised lost working draft— that is, the manuscript text which is latest in the genetic series making up the process of composition.

It may seem a small, even a theological, point to worry over a technical term, and about its application to Gabler's edition. But we shall see that the problem of copytext in this edition focuses attention upon everything in the edition which is most interesting and important.

AN EDITION like Gabler's is inconceivable for any author before the modern period. For pre-nineteenth-century authors the documents that might be assembled for a genetic text of this sort simply do not exist. The earliest example of a comparable kind known to me is the case of Byron's *The Giaour,* for which we have an enormous archive of early and working drafts, fair copies, proofs, and various post-publication states of the text. The past two hundred years have witnessed a growing effort not merely to recover lost documents of earlier periods, but to preserve the documents being produced by contemporary producers and reproducers of texts. The development of textual theory, as already noted, underwent a massive renascence during this period, and Gabler's edition testifies to the continuation of this theoretical process.

The theory of copytext was initially deployed in order to deal with editing situations where certain key documents are lacking. As editors began to encounter situations—they are typical of the modern period—where the basic lines of textual transmission are clear and relatively unambiguous, the theory of copytext as rationalized by Greg underwent a slight but important modification. Whereas critical editors of earlier works tried to reconstitute some (now lost) state of the text—ideally, the earliest possible or "original" text—critical editors of modern works are already in possession of the kind of "original" text which those other editors were trying to recover. For modern works, therefore, editorial attention turned to a minute examination of prepublication documents in an effort to recover what has since been termed "the author's final intentions." Greg's theory of copytext, on the other hand, has nothing to do with authorial intentions as such. For editors of works like *Ulysses,* so much authorial material has been preserved that an editor can imagine the production of a "genetic" text which mirrors the actual process of authorial composition. The "genetic" text for an editor of Lucretius, on the other hand, represents a postauthorial process of transmission rather than a prepublication process of composition.

Gabler's "continuous manuscript text" is a hypothesized reconstruction of a text which displays Joyce working out what Gabler seems to regard as his final authorial intentions. For Gabler, "the final state of the text's development is considered reached when it is last fully and correctly written out in the author's hand" (1901). Since all the pertinent authorial manuscripts are not forthcoming, the editor has to reconstruct critically the missing manuscripts and their readings. Once the synoptic "continuous manuscript text" is assembled and has been critically edited, the reading text can be produced. The latter reconstitutes, in a completed rather than in a genetic form, the text of "the author's final intentions."

In assessing the significance of this achievement, we must understand that Gabler did not *have* to proceed in this way. He could have aimed to produce a critically edited corrected edition of the original publication of 1922. In this respect, Hugh Kenner's interesting and otherwise admirable review of the edition has misunderstood the situation:

> Given the complex history of transmission, it is pointless to think of starting from an extant text and "correcting" it. Efforts in that direction have been made, with the result that all available texts contain approximately the same number of errors, the cost of each correction being some novel botch. The technique of the new edition was instead to build up the complex text as it was built up originally, and so arrive at a final version that would have been arrived at in 1922 if no one had made any mistakes.[9]

In the first place, Gabler's edition is not the "final version that would have been arrived at in 1922 if no one had made any mistakes." Gabler's edition alters the text of 1922 in more than five thousand instances, but the 1922 text does not contain more than five thousand mistakes, nor anywhere near that number.[10] The number of errors in the first edition is several hundred at the most, and the vast majority of these are relatively minor.

In the second place, the goal of producing a corrected version of the original publication is quite within the possibility of a critical edition. Far from hindering such a task, the "complex history of transmission" makes it easier, for that history is written in the massive surviving documentation. The fact that the intervening editions between that of 1922 and Gabler's have compounded corrections of the text with new corruptions merely testifies to the unsystematic (and careless) mode of correction. A scrupulous critical editor could—and probably should—produce a fully corrected edition of 1922. It would differ in notable ways from Gabler's edition.

Gabler understands this situation very clearly. "The first edition," he says, "comes closest to what Joyce aimed for as the public text of *Ulysses*." Were an editor to produce a fully and systematically corrected edition of 1922, then, the result would clearly be the work which Joyce "aimed for as the public text of *Ulysses*." That text would differ from Gabler's text in many more than four thousand readings, though most of these would be minor. Nevertheless, such an edition would represent a "correct" text of *Ulysses*. Would such a text mean that Gabler's text is "incorrect"?

The answer is no, for the simple and obvious reason that we are dealing with two different conceptions of "the text of *Ulysses*." Gabler's is an imagination of Joyce's work and not its reconstitution. Gabler invents, by a process of brilliant editorial reconstruction, *Joyce's Ulysses* (as it were), a work that existed, if it ever existed at all, for Joyce the writer rather than Joyce the author.[11] Gabler's edition does not give us the work which Joyce wanted to present to the public; rather, it gives us a text in which we may observe Joyce at work, alone, before he turns to meet his public. Given his purposes, then, Gabler is correct to declare the synoptic text to be the most important feature of his edition. The "reading text" is of secondary importance.

The most important consequence of Gabler's edition, therefore, in my view, is not that it has removed the accumulated corruptions from the text. What his edition has done is to reveal, in a precise and concrete way, what can be (and therefore what cannot be) entailed in the idea of textual instability. Gabler has shown that another text of *Ulysses* can be imagined and concretely rendered—a text that does not simply offer a large mass of minor textual variations from the previously conceived text, but that completely overhauls *the way we might think about the text as a whole*. By giving priority of importance to the "synoptic" text over the "reading" text, Gabler forces us to think of *Ulysses* as something other than a given object of interpretation on the one hand (which is the traditional and New Critical view) or as an invention of interpretation on the other (which is the common poststructural view).[12]

A number of different *Ulysses* begin to occupy the space of critical possibility. They are finite in number, and although new ones will become possible as time and circumstances change, all must take their orders from preestablished and determinate textual configurations. Some of these *Ulysses* will represent themselves, at the surface, as more stable than others. Gabler's "reading text" seems stable, whereas his "synoptic text" seems processive, but the appearance is merely a function of certain conventions of reading which have or have not been mastered. The diacritics in Gabler's edition are a grammar of an artificial language and should present no serious problems for readers of imaginative works, which are always mediated by artificial grammars of various kinds. When we have learned to "read" the synoptic text as we read the reading text, we shall have gone a long way toward understanding the nature of texts in general. Such an experience should remove forever that illusion of fixity and permanence we normally take from literary works because they so often come to us wearing their masks of permanence.

The appearances of stability or instability are only formal relativities, as the relations between Gabler's "synoptic" and "reading" texts so clearly show. In fact, all texts are unstable to the extent that they are all processive and (in Gabler's terms) "continuous." At the same time, all are fixed within certain real, determinable limits, and they assume certain specific forms. The fact that the texts have always to be re-viewed in terms of shifting historical perspective does not alter their status as specific things. We should probably think of them— to borrow a metaphor from Modernism—as "vortices."

Gabler's edition helps one to see the formal limits which always constrain the generation of texts. Besides the class of "reading" texts, there is the class of "genetic" texts, and the latter may be conceived either as mirrors of composition or mirrors of production. After Gabler I begin to imagine an entirely different genetic text of *Ulysses,* one which would represent the history of the work's initial *production* rather than its initial composition—the author's rather than the writer's *Ulysses.* This would be the synoptic text that would lie behind, or serve as the basis for, the "reading text" we would then call "the edition of 1922, critically emended."[13]

At the same time Gabler's work shows that any other imaginations of the text of *Ulysses* must be either versions of the foregoing or postproductive acts of translation—like Bowdler's or Lamb's Shakespeare. Instability in a text may take many forms, but the forms can and must be *determinate.* In addition, when we are dealing with texts as genetic constructs, we shall have to understand that only two *forms* of text are conceptually possible: either the text that is composed or the text that is produced. Any number of instances of those forms is hypothetically possible, but that number will always be a small number *in actual fact.*

Gabler's edition also calls one's attention to a peculiar generic quality of modernist writing: that its subject is often the act and process of writing itself. The fluid, not to say unstable, character of poetic and fictional work since the time of Wordsworth and Byron has often been remarked, but almost always in vague and general terms. Gabler's edition calls attention to the necessity of determining what forms of instability we are dealing with. Wordsworth's *The Prelude* is an oft-cited example of an undecidable text because Wordsworth generated, if only provisionally, several distinct versions, all (and none) of which can make a claim to authority. But Wordsworth never brought this work to its productive phase—that is, he never oversaw its appearance in print. In this respect, the instability of *The Prelude* is quite unlike the instability of Byron's *The Giaour* or *Don Juan*. In the latter two instances, instability is a problem not of composition but of production.

Further specifications of textual indeterminacy are possible and necessary. I instanced *The Giaour* and *Don Juan* because each epitomizes a different type of productive indeterminacy. In *Don Juan* the text's fluidity is largely a function of Byron's struggle with various censors. Byron agreed to modify his original work in a number of ways, sometimes reluctantly, sometimes unwillingly, sometimes actively, sometimes passively. He did so in response to various external pressures. Furthermore, deliberate changes were sometimes made in his texts without his knowledge, and these may or may not have gained his subsequent agreement. Finally, the whole phenomenon of pirating *Don Juan* is part of the poem's special type of productive indeterminacy. The pirated texts of the poem differ only in minor verbal ways from the early editions, but they constitute a major—indeed, a radical (in several senses)—shift to a whole new text of Byron's epic.[14]

The situation is different for *The Giaour*. In this case fluidity is a function of Byron's willingness to seize the opportunities offered by the productive medium itself. As the poem moved through successive editions, he revised and augmented it until it grew to four times its original length. The case shows how an author can utilize the media of production to extend the process of composition—something that Tennyson, for example, did repeatedly and in various ways.[15] More significantly, it calls attention to the possibility that several authorized versions of a work may be produced (not simply composed) for different purposes and perhaps readerships. The English and American editions of *Moby-Dick* are quite distinct; the early cantos of Pound are printed in a number of different versions, as are various poems by Auden; indeed, even the appearance of an author's work in an anthologized format exerts an important change in the status of the text (not merely the document).[16]

All of these are real and realized distinctions which, when kept in mind, enable us to deal more precisely with the so-called "instability" of the text. Gabler's work reminds us that fictive works do not exist in "definitive" forms (or editions); by the same token, it also reminds us that the indeterminacy of texts is a determinate and determinable matter. Like Humpty Dumpty, anyone can make a text to his or her liking, but that act itself will always be of a determinate sort and will be carried out within certain structures of possibility that are licensed by specific material conditions which are at once social, institutional, and technological. The significance of any act of textual making (which includes, of course, textual interpretation) is always concrete and specific, and it emerges to critical view when its conditions of existence are made clear. The significance of Gabler's work is clear because he has so fully specified the conditions which made his work possible, and perhaps even—at this point in time—necessary.

WHEN THEORISTS AND CRITICS speak of the "undecidable" or "indeterminate" text, they mean to indicate that various interpretations can be produced for particular passages or whole works, and hence to argue that "meaning" is not something which resides "in" a literary work but is rather something which is "brought to it" or "laid upon it" by the reader, who is now called—by metaphoric license—"the writer." No one has put the case for such a procedure more forcefully than Stanley Fish, particularly, perhaps, in his well-known essay "Interpreting the *Variorum*."[17] I do not wish to address the entire set of arguments put forth in this essay but merely to point out one of its salient features which is characteristic of this kind of approach. Fish's essay centers in the interpretive possibilities which are left open by a series of texts from Milton. Fish is interested in what he calls the "interpretive crux" (148), or those passages where interpreters have carried on (often prolonged) disputes about the meaning of the text.

In his examination, however, Fish acknowledges two types of cruces. The first are purely "interpretive": "what is the two-handed engine in *Lycidas?* what is the meaning of Haemony in *Comus?*" (148). Fish then glances at "still others" which are, however, "of interest largely to those who make editions: matters of pronoun reference, lexical ambiguities, punctuation." In this case he calls attention to those various matters of textual fact where the issue of what is correct and what is incorrect always impinges, if it often remains insoluble. The texts of antiquity are strewn with passages which we know to be, in their received state, corrupt, wrong, incorrect, but which we also are unable to set right. Modern texts, like *Ulysses,* exhibit similar, though usually less serious, textual problems: less serious only because we are not normally left without any idea about the correct reading, but with alternative possibilities.

In making his case for the indeterminacy of meaning, Fish never deals with a textual crux that involves a matter of fact. He avoids this sort of problem because his principal point is that textual inde- terminacy is a function of the "reader" rather than of the "text." So far as Fish is concerned, the factive (rather than the fictive) dimension of a text is a documentary matter which is to be set aside when the question of interpretation is raised. Fish wants to take the text as physical object at face value. For him there are, on the one hand, "no fixed texts" because various "interpretive strategies are always being deployed" (172); on the other hand, there are the stable "documents," the physical objects which the interpreter simply takes, for the nonce at any rate, as given. This is the structure of Fish's distinctions between the "editor" and the "interpreter" and between the "text" and the "document."

One has to realize, however, that Fish's distinction between a text and a document is not at all the distinction which textual critics intend when they make a similar verbal distinction between the terms. Vinton Dearing is the contemporary scholar most associated with this dis- tinction, which in textual criticism separates two different kinds of physical objects.[18] For Fish, however, a "text" is an *ideal* object from which we can—indeed, from which we must—abstract out its em- pirical aspects.[19] For modern hermeneutics, meaning is a function of the act of interpretation and not of something antecedently "in" the "text." This view is correct, however, if and only if we take "text" in an ideal sense, that is, if and only if the text is angelic rather than human. In the latter instance, the interpretive act "constitutes mean- ing" (as we now say) only in terms that are licensed by the received sociohistory of the text. And that sociohistory, for *texts,* is constituted at its most elementary level as a set of empirical documents whose meaning is intimately bound up with the sociohistory of the docu- ments.

In this context one may begin to understand more clearly the sort of illusions which lie behind the indeterminacy principles of much contemporary theory and criticism. "Rather than restoring and re- covering texts," Fish says, "I am in the business of making texts and of teaching others to make them" (180). The main thrust of this deliberately amusing and paradoxical remark is to suggest that texts are "made" not by the originary authors (Milton, Joyce, Byron) or by their editors but by their "interpreters." But the participial clause contains a related position which exposes the full significance of what Fish is saying. He draws a distinction between "making" texts and "restoring and recovering" them. What he *ought* to have said was: "Rather than restoring and recovering documents, I am in the business of making texts." In fact, however, the word "text" is repeatedly allowed to slip its moorings, as it does here, and carry a documentary meaning. This is a common feature of those interpretive strategies which do not deploy a sociohistorical empiric in their discussions of "textual" indeterminacy.

The word "document" is never used by Fish in a similarly ambiguous fashion. "Document" for him means the physical and received object. But whereas Fish and critics like him want "text" to mean the "ideal" and the "made" thing, the "meaning" rather than the "medium" of the message, they cannot preserve the distinction intact. This is because, quite simply, no message is possible outside a concrete medium of some specific kind; indeed, the medium (documentary) is constitutive of the message itself. "Documents" are no more stable— or unstable—than "texts."

What Gabler's edition shows is that unstable "texts"—texts that are "in process" or "indeterminate"—always appear in material forms that are as determinate as the most "stable" text one might want or imagine. Gabler's edition also shows that these determinate forms of indeterminacy are always limited and, furthermore, that the limitations are *determined* by certain material, institutional, and historical conditions that can be concretely specified. Criticism, whether in an analytic or a synthetic mode, is not "free play" and endless possibilities; it is structured play and certain particular possibilities. Gabler's own synoptic "continuous manuscript text" is an instance of one of two large and governing models for a process text (the other being what I earlier called the "continuous production text").

I should point out that Gabler's work exemplifies a discernible trend in European theoretical and textual studies. This movement is most directly associated with a series of editions which have been structured as "genetic" texts wherein the process of writing and producing is conceived as the editorial object. Rather than aiming to produce a "definitive edition" or an edition which reflects the author's "intended" work, these editions seek to illuminate—in an imitative textual structure—one or another phase or aspect of the writer's productive activity.[20]

It is highly significant that this work has been spearheaded by editors and textual critics rather than by hermeneuts and theoretically oriented "readers." When matters of *textualité* are raised within an interpretive discourse, a certain abstractness or blurring of focus often occurs. We are all aware of the discontent which so much postmodern and poststructural theory has stirred up in various quarters, even in the academy. In the present instance, however, the idea of textual instability or indeterminacy will always assume a specific and determinate form. The European editions I have alluded to—those of Hölderlin, Kafka, Flaubert, Klopstock, and Proust, for example—have already made an important practical and theoretical impact upon the direction which postmodern literary work will have to take. In them we see, with unmistakable clarity, that the study of texts cannot acquire precision unless it is carried out within firmly defined material and technological conditions, and in relation to the particular social and historical structures which are embedded within those material conditions.

Because Gabler's edition is the first English-language work to illustrate these new European lines, it needs to be carefully pondered by English and American scholars, and especially by theorists and literary interpreters. The edition argues, for example, that textual meaning may not be an "idea" or an interpretive function—may not be, that is to say, merely a textual "supplement." Textual meaning is always materially constituted *as* some particular text (in the documentary sense). Later glosses or supplementary moves on earlier texts will not reconstitute the earlier text—they will remain, sometimes literally, "in the margin"—until they constitute themselves, with clear self-consciousness, as a specific material formation.

So we study Gabler's volumes and are forced to conclude that they represent a postmodern *Ulysses*. The concrete formatting of these books, where the synoptic text is given highest priority, is the most dramatic representation of the work's postmodern textuality. In an earlier edition the "clear text" on the rectos would have been the editor's ultimate object of interest. In Gabler's work, on the contrary, it has to be regarded as a supplementary aid in the reading of the synoptic text, which is this edition's chief goal and ultimate concern. Furthermore, this "text" of Joyce's original work is enmeshed within an editorial network that is extremely conscious of itself. That is to say, Gabler seeks actually to specify the material, institutional, and historical conditions which are embodied in his edition. Of course he does this from a particular vantage; his chief point of view is that of an internationally mobile scholar, with postwar graduate training in English studies at the University of Virginia, influenced by the Greg-Bowers line of textual criticism, and with expertise in computer-based word processing and access to the computer facilities at the University of Tübingen. (What does not form a part of that point of view is as pertinent to understanding it as what does.) This set of determinants engages with another large set—those established as the institutional history of Joyce scholarship up to the present time. Gabler's edition takes a concrete form which replicates the conditions of its production. The elementary bibliographical data on Gabler's edition is no less than a coded set of interpretive clues for understanding, and using, the work.

The same is of course true for other literary works, whose meanings are a function of their material, institutional, and social histories. When Fish speaks of "interpretive communities" he has these determinate structures in mind. Unlike Gabler, however, Fish—in this respect he represents the dominant tradition of contemporary hermeneutics, especially in the United States—leaves those structures as undecided as the meanings he deploys in his *explications des textes*. As a consequence we get no clear presentation of those "interpretive communities" where meanings are founded: neither of Fish's own (empirically concrete) interpretive community, nor of the conceptual category itself. All communities, even interpretive ones, are social structures with specific histories. Fish's "interpretive community," on the other hand, is a purely nominal category, a notional rather than a theoretical structure. In it, "meaning" takes the determinate form not of the *in*determinate, but of the *non*determinate.

Gabler's edition of *Ulysses* provides an extremely useful point of contrast. The synoptic continuous manuscript text is an exhibition—a concrete and particular presentation—of a self-deconstructing and unstable text. Unlike a hermeneutical (that is, critically mediated and narrativized) presentation, however, Gabler's procedures make the structure of fluidity—its finite limits—very clear. Consider the following well-known passage from Episode 8 (Lestrygonians) in Gabler's rendering. With or without a knowledge of the diacritical marks, a reader of this passage might well take it for a L = A = N = G = U = A = G = E poem out of San Francisco or New York. In fact, Gabler's *Ulysses* is a distinctly postmodern text: the style is impersonal and maintained in a surface mode ("languaged"); the procedure is intertextual and self-referencing; the form of order is stochastic. None of these characteristics dominates the "reading text" offered on the rectos in Gabler's edition.

The passage reproduced on page 190 can be "translated" (or "read") if one understands the use of the diacritical marks. It opens with a textual revision in which the initial word changes from "Squatted" to "Perched." All the words in full brackets (angled or square) indicate some type of revision or cancellation, and the various superscripts tell the reader at what stage of the composition process the revisions were carried out, and where (in the manuscript material) they are to be found. Carets indicate passages that are added as an "overlay" (for example, an interlinear insertion) to a particular document, and the superior half-brackets mark off material that has been added to the continuous manuscript text at some "level" of the continuum. The degree sign signals that a textual note at the foot of the page must be consulted in order to understand a relevant but collateral (that is, nonmanuscript) process of revision. Finally, superscripts in parentheses indicate that the initial phase of the reading is being critically reconstructed from a hypothesized, but missing, document.

The reading text provided to the right of the synoptic text is a help in reading the latter because the reading text represents the ultimate stage reached by the continuous manuscript text. Beside the synoptic text, however, it is a pallid, chill, and drear document—disappointingly abstract, simple, and one-dimensional where the other is rich, complex, and many-leveled. Perhaps the most remarkable quality of the synoptic text is its capacity to preserve both the facts and the relationships of many kinds of detail, from the most dominant to the most marginal and tenuous. It is a text which Foucault would have admired, a text which re-presents a sociohistory of Joyce's *Ulysses* (not *the* sociohistory, of course).

One other thing might be noted about this passage. It contains a textual crux in line 17. The word "gums" does not appear in the first

—Jack, love!
—Darling!
—Kiss me, ⌐ᶜ[Reggie!] Reggy!ᶜ⌐
—My boy!
5 —Love!

His heart astir he pushed in the door of the Burton restaurant. Stink gripped his trembling breath: pungent meatjuice, ⌐ᶜ⌐[slop] slush°⁽ᶜ⌐ of ^(vegetables.) greens.^ ᴰSee the animals feed.ᴰ

Men, men, men.

10 ⌐ᴮ⌐[Squatted] Perched⁽ᴮ⌐ on high stools by the bar, hats shoved back, at the tables° calling for more bread° no charge, swilling, ^(chewing) wolfing^ gobfuls of sloppy food, their eyes bulging, wiping wetted moustaches. ⌐A pallid ⌐suetfaced⌐ young man polished his tumbler knife fork and spoon with his napkin. New set of microbes.⌐ A man with ^(a) an°

15 infant's^ ᴰsaucestainedᴰ napkin tucked round him ᴰ[spooned] shovelledᴰ gurgling soup down his gullet. ᴰ[ˈSpoonfed.]ᴰ A man spitting back on his plate: ⌐halfmasticated⌐ gristle: ⌐ᶜ⌐gums:°⁽ᶜ⌐ no teeth to ⌐[chew] chewchewchew⌐ it. Chump chop ⌐[he has.] from the grill.⌐ ᴰBolting to get it over.ᴰ Sad booser's eyes. ᴰBitten off more than he can chew. Am I like

20 that? See ourselves as others see us. Hungry man is an angry man. Working tooth and jaw.ᴰ ⌐Don't! O! ^A bone!^ That last pagan king of Ireland Cormac in the schoolpoem choked himself at Sletty southward of the Boyne. Wonder what he° was eating. ^Something galoptious.^ Saint Patrick converted him to Christianity. Couldn't swallow it all however.⌐

25 —Roast beef and cabbage.
—One stew.

Smells of men. Spaton° sawdust, sweetish warmish cigarettesmoke,° reek of plug, spilt beer, men's beery piss, the stale of ferment.
^Hisᶜ gorge rose.²^

30 Couldn't eat a morsel here. ᴰFellow sharpening knife and ⌐[fork,] fork to eat all before him,⌐ old chap picking his tootles. ⌐Slight spasm, full, chewing the cud.⌐ Before and after. ⌐Grace after meals.⌐ Look on this picture ^(and) then^ on that. Scoffing up stewgravy with ⌐sopping sippets of⌐ bread. Lick it off the plate, man!ᴰ Get out of ⌐[it.] this.⌐

35 He gazed round the stooled and tabled eaters, tightening the wings of his nose.

---

7 slush] *STET* LR; slop aD *PCU*   11 tables] (aW):tC; tables, aR   11 bread] (aW):tC; bread, aR   14 an] (aW):tC; a aR *UNCHANGED*   17 gums:] *STET* LR; *ABSENT* aD *PCU*   23 he] a4;

or any of the later standard editions. It appeared in the *Little Review* printing, and Gabler's superscript "(C)" tells us that in his view the word must have been added to the (now lost) typescript which served as printer's copy for the *Little Review* printing. The textual note signaled by the degree sign also tells us, however, that the word is not present in the author-corrected and extant typescript which was printer's copy for the first edition. If we turn to Gabler's reading text we find that "gums" is present in the text; as such, it gets numbered among the more than five thousand "corrections" to the received texts.

But Gabler's own procedures tell us something else, tell us that the text of *Ulysses* is "correct" with or without "gums." Gabler hypothesizes an "error" and a "correction" here when in fact what we have are two different readings, each of which is possible, and neither of which can be shown to be more or less "correct" than the other. This is an "undecidable" matter, and the specific character of its undecidability can be—has already been, by the synoptic text—determined. We understand this if we contrast it with the case of the word "chewchewchew" in line 18. This replaced the word "chew" at the stage of the first placard (the first proof level), which is to say that the word "chew"—authorized through several levels of manuscript and typescript—was superseded at a later, intermediate level of composition. The correction maintained its authority through all the subsequent levels of composition and production—an important point to bear in mind, since this is by no means always the case.

Gabler's synoptic text shows us, in this instance, two types of textual instability. In the case of "chew" versus "chewchewchew" we observe a process by which one reading is marginalized by another. Gabler's *Ulysses* does not erase the marginalized reading, however, but merely places it in its appropriate historical position. The dominant reading, moreover, is also historically located (more or less midway along the complex length of this text's process of composition); as such, its fragility—emphasized nicely by the surrounding diacritics—serves to epitomize the kind of text we are dealing with, where marginality and dominance are distinctly relative terms. In the case of "gums," on the other hand, instability is a function of equivalent authority rather than of dominance and marginality. The effect, in each instance, is very similar, for we are perforce made conscious that this text is to be fundamentally characterized as a thing of many real and concrete details which are, at the same time, extremely fragile, and put together in strange, stochastic orderings.

"Gums" and the lack of "gums": a small matter in the large scheme of things (of the world, of *Ulysses*), yet not an insignificant matter by any means. The world and the world of *Ulysses* are constituted by myriads of just such matters. Is not this one of the central "meanings" of *Ulysses*, and have we not been told so over and over again for more than sixty years by many literary scholars and ordinary readers as well? We have, but Gabler's *Ulysses* explains those meanings for us anew, and more clearly because his explanation has taken a peculiarly appropriate postmodern form. The appropriate modernist *Ulysses* is the 1922 first edition—a limited edition and supported by subscriptions of the literati. Its "perfect" form would be a corrected text of this edition. But the postmodern *Ulysses* is Gabler's edition: a product (1) marketed by Garland Publishing Inc., a highly specialized house which features academic books but which locates itself in the world of commercial publishing rather than in the world of the university presses; and (2) electronically typeset by pagina GmbH in Tübingen from the processed text generated by the editing program TUSTEP. In Gabler's *Ulysses* the finished and monumental text of Joyce's work is placed in a secondary—might one say marginal?— relation to that fascinating document called the "synoptic continuous manuscript text." Gabler gives us a particular, a *determinate* synoptic text; in so doing, however, he also indicates the limits which his text, and which all texts, necessarily defines and incorporates.

A CODA to the foregoing suggests itself and might be framed as the following question: "When shall we have an edition of the *Cantos* and what kind of edition will it be?" Gabler's work might lead one to imagine that something similar could be done for the *Cantos*. In fact, the assembling of the extant materials—even more complex and fractured than the materials of *Ulysses*—will best be done in computerized processes. But at that point the problems will have only begun in the sense that they will only begin to be framable in concrete and specific ways. Even now we can see that an edition of the *Cantos*— "corrected" of its "errors" (perhaps in several senses) yet representative of its fractured processes—will not be able to take a form like *Ulysses*.

For example, the fact that *Ulysses* accepts the linear conventions of the prose text, with margins, headers, and footers as physical limits to be filled out with text, distinguishes it from the *Cantos,* which uses the page both linearly and spatially. Margins, headers, and footers in the *Cantos* are a framework where words and word-strings are arranged in a kind of collage. Because of this arrangement, the form of the synoptic text in Gabler's *Ulysses,* which runs continuously from margin to margin down the page in sequences of numbered lines, is not really suited to a synoptic text of the *Cantos.* Some other resort will have to be arrived at (transparent overlays of various kinds?). At a recent conference on textual studies at the Clark Library, several people suggested that a corrected reading text of the *Cantos* might be produced in the usual book format with an accompanying computer disc. The latter would contain all the information for reproducing a continuous productive text of every page of the book's reading text. Given the character and capacities of word processors and editing programs, this option has much to recommend it. It would also put the scholarly material in a more appropriate format than the expensive one currently used for reproducing the continuous manuscript text of *Ulysses.*

Leaving aside problems of formatting and production, however, a question must still arise about whether a continuous *manuscript* text is what one should aim for. Perhaps some form of continuous productive text would be more appropriate since Pound, even more than Joyce, was alive to the interactive relations between the writer and the physical media which the work solicited and utilized. The marriage of text and document is extremely close in Pound, and the documentary life of the text is by no means to be principally located in the compositional manuscripts.

At the conclusion of her recent book on Pound, Christine Froula discusses this aspect of Pound's texts at some length. "The historical and collaborative authority of *The Cantos,*" she argues, "suggests that we must reconceive the text not as an object which the editorial project aims to perfect but as the trace of a temporal process which . . . is neither contained and bounded by the author during his life nor concluded and closed off by his death."[21] For Pound, if not for Joyce, the poem is at all points being conceived and—if the locution be permitted—"being practiced" as a continuously produced rather than as a continually composed text. At the conclusion to Canto I, for example, as Pound finishes his act of transporting (hardly translating) Homer into the early twentieth century, he calls attention to the fact that Homer is a social rather than a psychological text, as we have already noticed. Homer's voyage is continued and repeated by many persons and in many related ways: by Andreas Divus, by Pound, by printers and booksellers and many others who, like Odysseus, are men "of no fortune, and with a name to come." Pound's art deliberately incorporates and makes use of that entire productive world. When scholars finally get around to the inevitable project of "editing" his great poem, these matters will have to be taken into account.

PART III ❧

Literature and the Future of History

When human beings become autonomous they discover around themselves a false and empty world . . . The vast results of long centuries of struggle, or prodigious military or material conquest, have always led conquering peoples . . . to a failed and disappointing world, flattened by interminable crises. Through an extreme malaise and through a confusion in which everything appears vain and nearly disastrous, there grows the obsession with *The Recovery of the Lost World.*

Georges Bataille, "Nietzschean Chronicle"

10 ⟡

Contemporary Poetry,
Alternate Routes

Opposition is true friendship.

> William Blake,
> *The Marriage of Heaven and Hell*

that the vanishing point might be on every word.

> Lyn Hejinian, "Gertrude Stein: Two Lectures"

WHAT IS THE SIGNIFICANCE of that loose collective enterprise, which sprang up in the aftermath of the sixties, known as L=A=N=G=U=A=G=E Writing? To answer this question I will be taking, initially, a somewhat oblique route. And I shall assume an agreement on several important social and political matters: first, that the United States, following the Second World War, assumed definitive leadership of a capitalist empire; second, that its position of leadership generated a network of internal social contradictions which persist to this day (as imperialist demands collide with American traditions of isolationism and revolutionary nationalism); third, that this postwar period has been characterized at the international level by an extended Cold War shadowed by the threat of a global catastrophe, whether deliberate or accidental. Whatever one's political allegiances, these truths, surely, we hold as self-evident.

Postwar American poetry is deployed within that general arena, and to the degree that it is "political" at all, it reflects and responds to that set of overriding circumstances.[1] In my view the period up to the present ought to be seen as having two phases. The first phase stretches from about 1946 (when *Lord Weary's Castle* appeared) to 1973 (when Lowell capped his career with the publication of *History*). This period is dominated by a conflict between various lines of traditional poetry, on the one hand, and the countering urgencies of the

"New American Poetry" on the other. In the diversity of this last group Donald Allen argued for a unifying "characteristic": "a total rejection of all those qualities typical of academic verse."[2]

Of course, this representation of the conflict between "tradition" and "innovation" obscures nearly as much as it clarifies. The New American poets were, in general, much more inclined to experimentalism than were writers like Wilbur, Hecht, Simpson, or Justice. But Allen's declaration can easily conceal the academic and literary characteristics of the innovators. Duncan and Olson, for example, key figures in the New American Poetry, can hardly *not* be called "literary" or even "academic" poets. If they opened certain new areas in the field of poetic style, no less could and has been said of Robert Lowell, even in his early work. And if Frank O'Hara seems the antithesis of academic work, Ashbery is, in his own way, its epitome. Yet both appear in Allen's *New American Poetry* anthology. Moreover, who can say, between O'Hara and Ashbery, which is the more innovative of the two, so different are their styles of experimentation.

The issue here is not stylistic, however, but ideological and ultimately political. We can see this more clearly if we recall that the "political style" of American writing between 1946 and 1973 is unmistakably liberal-left. This is as true, in general, for the traditionalists as it is for the innovators.

If we compare the period 1946–1973 with the years since, many of the same kinds of literary conflicts seem to persist. Nevertheless, this most recent period is sharply distinguished from the earlier one by one momentous difference: the dramatic shift to the political right which has taken place following the Vietnam War. Like every other part of society, the literary world registered these new social circumstances. Specifically, two new lines of work began to make their presence felt. The first of these might be called personal (not confessional) or localized verse, though Robert von Hallberg has called it the poetry of the suburbs. It is marked stylistically by a moderated surface urbanity and substantively by an attempt to define "social" and "political" within a limited, even a personal, horizon. Furthermore, one observes in this work a renewed interest in narrative forms—a significant stylistic inclination, as we shall see more clearly in a moment. Robert Pinsky is perhaps the most conspicuous practitioner, and promoter, of this poetic mode, but it includes a large and heteronomous group of other, chiefly academic poets. Its spokesmen are Richard

Howard, Helen Vendler, and—most recently—von Hallberg. "The poetry I admire [from the last forty years]," von Hallberg says, "is fairly spoken of as one of accommodation rather than opposition."[3]

The other line is L=A=N=G=U=A=G=E Writing. Here a conscious attempt has been made to marry the work of the New American Poetry of the fifties with the poststructural work of the late sixties and seventies. As Frost, Yeats, Auden, and Stevens are the "precursors" of the poets of accommodation, Pound, Stein, and Zukofsky stand behind the L=A=N=G=U=A=G=E writers. Oppositional politics are a paramount concern, and the work stands in the sharpest relief, stylistically, to the poetry of accommodation.[4]

In a sense, the period from 1973 to the present appears to repeat the central struggle of 1946–1973 between the "academics" and the "New American Writers." L=A=N=G=U=A=G=E Writing is distinctively experimental, while poets like Robert Pinsky, Louise Glück, and John Hollander are traditionalists; and whereas the L=A=N=G=U=A=G=E writers are almost *all* situated—economically and institutionally—outside the academy, their counterparts—critics and poets alike—occupy important scholastic positions. The difference between pre- and post-1973 American poetry lies in the extremity of the ideological gap which separates the traditionalists from the innovators in the later period. As will be very clear from the discussion that follows, L=A=N=G=U=A=G=E writers typically emphasize their oppositional politics in ways that the New American Poets did not. The latter were more socially disaffected than politically opposed.

The two divergent lines in American poetry since 1973 are usefully contrasted in terms of the shape of John Ashbery's career and their relation to it. Throughout the seventies and even into the eighties, Ashbery has been the single most influential figure in American poetry. But there are certainly two Ashberys to choose from. For L=A=N=G=U=A=G=E writers, all of his work should be read out of—by means of—the experimental projects developed from *The Tennis Court Oath* (1962) to *Three Poems* (1972). Not that he has ceased to write important work since, but in those early years his innovative stylistic repertoire was fully deployed. Indeed, Ashbery's style—established in the sixties—has come to seem an early example of a postmodern sensibility. As such, it was (properly) taken as a swerve away from the poetries of the fifties and sixties—a presage of things to come.

The problem, however, is the political significance of Ashbery's "postmodern" stance. The heated controversy which has developed around the idea of the postmodern—is it or is it not a reactionary social phenomenon?—throws the problem of Ashbery's work into sharp relief.[5] His unmistakable style has been read as the poetic equivalent of a deconstructive mode; yet deconstruction in America, though seen in many traditional quarters as a socially subversive movement, has been centered in the Yale school, which has never made any effort to develop or practice an oppositional politics.[6] A similar type of "nonpolitics" is discernible throughout Ashbery's career—even as his work has been used by many younger writers whose oppositional politics are clear. But Ashbery himself has not exploited his own work's "oppositional" features and potentialities; and in the period from 1973 to the present his work has moved instead along lines that parallel the suburban and personal interests of poets like Pinsky, James McMichael, and Turner Cassity (for example, Ashbery's *Vermont Notebook* [1975], *Houseboat Days* [1977], and *As We Know* [1979]).[7]

Ashbery's avoidance of a conscious political position defines the style of his postmodern address. Not without reason has his work been canonized in academic discourse about contemporary poetry. As earlier Lowell became the exegetical focus of high/late New Critical discourse, Ashbery has become the contemporary touchstone for deconstructive analysis. What we confront here, however, is not so much an issue of poetic style or poetic quality as it is a problem in ideology—the kinds of cultural ideas that are to be propagated through that crucial ideological apparatus, the academy. In postmodern work we become aware of the many crises of stability and centeredness which an imperial culture like our own—attempting to hold control over so much, and such widely dispersed, human material—inevitably has to deal with. The response to such a situation may be either a contestatory or an accommodational one; it may move to oppose and change such circumstances, or it may take them as given and reflect, or reflect upon, their operations.

"The test of a 'politics of poetry,' " Barrett Watten has observed, "is in the entry of poetry into the world in a political way."[8] Watten has been a prominent L=A=N=G=U=A=G=E writer for some time, so for him "politics" means "opposition" rather than "accommodation." What we must recognize is that both types of writing, whether contestatory or accommodating, are political in character and represent a certain type of political stance toward life in imperialist America. Furthermore, from the vantage of a writer like Watten, the poetries of accommodation of the seventies represent a retreat from the critical responsibilities of art, and perhaps even an active celebration—properly hedged or refined—of immediate social and political circumstances.

One cannot write about these matters neutrally. Neutrality here in fact is a choice of the position of accommodation. And while I find much to admire in that kind of poetry, I think that by far the most important work is now being done elsewhere in American writing. Nor does the importance of that work lie solely in its "oppositional" politics. The most innovative work stylistically is now to be traced in the journals, chapbooks, pamphlets, and—increasingly—the books of various poets associated with L = A = N = G = U = A = G = E Writing. The eventuality is hardly a surprising one, for this work has been actively forging, over the past ten or fifteen years, writing procedures which seek a *comprehensive* account of the American experience during that period.

Of course, much of this work is weak, some of it is trivial, and a great deal has only a formal or aesthetic significance, despite its political urgencies. My interest here, however, is not in such matters. Rather, what I want to indicate is the kind of intervention L = A = N = G = U = A = G = E work typically seeks to make—*how* it tries to enter the world in a political way, and what it means to carry out through that entrance.

In the eyes of eternity—if eternity is interested in art—Wordsworth and Blake will each take their appropriate place, and later ages will find in each various resources appropriate to a later moment. But between 1789 and 1815 the work of Wordsworth and Blake entered the world very differently, and their art stood for two correspondingly different "politics of poetry." Each is part of the same cultural structure, but each imagined that culture—its past, present, and future alike—in radically different ways. When they produced their work they were carrying out a struggle of the imagination, ultimately a social and political struggle. Just so is all writing engaged in immediate disputes that have broad and long social implications—in contests of the present for the resources of the past and the possibilities of the future. And we too have choices to make. Histories of our moment are currently being written by various poets, and within those histories alternative histories of poetry are being carried out. Because I believe that the history which is $L=A=N=G=U=A=G=E$ Writing is extremely important, I want to indicate here, in a brief and polemical way, the context and import of its ventures.

I SHALL BEGIN this inquiry at a tangent, by looking at a passage from a recent essay by Richard Rorty. The essay as such has nothing to do with contemporary American poetry.

> There are two principal ways in which reflective human beings try, by placing their lives in a large context, to give sense to those lives. The first is by telling the story of their contribution to a community. This community may be the actual historical one in which they live, or another actual one, distant in time or place, or a quite imaginary one... The second way is to describe themselves as standing in immediate relation to a nonhuman reality. This relation is immediate in the sense that it does not derive from a relation between such a reality and their tribe, or their nation, or their imagined band of comrades. I shall say that stories of the former kind exemplify the desire for solidarity and that stories of the latter kind exemplify the desire for objectivity.[9]

Rorty, as we know, is committed to "stories" of what he calls "solidarity"—"pragmatistic" stories of the here and now. Or we should rather say that he *reads* all the stories that interest him out of the framework of his "cultural peers," the group he also calls "postmodern bourgeois intellectuals." This is the locus of his allegiances and conscious "solidarity." Though I shall later have some comments on Rorty's ideas about postmodernity, I must first call attention to the privilege Rorty gives to narrative itself. Rorty assumes—the passage is, in this respect, typical of all his work—that "human being" is fundamentally a social rather than a rational function. He goes on to say that we "give sense to" our human being in only two communicative forms. This thought is striking enough, but even more so is the idea that both of these forms are narrative ones.

As Michel de Certeau and others have pointed out, narrative is a form of continuity; as such, its deployment in discourse is a way of legitimating established forms of social order, as well as the very idea of such established forms.[10] Within discourse structures, critical alternatives to the orders of narrativity characteristically emerge from various types of nonnarrative and antinarrative. Such forms have grown especially prominent in the discourses of postmodernism. As we shall see more particularly in a moment, however, while both nonnarratives and antinarratives move counter to regularized, normative, and "accommodating" orders, they exemplify distinct forms of discourse. Antinarrative is problematic, ironical, and fundamentally a satiric discursive procedure. It *engages* a dialectic, and its critical function is completed in a structure of antithesis, which may include the double irony of a self-antithesis. Nonnarratives, on the other hand, do not issue calls for change and alterity; they embody in themselves some form of cultural difference. To adapt (and secularize) the terminology of Blake, nonnarrative is the "contrary" (rather than the "negation") of narrativity. Its antithesis to narrative is but one dimension of a more comprehensively imagined program based in the codes of an alternative set of solidarities. Byron's *Don Juan* is one type of antinarrative and Blake's *Milton* is another type. *The Marriage of Heaven and Hell,* on the other hand, is decidedly nonnarrative.

The special relevance of nonnarrative and antinarrative lies within the horizon of postmodernism, when such forms (and their correspondent terminologies) began to be elaborated. Nevertheless, because nonnarrative and antinarrative were not contemporary inventions, their presence in certain previous literary works can help to define their special currencies. Consider antinarratives, for example, whose structures depend upon, reflect, and thereby maintain the forms of narrative continuity which they bring under critical examination. The digressive structure of *Don Juan,* for example, is intimately connected to the fate of that poem's narrative—which is, fundamentally, the recollective narrative of Byron's own life told via several displaced and putatively fictive narratives involving the poem's hero Don Juan. Similarly, Blake's *Milton* is a critical examination of English history between approximately 1640 and 1810. That history is presented as a system which replicates itself in its various subsystems (for example, the events of Milton's life, the events of Blake's). Furthermore, these histories are placed within the context of the more comprehensive narrative of human history as set forth in the redemptive mythos of Jewish-Christian polemics. The critique of history in *Milton* appears as a secret narrative moving antithetically to the known and apparent narrative: Blake represents this structure as a pair of cogged wheels, with the destructive wheel (of nature) turning in one direction, and the redemptive wheel (of art)—attached to it—turning in the other.[11] That image itself suggests the intimacy of the relation between narrative and antinarrative.

Nonnarrative is different—for example, Blake's *Marriage of Heaven and Hell*. Among all of Blake's works it most closely resembles the *Songs of Innocence and of Experience* in terms of both its ideas and its form. Both works explore the significance of what Blake calls "contraries." Furthermore, both are collections of diverse materials—anthologized structures where the relations between the parts are not determined by narrativities. This odd character of the *Marriage* in particular is underscored in several ways. The work opens with an "Argument," which ought, by poetic convention, to be a brief summary of the work to follow. But the "Argument" is a small narrativized unit whose relation to the rest of the *Marriage* can only be arranged by the reader's ingenuity in drawing different kinds of verbal and tropical analogies of the "Argument" (and parts of it) with other parts and pieces of the work. The *Marriage* contains as well a number of other brief narrativized units, but all are self-contained; their interrelations, once again, have to be consciously constructed because the work as a whole is not organized as a narrative.

This fact about the internal form of the work is emphasized by the heterogeneity of the particular writing-units. Some are narrativized, one is a collection of proverbs, and four others are expository presentations of different kinds of ideas. Furthermore, the subject matter taken up in these different textual units is equally heteronomous. The "Argument" (plate 2) is a spare allegorical narrative based in the biblical mythos; the "Song of Liberty" (plates 25–27), also narrativized, is a polyglot piece whose primary location is in contemporary history; and the other narrative units (for example, plates 12–13, 15, and the two narratives embedded in plates 17–23) are equally diverse with respect to type and subject matters. The differentiating inertia of the *Marriage* operates as well within the specific textual units. Plates 12–13, for example, narrate a personal anecdote, but the location of the event—in some kind of spiritual hyperspace—forces a reorientation of certain fundamental categories of thought (spatial, temporal, social).

Finally, one must observe the variable order of the text as a whole.[12] Most copies of the *Marriage* are arranged in the sequence plates 1–27, but copies E and G deploy perfectly acceptable alternative orders, and copy G was in fact foliated by Blake himself. The shifting plates are 4, 14, and 15, which are so moved that two other orderings are created for the work. One should note here that a similar indeterminacy of textual relations is found throughout Blake's work: no copy of the *Songs* has an order which corresponds to that of any other copy, and variations are the rule in almost all of his engraved works. There is no doubt that these variances in sequencing are deliberate, and there is every reason to think that he was encouraged to this kind of textual experimentation by recent biblical and classical scholarship.

Whatever the order of this wild diversity of material, then, it is clearly not a narratological one. Indeed, narrativity is short-circuited from the moment that the reading process is spatialized as a field of illuminated printing. It is not simply that the "text" is illustrated or illuminated; rather, the verbal discourse evolves *as a set of images, decorations, and pictures*. To say that one "reads" Blake's works is to invoke a metaphor, as one does when one speaks of "reading" a painting. Of course, if Blake's work is delivered over to us simply in typographical forms we are likely to end up as nonmetaphoric "readers" of the "texts." This commonly happens when Blake is "taught," but it is a type of misreading—an abstracted form—which has nothing to recommend it as an imaginative activity. In short, Blake ought to be "read" in facsimile.

What, then *is* the order which pervades a work like the *Marriage?* Blake called it the order of Imagination—the order generated through the faculty or process which discovers previously unapprehended relations of things. The most striking aspect of the highly differentiated material in the *Marriage* is that it encourages the reader to draw out unusual substantive and grammatological relationships which convention will normally miss or avoid. Antinarrative calls those conventions into question and develops the premonitory conditions for imaginative activity. Indeed, antinarrative frequently generates imaginative localities and incommensurate particulars which escape the imperialism of narrativity. But nonnarrative alone will establish, among the kingdoms and principalities of narrative, the proper world of what Blake called Imagination.

Once again we must ask, however, what is the order of that world? An answer may be glimpsed if we reflect for a moment on one of the most striking variations in the plate sequencing. Plate 15 (the Printing House in Hell episode) comes last in copy E of the *Marriage*, immediately after the "Song of Liberty," which is the work's traditional conclusion. This dramatic placement clearly calls attention not merely to the work's own productive processes, but to the satanic view of what all knowledge, imaginative or otherwise, must be: mediated language forms generated through specific social—specific material and institutional—processes. In all copies of the *Marriage* the subject of Blake's own productive processes is prominently and recurrently treated. This subject calls attention to the inherently material and social character of imaginative work. Placing plate 15 at the end is one way of giving such ideas paramount and conclusive importance.

A poem like the *Marriage,* then, urges us to see that the order of nonnarrative is the order of production (as opposed to the orders of reflection and reproduction). This order is emphasized in the *Marriage* through the pervasive thematic of the printing and engraving processes: the meaning of the *Marriage* is its means and modes of production. It is, as one might say, "a poem about poetry," but not about the "idea" of poetry. The *Marriage* is "about" poetry in the sense that poetry is understood as a set of socially engaged material practices. In the *Marriage* poetry "practices itself," poetry is carried out; and this work of poetry as a productive social practice is self-consciously brought before the attention of the "reader." This sort of thing happens in Blake's work all the time—for example, in *Jerusalem,* part of whose wit involves the understanding that Albion's "emanation" is in literal truth the work Blake produces and calls *Jerusalem.*

This example of Blake is a useful point of departure for considering a large and important body of contemporary writing in which anti-narrative and nonnarrative figure prominently. Blake is useful not merely because his example is familiar, but perhaps even more because his is a problematic case. In the *Marriage* a redemptive myth is essayed which is based in forms of creation rather than forms of atonement. Within the general framework of Judeo-Christian culture, a production-based redemptive order is unusual, and extremely difficult to maintain. Blake's work is most emphatically carried out within a Judeo-Christian culture, and although the work moves at a strange diagonal to that culture, it never wholly escapes its gravitational field. Atonement, rather than creation, is a form of thought—a mode of action—which recurs throughout the work, most prominently, I suppose, in *Milton* and *Jerusalem.* To the extent that Blake is interested in creation rather than redemption, he is hostile to the theory of atonement. In the end Blake arrived at a compromise: he rejected the traditional theory of atonement, but he embraced a heterodox theory which held, essentially, that a general redemptive scheme would emerge through the practice of continuous self-atonement.

INSOFAR AS WORKS like the *Songs* and *Marriage* are nonnarratives which do not involve themselves in forms of atonement, they resemble various kinds of poststructural discourse, in particular the work now commonly known as L=A=N=G=U=A=G=E Writing. Since antinarrative and nonnarrative forms abound in this work, it exemplifies a significant strand of postmodernist writing. But unlike certain other forms of postmodernism—prototypically the academic postmodernism associated with the Yale school, on the one hand, and with Richard Rorty on the other—L=A=N=G=U=A=G=E Writing typically deploys a consciously antithetical political content. It situates itself, therefore, to the left of Rorty's "postmodern bourgeois intellectuals."

Though an extraordinarily diverse group, L=A=N=G=U=A=G=E writers are involved with writing projects which fracture the surface regularities of the written text and which interrupt conventional reading processes. Thus Richard Foreman writes a theoretical essay carrying the imperative title "Trying to be Centered . . . On the Circumference."[13] If the Word of God issues from that famous circle whose center is everywhere and whose circumference is nowhere, these new words come from a circle of human writers whose circumference is everywhere and whose center is nowhere. Abigail Child declares, in an aphoristic manifesto, that the poetic object is to set "UNITS OF UNMEANINGNESS INCORPORATED ANEW//vs. A COMMUNITY OF SLOGANEERS" (94). The sense is that poetry and writing generally have been colonized by imperial forces, and that the power of this monopoly has to be broken. The object of writing must be to set language free, to return it from the domains of the abstract and the conventional (the communities of SLOGANEERS, whose name today is Legion) to a world of human beings and human uses.

The program of these writers, consequently, has a strong, usually an explicit, social and political orientation. I want to leave that aside for the moment, however, in order to concentrate on its more local and even technical aspects: for example, on Tina Darragh's forms of "procedural writing" which she adapts from the work of Francis Ponge. Darragh produces arrangements of textual forms—they are literally unreadable, as is much other L=A=N=G=U=A=G=E poetry—by selecting, via an orderly but arbitrary plan, sequences of verbal materials that appear on a single page of a dictionary. The point of this kind of operation becomes very clear if we read a few of Bernadette Mayer's practical writing injunctions as set forth in her mini-manual "Experiments":

> Systematically derange the language, for example, write a work consisting only of prepositional phrases, or, add a gerundive to every line of an already existing piece of prose or poetry, etc.
>
> Get a group of words (make a list or select at random); then form these words (only) into a piece of writing—whatever the words allow. Let them demand their own form, and/or: Use certain words in a set way, like, the same word in every line, or in a certain place in every paragraph, etc. Design words.
>
> Write what cannot be written, for example, compose an index. (Read an index as a poem).
>
> Attempt writing in a state of mind that seems least congenial.
>
> Consider word & letter as forms—the concretistic distortion of a text, for example, too many o's or a multiplicity of thin letters (lllftiii, etc.)
>
> Attempt to eliminate all connotation from a piece of writing & vice versa. (81–82)

The final injunction in Mayer's list of writing experiments is appropriately, summarily, placed: "Work your ass off to change the language & don't ever get famous" (83). The message is clear: the celebrated writing of her time appears in digestible and accepted forms; indeed, at this time (at any time, one wonders?) fame, conventionality, and the regularities of narrativized discourse are functionally related to everything that must be judged unpoetical, inhuman, a failure—even perhaps, a betrayal. To revive poetry, "to change the language," means trying to "write what cannot be written," to produce what cannot be "read" (an "index," a "multiplicity of thin letters")—in short, to "derange the language" from its current (truly "deranged") conventionalities.

Mayer's "Experiments" speak very clearly about a number of the most important characteristics of L=A=N=G=U=A=G=E Writing. In the first place, writing is conceived as something that must be done rather than as something that is to be interpreted. The vantage is Horatian rather than Plotinian. The "meanings" sought after in this work are neither ideas which lie behind (prior to) the texts nor residues left over from their operations. Meaning occurs as part of the process of writing—indeed, it *is* the writing. Thus Charles Bernstein says of such poetry that it "emphasizes its medium as being constructed . . . designed, manipulated, picked, programmed, organized" (39). "Whatever gets written gets written in a particular shape, uses a particular vocabulary & syntax, & a variety of chosen techniques . . . Sometimes this process takes place intuitively or unconsciously . . . Sometimes it is a very conscious process . . . In either case, various formal decisions are made & these decisions shape the work" (43). This kind of statement—it appears repeatedly in the manifestos of L = A = N = G = U = A = G = E Writing—argues that discourse, including poetic discourse, is not meaning-referential but meaning-constitutive. Writing is an event, a praxis, and in our day one of its principal operations involves the dismantling of the ideology, reified in so much that passes for "writing" (the SLOGANEERS), that language—which in this context means producing and reproducing texts—is an object, an icon. "The signs of language . . . are not . . . mere structures," Bernstein says; "They do not sit, deanimated, as symbols in a code, dummies for things of nature they refer to" (41). We are to think of poetry as "making a path" rather than "designing a garden" (39). "Texts are themselves signi*fieds,* not mere signifiers. TEXT: it requires no hermeneusis for it is itself one—of itself" (34).

A second crucial feature of the L = A = N = G = U = A = G = E approach to poetry and writing centers in its preoccupation with nonsense, unmeaning, and fragmentation. These writers practice language experiments which generate and promote such conditions. As readers, their approach is archaeological. Their reviews and critical comments on poetry display little concern with "interpretation;" rather, they elucidate as it were the behavior, the manners, the way of life that various kinds of writings perform and live. When Alan Davies and Nick Piombino see poetry as a locus of "indeterminate intervals," they develop a method for encountering and illuminating texts which they call "Field Reading."[14] One recalls Tina Darragh's work with "procedural writing" whereby the page of a dictionary is suddenly exposed as a field of strange and unrecognized deposits—odd bits and pieces scattered across a surface whose depths and layers and correspondence escape the notice of the dictionary's ordinary users.

This archaeology of knowledge represents a deliberate intervention in and through the processes of writing. Field reading and procedural writing are stochastic immediate events that intervene with writing deposits, equally stochastic, which are already situated. What is crucial to the immediate acts of intervention, however, is that they are conscious of their own relative status. These writers deploy an archaeology which does not stand in an objective and superior relation to the fields they are exploring. There is a "transmutative effect" (49) between writings and readings, feedback loops that persist and expand their operations as the random and the deliberate intersect in the dynamic field of language use: "There's a place that you're going from and a place that you're going to; to get to that place, that tracking, is as worthwhile as the endpoint of going, because while you're going there you find other things and those things are related to the final place; that helps to define what it is when you get there. New combinations and connections are experienced. In finding your locus you redefine it again each time, systematically finding new coordinates."[15]

This passage reminds us that, in the view of L=A=N=G=U=A=G=E Writing, the time is always the present. Nevertheless, past and future are permanent concerns of these writers, whose work would be travestied if it were represented as the imperialism of the here and now, or the immediate self. The textual activism that is promoted in L=A=N=G=U=A=G=E Writing places the writer inside the writing process. The writer manipulates and deploys his or her texts, but in so doing the writer is also, necessarily, made subject to their inertia as well. "Texts read the reader," Bruce Andrews observes (36), which means, in this program, that they read the writer as well. The activist writer/reader, by operating on and in texts, undergoes the limits and the significance of that activism. As a consequence, "meaning" emerges not as an appropriation or institution of truth but as "the enabled incapacity to impose a usage" (35). The program is conceived to reveal the power of writing and the production of meaning as human, social, and limited in exact and articulable ways. Indeed, it is designed to demonstrate and *practice* such a conception.

Thus we can see the general context—political and stylistic alike—within which the antinarrative and nonnarrative procedures of L=A=N=G=U=A=G=E Writing are deployed. Narrativity is an especially problematic feature of discourse, to these writers, because its structures lay down "stories" which serve to limit and order the field of experience, in particular the field of social and historical experience. Narrativity is, in this view, an inherently conservative feature of discourse, and hence it is undermined at every point. Charles Bernstein's poems, for example, typically begin with an attack upon conventional "beginnings." In traditional texts the "beginning" signals the text's sense of itself as a "unitary document" within which "continuity is possible."[16] Because the fundamental codes of the reading procedure are established at every beginning, Bernstein's poems typically start by throwing up barriers and creating problems. His initiating codes are always antithetical, as we see at the outset of one of his most astonishing poems, "For Love has such a Spirit that if it is Portrayed it Dies":

> Mass of van contemplation to intercede crush of
> plaster. Lots of loom: "smoke out", merely
> complicated by the first time something and don't.
> Long last, occurrence of bell, altitude, attitude of.
> The first, at this moment, aimless, *aims*. To the
> point of inordinate asphalt—lecture, entail.
> These hoops regard me suspiciously.[17]

From this apparently scattered set of texts one scarcely knows how to proceed. We are at the outset of a "poem"—this much we know, from having decoded other attendant bibliographical conventions—and hence we assume that "continuity is possible." Bernstein counts on that assumption and then attacks it. To "go on" with this text means that the reader has assented to the justice—the poetic justice—of Bernstein's initial move. And if we *do* in fact go on with his text, we will discover that relationships and forms of order can be had only if they are actively made by the reader. We will also discover that such relationships and forms of order are multiple and that they shift from reader to reader and from reading to reading. Continuities do not lie in wait for us, and the idea that we should expect continuities is specifically rejected.

This is the antinarrative mode of L=A=N=G=U=A=G=E Writing and it is Bernstein's most typical form of stylistic address. The nonnarrative mode is perhaps best displayed in the elaborate forms of serialized writing produced by Ron Silliman. This is how *Tjanting* begins:

> Not this.
> What then?
> I started over & over. Not this.
> Last week I wrote "the muscles in my palm so sore from

halving the rump roast I cld barely grip the pen." What then? This
morning my lip is blisterd.
    Of about to within which. Again & again I began. The gray
light of day fills the yellow room in a way wch is somber. Not this.
Hot grease has spilld on the stove top.
    Nor that either. Last week I wrote "the muscle at thumb's
root so taut from carving that beef I thought it wld cramp." Not so.
Wld I begin? This morning my lip is tender, disfigurd. I sat in an old
chair out behind the anise. I cld have gone about this some other way.[18]

In an important essay, "Narrating Narration," on Silliman's work,
Bernstein points out that Silliman's nonnarratives consciously work
against "the deep slumber of chronology, causality, and false unity
(totalization)."[19] He elaborates this idea in a general comment which
might well serve as the basis for a particular exegesis of the passage
I just quoted: "Detail is cast upon detail, minute particular on minute
particular, adding up to an impossibility of commensurable narrative.
With every new sentence a new embarkation: not only is the angle
changed, and it's become a close-up, but the subject is switched. Yet
maybe the sound's the same, carries it through. Or like an interlocking
chain: A has a relation to B and B to C, but B and C have nothing
in common *(series not essence)*."[20] Silliman's text commits itself to
the "Not this," to a productivity that starts over and over again. But
while the work is clearly a processive text, its movement is not governed by a narrativized totality. At the same time, if the work is
oriented toward "the future," toward "what comes next," it grounds
itself in both the present and the past: what it denominates, in its first
two sentences, as the "this" and then "then." The chief effect is a
brilliant sense of immediacy which is not, however, fixed or formal-
ized. The text is restless in its presentness, restless in a presentness
which at all points vibrates with its relations to the past and its
commitments to the future. In fact, Silliman's energized presentation gradually shows that the past and the future are themselves
open to many possibilities. "I cld have gone about this some other
way," he writes, and in that very statement we observe a change of
direction.
    In a work like *Tjanting* language is carrying out—dramatizing—
certain fundamental realities of social space and social relations. Silliman's text is a vast trope of the human world. Events in the past
continually impinge upon the present and possibilities beyond the
present: words and phrases recur in slightly altered forms and cir-

cumstances, as do syntactical forms, images, and sound patterns. As a consequence, we confront time, or the sequence of eventualities, in a highly pressurized state. The shifting forms of the repetitions open the textual field to greater possibilities. They also locate startling interventions in the text's immediate moments:

> The yellow room has a sober hue. Each sentence accounts for its place. Not this.[21]

But perhaps most remarkable of all is the translation of the past— that is to say, earlier textualizations—out of this generational process. So, while "earlier" textual forms appear in various "later" transforms, a reciprocal transformative process operates backward, as it were, changing the "earlier" texts within their memorial "later" constitutions. Thus in the next paragraph of *Tjanting*, when we come upon the statement "Each sentence accounts for all the rest,"[22] the "rhyme" of the sentences forces a new perspective on the earlier form "Each sentence accounts for its place." Minimally we observe that the particular "places" of "Each sentence" are functionally integrated with "all the rest." Out of the play of language emerges an idea of history as profoundly dialectical—as dialectical as Silliman's textual presentation. The "past" is no more fixed than the present or the future. All time is open to transformation.

Silliman's poem, in its largest sense, aims to represent through textual enactment a redemption of the *localities* of human history. Marxist in its orientation, Silliman's politicized writing has passed through the filtering critique of the Frankfurt school, and especially through the work of Benjamin. His Marxism is "western" in the concrete sense that it is carried out within the arena of advanced capitalism and American political imperialism. His struggle against these exploitive social formations appears as a critique of the modes of language which produce and reproduce the "reality" of a capitalist world and history.

Silliman is especially interested, then, in that paradigmatic bourgeois form of writing, the novel, along with those correspondent breezes "referentiality" and "narrative." He does not attack "reference" in language—all language is social—but that deformed and repressive form of reference called referentiality wherein language is alienated from its use-functions:[23] "What happens when a language moves toward and passes into a capitalist stage of development is an anaesthetic transformation of the perceived tangibility of the word, with corresponding increases in its descriptive and narrative capacities, preconditions for the invention of 'realism,' the optical illusion of reality in capitalist thought. These developments are tied directly to the nature of reference in language, which under capitalism is transformed (deformed) into referentiality" (125). Silliman calls poetry "the *philosophy of praxis in language*" (131) because its procedures are performative, "gestural," and nonnarrative. Poetics is, therefore, the critical instance through which narrativized forms are to be understood. In every novel is concealed its true poetic screaming to get out: "Repression does not, fortunately, abolish the existence of the repressed element which continues as a contradiction, often invisible, in the social fact. As such, it continues to wage the class struggle of consciousness" (126). But the novel, dominated as it is by referentiality and narrativity, is always moving within the medium of its own self-occlusion. The function of poetry is to provide an example of language in conscious pursuit of complete self-transparency. At this particular juncture of late capitalism, poetry represents the "social function of the language arts" as a liberating rather than a repressive structure: "to carry out the struggle *for* consciousness to the level *of* consciousness" (131).

Because "all meaning is a construct" (168), however, this self-transparency of the word is not an Idea or *a priori* form which the poem tries to accommodate. Self-transparency, like social justice, is a practical matter—a form of accomplishment rather than a form of truth. It has to be carried out. In Silliman's writing, this "constructed" procedure appears most frequently in his resort to various artificial numbering systems to order his work. Two procedural rules govern the form of *Ketjak* (1977), for example. First, the work moves by a series of paragraphs in which each successive paragraph has twice the number of sentences as the previous one. Second, each new paragraph must contain, somewhere, all the words used in the preceding paragraph. The method is designed to generate a network of accumulating and interconnecting details. New material is continually being generated, but always within the context of the body of materials which has already been developed.

Of *Ketjak* Bernstein has acutely noted that "the narrative rules are not taken to be of intrinsic interest."[24] Indeed, these are not "narrative rules" at all, but generative ones. Furthermore, they do not occupy the reader's attention as such, they provide the framework within which acts of attention are carried out. Therefore Bernstein observes, in a brilliant turn of critical wit, that "definition is a posteriori" in Silliman's work, "arising from a poetic practice in which the reader is acknowledged as present and counting."[25] What "counts" are the multiple perspectives processed through the text along with the reader who takes part in that processing. This is why Bernstein says that a Silliman poem is "not reductive to a single world viewed" but is "participatory, multiple."[26]

Yet in *Tjanting,* written four years after *Ketjak,* Silliman deployed a numerically based rule for generating his materials which clearly held something more than a procedural interest for him. The work, he has said, grew out of a problem he had been pondering "for at least five years: what would class struggle look like, viewed as a form. Would such a form be useable in writing?"[27] The answer was that it would look like the Fibonacci number series—that is to say, the series in which each term is the sum of the preceding two. "What initially attracted me to the series were three things: (1) it is the mathematical sequence most often found in nature, (2) each succeeding term is larger, and (3) the quantitative difference between terms is immediately perceptible, even when the quantities are of syllables or paragraphs."[28] Such a sequence came to embody for Silliman an *objectively based* dialectical process: "The most important aspect of the Fibonacci series turned out not to be those gorgeous internal relationships, but the fact that it begins with two ones. That not only permitted the parallel articulation of two sequences of paragraphs, but also determined that their development would be uneven, punning back to the general theory of class struggle."[29] But what must be noted is that *Tjanting* does not tell the/a "story" of "class struggle." It does not reflect the operation of "the general theory of class struggle" in a projected "fiction" (first-person or otherwise). Rather *Tjanting* is a localized instance of class struggle itself: not merely Silliman's personal act of struggle, but his deployment of an artistic occasion within which such struggle may take place. In the end, as Bernstein observed, it is the reader in the poem who "counts."

As with other L=A=N=G=U=A=G=E writers, Silliman's work engages adversely with all that means to appear authoritative, fixed, and determined. These antithetical projects function within the world of language because language is taken as the representative social form per se—the social form through which society sees and presents itself to itself. Thus, the "languages" within which these writers live and move and have their being are quite specifically the "languages" of the Cold War west after the debacles of the Korean and Vietnam wars. This is important to realize for it helps to explain the extremity of their work. In them poetry appears at a crisis of its traditional modes of expression. So false and self-conflicted seem the ordinary public forms of discourse—in the media, the policy organs of government, and the academic clerisy—that the artistic representation of such discourse must either be subjected to their one-dimensionality or activate a critical engagement.

That L = A = N = G = U = A = G = E writers have chosen the alternative is clear not only from their poetic practice, but from their theoretical and exegetical work as well. Though they discuss and comment upon one another's work quite frequently, these discussions almost never take the form of "interpretation." Interpretive remarks are of course embedded throughout the commentary, but they are subordinated to various types of pragmatic and performative modes of discussion. As often as not the "commentary" will take the form of another poem or poetical excursus, or of an explanation of how some particular text "works" (rather than what it "means"), or, as we have already noticed in the work of Tina Darragh and Bernadette Mayer, of a set of directions and procedures, a mini-course in how-to-write.

THE SPECIAL CHARACTER of Silliman's nonnarrative texts is nicely dramatized if we set a work like *Tjanting* beside an academic text like John Hollander's *Reflections on Espionage* (1976).[30] This may seem an odd comparison, but it is in fact quite apposite. In the first place, both poems are fully conscious of their placement within the sociohistorical field of Cold War America. Correlatively, both imagine and reflect upon the function of poetry within such social circumstances. Finally, both resort—in an extraordinarily odd conjunction of purposes—to the Fibonacci number sequence as an important procedural device within which their poems' meanings are carried out.

Reflections on Espionage is a narrativized text made up of a series of code messages sent by the spy Cupcake to various other persons in his espionage network. The poem tells the story of Cupcake's increasing psychic disaffection—partly concealed even from himself— with his work as a spy. Eventually Cupcake comes under the surveillance of his own organization's internal security apparatus, and at the end—his reliability as a spy hopelessly compromised—the organization calls for his "termination."

The story involves, of course, an elaborately executed allegory in which "spying" is equated with "being a poet," and vice versa. The text is full of coded references to American poets and writers, mostly Hollander's contemporaries. Its distant progenitor, Browning's "How It Strikes a Contemporary," underscores by contrast the special character of *Reflections,* for Hollander's story—like his hero—is dominated by nostalgia and a pervasive sense of social anomie. The poem's world is graphed along an axis of "them" and "us" which reflects both the political situation of the Cold War and the typical antagonisms and divisions between "schools" or groups of poets. All this would be merely amusing were it not that Hollander's hero continually reflects upon the social function of poetry; from these reflections he draws the most mordant and disheartening conclusions. In fact, *Reflections* argues, or rather demonstrates, that poetry under the social circumstances "reflected" in this poem has, like spying under the same circumstances, only an alienating effect. This poetry of "reflection" preserves, and ultimately reifies, the world-as-alienation, and it does so by failing to imagine that poetry might struggle with, rather than merely reflect (upon), its world.

Cupcake's meditations on his work as spy/poet lead him to a sharp sense of his own isolation. In his loneliness he calls into question the whole enterprise to which he has given himself:

> What kind of work is this
> For which if we were to touch in the darkness
> It would be without feeling the other there?
> It might help to know if Steampump's dying
> Was part of the work or not. I shall not be
> Told, I know.   (3–4)

Cupcake's question is rhetorical and will not—cannot, in his imagination of the world—be answered. This social alienation mirrors a correspondent crisis of the personality.

> Names like ours leave no traces in
> Nature. Yet what of the names they encode, names
> One's face comes in time to rhyme with, John or James?
> The secret coded poem of one's whole life rhymes
> Entirely with that face, a maddening
> Canzona, every line of which sings in the
> Breaths we take and give, ending with the same sound.
> As with the life, so ridiculously, with

> The work. But, after all, which of them is the
> Enciphered version of the other one, and
> Are we, after all, even supposed to know?   (28)

In the end Hollander's "master spy" will watch the system he has served send out a broadcast order for his execution. His final coded transmission is a frightening poem constructed partly on the use of the Fibonacci number series. Its principal message, secreted away in the poem's initial and terminal syllables, is revealed by using the Fibonacci number sequence as an index to those syllables. It is a plea for death, and it is answered in the poem's final line—a series of Xs which, decoded, translate: TERMINATE CUPCAKE.

Silliman's imagination, as we have seen, found in the Fibonacci numbers an image of class struggle and social dialectics. The numbers confirm his search for signs and modes of social dynamism. But when Cupcake uses the Fibonacci series in his final transmission, he interprets his own usage in these terrible terms:

> and I have sat watching
> Key numbers in their serial dance growing
> Further apart, outdistancing their touching,
> Outstretched arms.   (71)

Hollander's alter-ego "editor" of Cupcake's story supplies a gloss to Cupcake's final transmission. The exegesis remarks on the desperation of the passage but can only replicate the master spy's own sense of helplessness:

> This disturbing and disturbed transmission seems to be a kind of cry
> for help. But to whom?   (75)

The interpretation here is congruent with the poem's self-conception. Hollander characterizes Cold War America and its poetry as a world of desperate (rather than rich) ambiguities. It is a poetic world whose own highest value—close interpersonal relations—is contradicted by the social structures and practices it takes for granted. To Hollander, the march of the Fibonacci numbers is the apocalypse of such a world, the prophecy of its desperation and its even more fragmented future.

Hollander's poem imagines what it knows (or thinks it knows) about poetry and society alike. Such an imagination, however, can mount no effective resistance against its own terrible revelations: vacancy in luxurious words, dismemberment in the way we live now. It is all mirror and meditation, a story and a set of reflections on the story. In this respect the contrast with writers like Bernstein and Silliman is striking and unmistakable. In them antinarrative and non-narrative continually work against and move beyond the enchantments of what has been given and what is taken to be "real." They are the inheritors of Blake's early attempts to dismantle those prisons of imaginary beauties: social and personal life in its cruel apparitions, and art as what reflects upon such things. Hollander's poem is a work of decadence in that it refuses to press the charges called for by its own investigation. Pleading "no contest," it is properly found guilty. *Reflections on Espionage* is anything but a trivial poem, however. Its analogues are, for example, Fitzgerald's *Rubaiyat* and Rossetti's *House of Life* and all those works which deliver us over to luxurious and unlivable things. The highest form of such poetry is reached in the work of artists like Baudelaire, the mayor of the City of Pain, over whose gates is written the legend "Anywhere out of the World."

Poetry can and does offer alternatives to such desperate forms of idealism, however. I do not have in mind work which celebrates or reflects the "solidarity" of "postmodern bourgeois intellectuals," though we certainly have a great deal of that today. Charles Bernstein's "For Love has such a Spirit . . ." is too long to quote in full, or even at length, but it certainly represents such an alternative: a Shelleyan performance, not unlike "Epipsychidion" or the great "Life of Life" lyric, in which love burns through all the vests which seem to hide it from us.

> For love I would—deft equator.
> Nonchalant attribution of all the, & filled with
> such, meddles with & steals my constancy, sharpening
> desire for that, in passing, there, be favorite
> in ordinary, but no sooner thought than gone. My
> heart seems wax, that like tapers burns at light.[31]

This is a "deconstructive" poetry, fully postmodern in its style, but in its nervous erosions it moves the "Spirit" of a love that, settled in what is "ordinary" and given, will not settle for anything.

Silliman's nonnarratives are also exemplary alternatives, and a number of other significant writers might be named: Alan Davies, Lyn Hejinian, Susan Howe. They are all distinctive and distinguished writers. In each of them, however, writing is used to contest and disrupt those forms of order which are always replicated in the "realism" deployed through narrativities. These disruptions take antinarrative as well as nonnarrative form. In the latter, however, the critique of fixed orders ("reality") is carried out simultaneously with the deployment of new orders and "realities": "The mind evolves a blueprint out of what is already there, doesn't recognize where to go next, then explores and enumerates the possibilities . . . The odd connection permits a reexperience of what was originally recorded but not really experienced. The mind (language) reshuffles its fragments in order to attain the original hierarchy; reassembling it permits reprocessing from the new perspective."[32] This might have been a specific commentary on Silliman's *Tjanting,* for the process sketched here is precisely what we discover in Silliman's poem. But Davies and Piombino are making a general statement about $L=A=N=G=U=A=G=E$ Writing. It is well put. And though it does not talk directly of a "politics of poetry," the politics of such writing—the theory and the practice of it alike—are plain for anyone to see.

11 ⟨⟩

The Third World of Criticism

There is no freedom, even for masters, in the midst of slaves.

Lord Byron, *Letters*

This is a beautiful country. I had not cast my eyes over it before, that is, in this direction.

John Brown, from the scaffold, 1859

AT THE CONCLUSION of his great essay "Concerning Violence," Frantz Fanon argues that "the fate of the world depends upon" whether the first two worlds, especially the first world, are able to operate from a noncolonialist imagination.[1] To Fanon this means that the first world must realize its obligation not merely to allow the Third World its independent development, but also to assist actively in that development, with no strings attached.

The full argument is by this time a familiar one, though certainly no less important for that reason. What still surprises a western reader of this essay is its exclusive rhetoric. Fanon's essay addresses the people of the Third World; indeed, not until the conclusion does he allow himself to think at all about the effect his words might have on the first two worlds. But at the end, for the first time in the essay, the people from those other two worlds are allowed in the room with Fanon and his audience, are allowed to listen, from the margin of Fanon's center, to the urgency of his message.

What we hear, from our corner of that room, is "what [the Third World] expects from those who for centuries have kept it in slavery." The message is "to rehabilitate mankind, and make man victorious, once and for all": "This huge task which consists of reintroducing mankind into the world, the whole of mankind, will be carried out with the indispensable help of the European peoples, who themselves must realize that in the past they have often joined the ranks of our common masters where colonial questions were concerned. To achieve this the European peoples must first decide to wake up and shake themselves, use their brains, and stop playing the stupid game of Sleeping Beauty."[2] From the vantage of the eavesdropping "European peoples"—ourselves—this involves awakening from certain luxurious and heroic dreams. We are to stop projecting those grand illusions which proceed from small imaginations. If we are hearing Fanon at all, we are hearing from his point of view—that is to say, from the point of view of a Third World, where the dialectic of the first two worlds is completely reimagined.

The problem here is not at all that we occupy a *different* world, but that in investing it with privilege we have generated the inertias of violence and domination which Fanon has spoken of. Nor is the problem simply that our heritage of violence has borne away an actual Third World. The problem is more acute, simple, and closer to home: that in our violent histories we have acquired a certain kind of imagination and that this imagination is written out in the treasuries of our kings and the gardens of our queens. Walter Benjamin, who had a Third Imagination, could not "contemplate without horror" the cultural treasures which descended into his hands: "There is no document of civilization which is not at the same time a document of barbarism. And just as such a document is not free of barbarism, barbarism taints also the manner in which it was transmitted from one owner to another."[3] This is the voice of a European person speaking to European peoples out of a Third Imagination. Benjamin's "Theses on the Philosophy of History" deploy the rhetoric of the second world frequently, but in fact he lived an uneasy existence at the margins of both of the first two worlds. For when he says that the task of the "historical materialist" is "to brush history against the grain,"[4] he cannot except the atrocious histories of the second world as well, where the violence of the first world has met its match.

What would it mean, then, to acquire a Third Imagination? On this question Fanon is clearer than Benjamin, even for European persons like ourselves. He sketches an answer (it is not written for us, but we can read it with profit) in his essay "On National Culture." According to Fanon, in the context of imperialism a national culture develops in three phases. (Fanon, of course, writes of these matters from the perspective of an actual citizen of the actual Third World; his analysis reflects on circumstances in the first two worlds as well, however, since the latter live through, by carrying out, the imagination of violence visited upon the Third World.) In the first phase of its development a cultural mode of violation is established and assimilated. In the second phase, when the violation is discovered, an effort is made to find a world elsewhere, an inviolate world: "Past happenings of the byegone days of . . . childhood will be brought up out of the depths of . . . memory; old legends will be reinterpreted in the light of a borrowed estheticism and of a conception of the world which was discovered under other skies."[5] This is a phase of enlightenment where the past is used to clarify conditions in the present. It prepares for the third phase, "the fighting phase," when one "turns himself into an awakener of the people," to "shake" them from their lethargy.[6] The imagery echoes Fanon's call to a similar awakening of the "European peoples" at the end of the essay "Concerning Violence."

In the third phase, past and present are conceived from the vantage of the future. In terms of an actual literary practice, the third phase means, for example, that "the storytellers who used to relate inert episodes now bring them alive and introduce into them modifications which are increasingly fundamental." "Conflicts" are brought "up to date and . . . modernize[d]," and "the method of allusion is more and more widely used": "The formula 'This all happened long ago' is substituted with that of 'What we are going to speak of happened somewhere else, but it might well have happened here today, and it might happen tomorrow.' "[7] What Fanon means is that an imagination of the future, of what the future should be, determines both the writing and the reading of the texts we inherit and create. This third phase, which is one with the Third World, is the Third World's gift to "the whole of mankind"—an objective and precisely an *alienated* perspective on the dialectic of violence of the first two worlds and all the "inert episodes" which we fondly call our literary and cultural inheritance.

For the nations of the first and second worlds, with their imperialist histories, the awakening Fanon speaks of would expose new ranges of historical possibility—new configurations of the past, different imaginations of the present and the future. Our cultural productions generally represent those histories in forms of beauty and sublimity, though in fact they are histories which, as often as not, are founded in shameful and barbarous deeds. A critical awakening would strip away such modes of deception (and self-deception); it would entail a refusal to read our cultural deposits on their own ideological terms, and a refusal as well to develop new readings (or writings) which merely modernize and update those ideologies.

Initially this requires that our cultural works be alienated from the tradition which represents them as the best that has been known and thought in the world. This alienation does not mean, however, that the works should be debunked. Neither an antithetical nor a third reading can afford to deliver any part of cultural history into the hands of an imperial imagination. Rather, the works must be raised up from their narrowly imagined totalities, must be seen as part of that larger context which emerges when they are *specifically* situated, when they are delivered over to their historical and social localities. That critical event—the islanding of history and its works[8]—establishes the possibility of a proper sphere of totalization—one that is horizontally international and vertically transcultural and transhistorical.

This islanding of the works of culture is especially crucial for readers in a western tradition, where the intertexture of our cultural works, in particular of our poetry, has woven a net that is strangling human imagination. The burden of the past that weighs like a nightmare on the brain of the west is an imperial burden, the anxiety that it might not all be of one piece, that secret histories, forgotten facts, other imaginations operate in all that we do and make, and that our massive ignorance of these Othernesses is working to undermine what we do. Like Napoleon moving inexorably toward the capture of Moscow, Great Traditions follow their difficult and equivocal victories of imagination to an ultimate destruction.

That destruction does not overtake the works of the past, it merely makes them inaccessible to people in the present who are unable to imagine them anew, objectively. Writers like Benjamin and Fanon call us toward that objectivity, to an imagining of poetical work in ways that will try to overcome the illusions those works themselves have helped to perpetuate. Every poem is an island that imagines itself a world, and it *is* a world—but not the world—because it is a world within and among other worlds. Its illusion of totality is a dream of a truth that can only come to be in the exposure of the meaning of the dream.

A work like the *Oresteia,* for example, dreams of a society to be founded forever in an imagination of justice and civil harmony. This utopian dream is then realized in Aeschylus' work, which we have since continued to interpret in terms that accommodate its own self-conception. Yet such interpretations visit a serious injustice upon the *Oresteia* and its utopian dream of a just and harmonious society. Justice here depends upon the exposition of the objective and alienated truths of Aeschylus' dramatic work. Such an exposition can never be completed, of course, but it will not even advance beyond a mirror-stage unless the work is seen objectively.

As we know, the *Oresteia* deals with the impasse which a retributive system of justice develops for itself. Or rather, it *imagines* such a system at an impasse—for in fact one could have imagined it otherwise, could have told a different story in which retribution falls upon the guilty by hands that are other than familial hands.

But Aeschylus wants to imagine retributive justice at an impasse because he wants to celebrate not simply a "universal" idea of justice, but the Athenian version of a universal idea of justice. The play is presented in Athens at a crucial and specific time, 458 B.C., shortly after the passage of the revolutionary Ephialtic reforms.[9] Scholars have long recognized this topical dimension of the *Oresteia,* and in more recent years have reached a certain broad agreement that Aeschylus, though generally conservative, must have supported a number of these new legal reforms. The trilogy makes a significant ideological intervention in the immediate aftermath of the struggle between the reformers (like Ephialtes and Pericles) and the traditional authorities (like Kimon).

The Ephialtic reforms were an attempt to replace the traditional oligarchic legal structure with democratic structures. As such, they were equally bound up with certain international issues, and most specifically with the uneasy relations (and alliance) between Sparta and Athens following the Persian War. Sparta, of course, was an oligarchy, and Athens' alliance with her was maintained and supported, at the crucial period of the reforms, largely through the authority of men like Kimon.

The context in which the reforms were passed is important if we are to understand the *Oresteia.*[10] Athens had been asked to send a supporting force to Laconia to aid the Spartans in putting down the revolt of their helots in 463. Kimon argued successfully, against strong democratic opposition, to send an Athenian contingent, but when the army arrived in Laconia, with Kimon at its head, it was ignominiously sent away by the suspicious Lacedemonians. Kimon returned to Athens in disgrace, the reforms were passed in 462/461, and Kimon was ostracized. But the reforms were not instituted without vigorous and widespread opposition and great civic unrest in Athens. Ephialtes himself was assassinated shortly after the passage of the initial series of reforms.

The *Oresteia* is clearly preoccupied with all these matters; indeed, one of its principal objects, as we see most clearly at the end of *The Eumenides,* is to promote an ideal of civic harmony, and (reciprocally) to warn of the dangers that beset a society torn by internal and civil discord. At the end of *The Libation Bearers,* with Clytemnestra and Aegisthus now dead at the hands of the avenging Orestes, and with Orestes pursued by the Fates, the Chorus—dismayed at the prospect of a ceaseless process of internecine death—prays for an end to the bloodletting:[11]

> Where
> Is the end? Where shall the fury of fate
> Be stilled to sleep, be done with?   (1074–1076)

The prayer recalls the refrain of the Chorus at the beginning of the *Agamemnon* ("Sing sorrow, sorrow: but good win out in the end") and anticipates the conclusion of the trilogy, when the judgment of Athena, at the trial and immediately afterward, produces the trilogy's final vision of civil harmony.

That vision is itself crucial to the resolution of the dramatic conflicts. After the acquittal of Orestes the Fates are at first implacable in their resentment, but Athena persuades them out of their wrath with benevolent promises. These are all founded in a conviction that Athens is destined for greatness:

> If you go away into some land of foreigners,
> I warn you, you will come to love this country. Time
> in his forward flood shall ever grow more dignified
> for the people of this city. And you, in your place
> of eminence beside Erechtheus in his house
> shall win from female and from male processionals
> more than all lands of men beside could ever give.   (851–857)

This is a social and a political vision, and it celebrates what the final courtroom scene dramatizes: Aeschlyus' conviction that the institutions of Athens are the glory of Greece—indeed, the glory of the world. Important to the meaning of the conclusion of *The Eumen-ides* is the fact that a stranger to Athens, a guest, should go there to seek justice. Athens took a justifiable pride in her legal institutions, and specifically in the two fundamental principles: that rule should be maintained by law and not by men, and that everyone—guest and citizen alike—should have equal protection under the law. The conclusion of *The Eumenides* is a celebration of those legal institutions.

But the play is also celebrating something else—a treaty of alliance with Argos made in 461 at the urging of the (now politically dominant) reform party. This second focus of celebration is closely allied to the first. It is a celebration not of Athens' political institutions, however, but of her economic and political power. The two celebrations are connected in the reality of Athens' circumstances in the period 463–458, when Athens arrived at a position of enormous economic, military, and political power and influence. This position was achieved gradually during the period following the Persian wars, but most dramatically between 477–463, that is, between the founding of the Delian League, with Athens at its head, and the subjugation by Athens of various members that tried to revolt from the league. The important island of Thasos was reduced in 463 after a two-year struggle. During this fifteen-year period between the foundation of the League and the Ephialtic reforms, Athens' empire came into being.

These matters bear upon the *Oresteia* because the treaty with Argos is the play's device for focusing our attention on Athens' position in the Greek world at the time. Aeschylus draws our attention to Argos immediately, at the opening of the *Agamemnon* (24), when we are told that the king is returning home from the Trojan War to Argos. According to Homer, however, Agamemnon was king of Mykenai, not of Argos. Scholars agree now that this change was made as a compliment to Athens' new ally.[12] The change was not an awkward one in any case since the Argives had recently conquered the ancient city of Mykenai and incorporated her into their domains.[13]

The conquest of Mykenai was the latest in a series of adventures which placed Argos in a position to rival Sparta for control of the Peloponnese. Athens sought the treaty with Argos—a defensive alliance against Sparta—immediately after the failure of Kimon's expedition into Laconia to aid Sparta. The alliance with Argos, in other words, was an international part of the democratic reforms being carried through by Ephialtes and Pericles. The alliance was meant to strengthen the Athenian empire against its chief rival for power in Greece, Sparta.

Aeschylus alludes to this treaty with Argos three times in *The Eumenides,* and in each case the passage imagines an alliance "for the rest of time" (291, 670). In the final passage Orestes, speaking as the mouthpiece of Argos, swears to fight with Athens against those who come against her and to be the "gracious spirit" of all those others, her tributaries and her allies, who "align their spears to fight beside her" (773–774). Orestes' oath of alliance is immediately followed by the scene in which Athena finally persuades the Furies to take up their office of benevolence toward Athens. Before the play concludes in its vision of civic harmony, Athena addresses the as yet unpersuaded Furies. "Do not," she warns them,

> engraft among my citizens that spirit of war
> that turns their battle fury inward on themselves.
> No, let our wars range outward.　　　　　　　　(862–864)

The prayer expresses at once Aeschylus' dismay at the recent civil discords in Athens between the rival democratic and aristocratic parties, and his confidence in the martial strength of the empire in face of her enemies. The confidence here is part of the trilogy's compliment to Argos, whose alliance added so much to Athenian power vis à vis the Lacedemonians.

Yet hidden in the splendor of the play's conclusion, with its grandiose imagination of social harmony, is a terrible truth which the ideology of Aeschylus's trilogy could not see, but which the dramas are nonetheless forced to confront. For the fact is that this very alliance with Argos, which seemed to promise so much good, was the triggering event behind the so-called First Peloponnesian War, and the first act in a tragic curve which would eventually plunge all of Greece into war and bring about the destruction of the empire so vaunted in the *Oresteia.* Athena, goddess though she is, cannot understand the full, tragic weight of her prayer for outward-ranging war. In its imagination of an end to the cycles of bloodshed, the *Oresteia* is prophesying an even greater cataclysm, and no end to the cycles of destruction. For the *Oresteia*'s imagination of justice and harmony are illusions, founded in a set of contradictory social structures (democracy and imperialism) which would only grow more extreme with the passing of time.

We do not understand how poetry works if we think that, because the Peloponnesian Wars took place after Aeschylus wrote the *Oresteia*, therefore the trilogy and those wars are not implicated in each other. We may imagine, rather, that the "meaning" of a poetical work is structured by the historical limit of the author's life; this imagining is all the more insisted upon when the "meanings" we seek are social and historical ones. But we are wrong in this imagining, because every poetical work casts itself along what Shelley called "futurity." In writing what amounts to an imaginative history of the present, every poem thereby constructs a past and a set of possible futures. One of the futures constructed in the *Oresteia* is "an upright course clear through to the end" (995) and "peace forever" (1046). But another future, more dreadful, is also constructed through the play *in the very illusions and contradictions which are borne along with that first, benevolent imagination of the future*. The tragic meaning of the *Oresteia* is not a mere quirk or irony of history; it is part of what it signified from the beginning, and what was most dramatically realized in the celebrations of the treaty with Argos.

Poems move out into many futures, which are their own real futures as well, unknown to themselves. The *Oresteia* today means both more and less than it meant in 458 because its meaning—which is always localized in the present—carries along the many histories of meanings which were only initiated in the trilogy's first appearance. These meanings are sometimes lost, often recovered, and always refashioned. If we read the *Oresteia*'s conclusion as an unequivocal celebration, we will be reading it in terms of its initial self-conception; and we will be reading *out* of the work that other dominant line of meaning which is so closely connected to the celebratory meaning and which is so intimately involved with the work's history—with the work as meaning in and through the history its own celebration calls our attention to.

We will, moreover, be reading in a way that projects a certain meaning into our own immediate circumstances. More clearly than most works of the past, the *Oresteia* seems to impinge upon ourselves and our present. This work and its significant history "all happened long ago," but Fanon's suggestion—that "it might well have happened here today, and it might happen tomorrow"—point toward the "formula" which all criticism, whether consciously or not, adheres to. The tales told in the *Oresteia* are certainly happening here today and will happen again tomorrow. The question is: how will we choose to read those tales—objectively, or in terms of their own (and our own) celebrations and self-conceptions?

Shelley wrote *Prometheus Unbound* as a response to the future bequeathed to him by Aeschylus' *Prometheus Bound* and the (subsequently lost) *Prometheus Unbound*, with its celebratory reconciliation of "the Champion with the Oppressor of mankind."[14] Shelley's play is a reading of the lost Aeschylean drama according to Fanon's "method of allusion" and "modernization": not an imitation but a remaking in terms of a more objective imagining of Aeschylus than the Greek dramatist would have intended. Aeschylean drama, however, like all poetry, lays down a rich deposit of incommensurate detail even as it follows its specific ideological commitments. In this way poetry always tells more than it knows, always carries within itself many opportunities for greater objectivity and truth.

Genesis, more than most texts, has worked assiduously to project a monomorphic image of its world; but even in Genesis the relics of a larger story remain, a story which includes many other cultures and civilizations as great and as barbaric as Israel's. The Israel of Genesis is an island in a greater world, and the more it insists that it is the center of that world, the more it gives us glimpses of the actual, the whole, the objective truth.

To relinquish an empire is no easy task, and it can be, as Pericles once argued, dangerous as well.[15] To maintain one, however, is not merely wrong, which Pericles observed, it is even more dangerous. The dangers are especially acute in the case of empires like the Athenian and the American—empires, that is to say, which were acquired in a brief period and only half purposefully, empires which developed in volatile political circumstances both at home and abroad.

To relinquish an imperial imagination is also difficult, and a no less urgent task. Empires are maintained by imperial intellects. Cultural studies, and literary work in particular, function either to build or to unbuild such minds. In this respect Blake's work is exactly a prophecy against empire, a model of how the poetic moves against the perpetuation of empires and toward the development of less exploitive societies, less alienated imaginations. Literary work is the art of multiplicities and minute particulars, the science of *un*buildings: one law for the lion and the ox *is* oppression.

In this context Shelley's famous words bear remembering:

We have more moral, political and historical wisdom, than we know how to reduce to practise; we have more scientific and oeconomical knowledge than can be accommodated to the just distribution of the produce which it multiplies . . . our calculations have outrun conception; we have eaten more than we can digest. The cultivation of those sciences which have enlarged the limits of the empire of man over the external world, has, for want of the poetical faculty, proportionately circumscribed those of the internal world; and man, having enslaved the elements, remains himself a slave.[16]

These are stirring words, and worthy of honor—not least because they are fully conscious that poetical work is not an aesthetic resort but an activity with real social investments and obligations. They are as well, however, words spoken out of that fundamental Romantic Ideology which is epitomized in the Kantian aesthetic, but which is equally operative in the anti-Kantian Romantic program first deployed by Blake. That is to say, Shelley—like Blake before him—takes it for granted that the redemption of the social order is the function of the "poetical faculty." For them, poetry and Imagination are not involved with the false consciousness of ideology.

Yet it is plain that this ascription of transcendent status to art and the Imagination is mistaken—indeed, is contradicted by the actual practice of Romantic artists themselves. Milton earlier established the model that, in place of a failed social order, one might establish the order of an inward paradise. But neither Blake nor Shelley—nor even Wordsworth, for that matter—accepted Milton's consolatory move. Their departures from Milton's model all differ somewhat, of course, but Blake's departure is especially significant because his work enacts an artistic practice that is committed to the transformation of society: the installation of the city of God (which for Blake means a *human* city) in England's green and pleasant land.

Blake understands that this will be a city of art, a place where all the work will be artists' work—work designed to move against (though it will never entirely defeat) what Shelley called "Fate, Time, Occasion, Chance, and Change." It will be a social order with no "corporeal war," an order entirely cleansed of "the Wastes of moral law" deplored by Blake. None of these imaginations are "inward" imaginations; they are emphatically political, institutional, even economic—as Blake's works repeatedly emphasize.

Blake's work is important in this context because it consistently foregrounds the material, social, and institutional bases of its productive modes. Unlike Shelley and the other Romantics, he took none of art's productive processes and institutions for granted. An imaginative and poetical transformation of the social order is carried out at all levels and in every form of that order. His illuminated poems are especially clear examples of his understanding that if art is to be an agent of change, its agencies will be operating at the earliest stages of conception and through all later productive, distributive, and reproductive phases. None of this must be allowed to escape poetry's concrete transformative deliberations.

If Blake's judgments about these matters went far beyond those of other artists of his time—and I think they did—the irony is that he became, nonetheless, the most ineffectual of that period's many angels. No one had less influence on his age than Blake, and it was not until many decades after his death that he began to gather a public. And now he is an academic subject, central to the curriculum.

It was not what he had in mind. In *The Marriage of Heaven and Hell* "the cherub with his flaming sword"—that is to say, the angel of the social apocalypse—"*is* hereby commanded to leave his guard at tree of life" (plate 14, my italics). But the angel of history did not appear to obey that poetic command, which Blake gave in this early poem and which he repeated in all his works throughout his career. (In fact, the command was obeyed as it was issued, only its accomplishment came in forms of truth which Blake had not thought of.) As with Aeschylus' *Eumenides,* the future of Blake's work would bear along with that work, and for that work, as much history as it had imagined, but far more than it knew.

Are they fortuitous, these discordant artistic futures, and irrelevant to the ways we should understand and use our poetic resources? I do not think so. When we think of poems "in their historical contexts," our historicist biases—even in their "New Historicist" modes—take those "contexts" to be located primarily in the past, or, if we have read our Nietzsche and Foucault with care, in the present and the past. And when we think even more deeply about such matters, we also understand that these historical contexts are multiple and conflicting: heteroglossial, as Bakhtin would say. But if it is true that all futures are functions of the past (and the present), then we must expect to find those futures being carried out in the works that seem to be speaking and acting only from the past.

Poems imagine more than they know. The *Oresteia* is a far greater work, in those future contexts of reality it had not discussed and did not desire, than it is when we read it merely in the context of its own grandiose—and mistaken—self-conceptions. Its greatness is intimately bound up with its own imaginative capacities, which solicit the total appearance of the human truth of things—that is to say, their social and historical truth, in all its contradictions and emergencies. And the same is true for Blake's work, which, like the *Oresteia*, looked forward to the advent of a New Jerusalem. But it did not come. The violent would bear it away, and Blake would play his part in the closet dramas of the academy and the struggles in the auction salesrooms.

Blake's distinctly nonradical reception history is an irony very like the one we saw in the future of the *Oresteia;* the irony is no more an aberration for Blake's work, however, than it was for Aeschylus'. There are more things in Blake's heavens and hells than he thought of in his philosophy. Though his mode of artistic production involved a conscious effort to avoid the machineries of mercantile capitalism, it also ensured that his work would be expensive, even in his own day. The provenance histories of the illuminated works show that they have, with few exceptions, been sought after and owned by rich people and art connoisseurs.[17] Thus, although Blake's ideas and goals looked to the material transformation of unjust and exploitive social conditions, the "vehicular forms" of these projects had, from the outset, small purchase among those who would be most interested in carrying out such social transformations. Unlike Shelley and Byron, for example, Blake was unknown to the Chartists. He was delivered into the aesthetic hands of the Pre-Raphaelites through quietist religious agencies: that is to say, through that pious circle of men who called themselves the "Ancients" and Blake the "Interpreter"—men like John Linnell, George Cumberland, Frederick Tatham, George Richmond, and of course Alexander Gilchrist.[18] Similarly, though we can see that in Blake's day the New Jerusalem Church and other dissenting sects drew their strength from the underprivileged, the character of religious nonconformity had changed drastically between 1790 and 1830. The Evangelical Movement in the first two decades of the nineteenth century moved closer to the ideological mainstream of English society —so much closer, in fact, that it had become an important reforming movement even within the Church of England by 1820.[19] We should not be surprised, therefore, that Blake asked to have the Anglican service read at his funeral in 1827. It may seem an odd turn of events in the career of this great antinomian figure, but he was first and last a Christian, and his own work remained open—as it still remains open —to those clerical interpretations which survive in the valley of their saying, which make nothing happen beyond what has been established as possible or acceptable.

Once again, however, this is a historical eventuality which lies hidden within Blake's own work. That his ideas and goals were partly mystified in themselves seems quite clear, and not simply from his sexist theory of the emanations,[20] or his decision to write in such a way that the figure of a privileged "Interpreter" would become so central to that correspondent entity known as "Blake Studies." Even more crucial to the historical meaning of Blake's work was his conviction, which he shared with every major poet of his age, that art is a nonideological agency. Of course Blake understood very well that imagination and poetry are human acts embedded in their times of conflicting vision and contested human interests. But he also, and contradictorily, believed that there could be—had to be—an originary Prophet of such Losses who would not be subject to those losses. A New Day would dawn with the Dawning of the Imagination, when the unfallen Zoa—Los, the Zoa of Poetic Creation—would assume an empire over the world. This idea—the Romantic Ideology of the Poet as Genius—is one of the last infirmities of those noble Romantic minds.

It was, in addition, a mental infirmity which they themselves recognized—in others. The Romantic "interpretation" of Milton—vulgarly, that Satan is the hero of *Paradise Lost*—is not something which, in their view, was laid upon Milton's work anachronistically. Blake's *Milton* argued the case against the great Puritan on the basis of English history, especially the history of English imperial interests as they developed between Milton's day and Blake's during the Napoleonic Wars. Blake's argument is that Milton's works contributed largely to the construction of that evil history; indeed, the famous "paradise within," which Milton preached, is revealed in Blake's revisionary poem as the "cold bosom" and corrupted heart of "Albion," who sleeps in righteousness on his "Rock of Ages."

> The Nations still
> Follow after the detestable Gods of Priam; in pomp
> Of warlike selfhood, contradicting and blaspheming . . .
> I will go down to the sepulcher to see if morning breaks!

I will go down to self-annihilation and eternal death,
Lest the Last Judgment come & find me unannihilate
And I be seiz'd & giv'n into the hands of my own Selfhood
(14:14–16, 20–24)

Milton's work constructs an image of the paradisal and the elect through a reciprocal definition of the hellish and the damned. It is an image founded, therefore, quite literally, in sin. Its consequence is an imperial history which, in political terms, reappeared in Blake's day as a dynamic of the Elect (England), the Reprobate (France), and the Redeemable (that which remains, the Third World). In such a scheme that Third World is to be appropriated to the missionary zeal of an Elected design. But to Blake such a design is not merely moral righteousness, it is actual political imperialism. To Blake it is a design founded in England, reinstituted in Milton, and thence dispersed across the world in a process of real historical events.

> Lambeth's Vale
> Where Jerusalems foundations began: where they were laid in ruins
> Where they were laid in ruins from every Nation & Oak Groves
>   rooted . . .
> When shall Jerusalem return & overspread all the Nations
> Return: return to Lambeths Vale O building of human souls
> Thence stony Druid Temples overspread the Island white
> And thence from Jerusalem ruins, from her walls of salvation
> And praise: thro the whole Earth were reard from Ireland
> To Mexico & Peru west, & east to China & Japan: till Babel
> The Spectre of Albion frownd over the Nations in glory and war
> All things begin & end in Albions ancient Druid rocky shore
(4:14–16, 18–25)

England's spectrous presence is called Babel in the context of these historical references because she works to build an imperial city and to sacrifice all other cities to that monomorphic empire. From the ruins of Jerusalem—a plural reality, as we know from the conclusion of Blake's last major prophecy—emerges Babel, the great figure of all the Buildings of Loss. Its more common name is the British Empire.

Blake deployed a poetical scheme for imagining all the buildings of loss as the Buildings of Los: as the city of art, "great Golgonooza," a place which opened out to the world of Eternity. And Eternity, Blake's ultimate object in several senses, stood apart from history and time and space because it incorporated, like a Hegelian dialectic, all of human history within itself. But *in truth* the Hegelian dialectic and Blake's "Eternity" are, like Kant's aesthetic, historical formations. Their historicity is revealed most dramatically when they enter the fullness of time, that is, when Blake's "Eternity" or Hegel's dialectic or Kant's aesthetic is viewed in the perspective of a more encompassing—a more objective—form of history. That is the perspective of the unknown and the possible, the perspective which alone reveals the multiple histories which lie hidden, and as often as not repressed, within the works where they have been imagined, but where they are not recognized. These futures, which may be either terrible or wonderful, are the instruments through which all of history—past, present, and future alike—is opened to change. Such an opening is what Blake supplied for Milton and his other cultural forebears. But while in this respect Blake, like Jesus, saved those others, of himself we have to think—it is one of the few (terrible) insights left to an imperialist imagination—that "himself he could not save." He could not, quite simply, because he had held back—because he had "saved"—a part of his work that was to be placed forever beyond the possibility of either fall or redemption.

In fact, there is nothing which can be set apart in that way, and the idea that Eternity exists outside of its various human imaginations (of which Blake's is only one) is an immortalist illusion. In Romantic art it reappears as the idea of an aesthetic, and while Blake fought against that idea, his own work ultimately submitted to its domination. Its illusory character, so far as poetic work is concerned, would not be fully and consciously (re)exposed until the twentieth century, in the unfolding of Ezra Pound's great poetical project, the *Cantos*. I say (re)exposed because the transcendentalizing of poetry and imaginative agencies is by no means characteristic of the cultural periods of the west—even the Christian west—before the coming of Romanticism.

Had Byron begun writing *Don Juan* when he began *Childe Harold's Pilgrimage* in 1809, and had he gone on with it all his life and lived until (let us say) 1870 or so, he might have produced something comparable to the *Cantos*. I sketch this literary fantasy because it calls attention to certain important similarities, and even more important differences, between *Don Juan* and Pound's epic. In the first place, both works were produced in a seriatim process. *Don Juan* was published in six separate parts over a five-year period, and the separate volumes reflect that passage of time and its circumstantialities. The work replicates the serial publication of *Childe Harold's Pilgrimage*, which was issued in three separate volumes between 1812 and 1818 and was written over a ten-year period. Byron's work refuses to proceed upon "system"; the horizon of *Don Juan*'s expectations is close and short, and the poem cultivates, as we know, a series of immediacies. "Note or text,/ I never know the word which will come next" (*Don Juan* IX, stanza 41). With this deliberate cultivation of inconsequence (the word should be taken in several senses), Byron defies the highest poetical canons of his age, most especially those of Kant, Coleridge, and Hegel. As he got further along with *Don Juan* he began to imagine a conclusion—the death of Juan on the guillotine in the Reign of Terror—and he seems to have begun to prepare for that event.[21] But in the work we have, the seriatim process persists to the end.

Unlike Byron, Pound began the *Cantos* with definite plans and preconceptions, and he did not put into question the Romantic criterion of Total Form. On the contrary, in setting out to write a *Commedia* appropriate to his epoch, Pound's plan was fairly dominated by the idea of Total Form. The idea captured him because, even more than the writers and poets of 1780–1830, Pound confronted an epoch—particularly from 1914, the year before he began the *Cantos*—that surpassed even Byron's age in its cultural fragmentation and social barbarity. "These fragments you have shelved (shored)" (Canto VIII:1): that theme directs the *Cantos* from the first. But Pound's initial articulation works some telling puns on the words "shelved" and "shored": in addition to their obvious primary meanings, both words suggest "fragments" that have come or been washed ashore, like Odysseus at Phaiakia or his other stopping places.

Pound's method for negotiating that treacherous world was what he called the periplum, or what he understood as point-by-point navigation. That method of proceeding is the equivalent of Byron's seriatim maneuvers, only in Pound's case it is initiated in concert with a quest for Total Form (social as well as aesthetic, it should be understood). As it turned out, the production history of the *Cantos* became a kind of periplum in time. Ten separate "books" of the work were printed from 1925 to 1969, and individual Cantos or parts of Cantos—some later revised or rejected altogether—were published in various magazines and journals. The first pieces of the poem appear in print in 1915, and to this day—Pound died in 1972—further previously unpublished fragments continue to appear.[22]

It has been wittily (and justly) said that "The eleven Pisan Cantos were written at a time [1945] when the poem including history found itself included in history."[23] In truth, however, the *Cantos* was *always* "included in history," as the production history of the poem emphasizes. The Pisan Cantos are special only because they dramatize that inclusion beyond any possibility of mistake or unawareness. For more than fifty years—1915 to 1969—the *Cantos* moved through the twentieth century, appearing at intervals to reflect the European/American mind back to itself. The effort was to bring (or restore) coherence to that mind. In the end—in the great tragic texts of *Drafts and Fragments* of 1969, a malebolge year of this century's western and imperialist wars—Pound echoed Byron's "Stanzas to [Augusta]":[24]

> Tho' my errors and wrecks lie about me.
> And I am not a demigod,
> I cannot make it cohere.   (Canto CXVI)

"I lost my center / fighting the world," he remarks in the "Notes for CXVII et seq."; for in this quest after a "paradiso / terrestre," Pound discovers that what initially appeared as fragmentation and contradiction was precisely that: "The dreams clash / and are shattered."

The greatness of the *Cantos* is in large part a function of its chronology, and its involvement in the real history which is schematized in that chronology. The poem begins with the goal of Total Form as it had been framed and imperially imagined in the west between 1780 and 1915. It then tests that imagination as it plays itself out, more brutally than it ever did in the nineteenth century, from the First World War to Vietnam. The great *artistic* benefit to a work that has been produced over such a long period is that time and circumstances—if the poem is honest with itself—will play havoc with its most cherished illusions. In the *Cantos* we finally see, fully displayed, the brutal truth of the western dialectic as Benjamin had framed it: "There is no document of civilization which is not at the same time a document of barbarism."

Of course, when the academy reads such a poem it has ways of avoiding its imaginations. One way is to celebrate the *Cantos* for its "beauties," for its local achievements and its grand aspirations. These things are accepted. Reciprocally, the poem will have its horrors denounced, deplored, or set aside: its antisemitism and racism, for example, or its unrepentant adherence to fascist programs. If one takes this way with the poem, all these matters are accepted at face value, as if the beauties were evidently beauties and the horrors, horrors, as if they were all understandable to persons of sympathy and taste.

Another way is more critical. It will argue that somehow the beauties and the horrors are functions of each other, that the former have been gained—insofar as they *are* gained—only through a concert with the latter. In this view the poem is internally self-contradicted and is to be read as a moral exemplum or cautionary tale.[25]

But in truth neither this poem, nor any other poem or cultural product, ought to be read from such a safe—such an imperial— distance. Not in the west, at any rate. The distanced reader is what Baudelaire knew to be a hypocritical reader. Pound's exposure of European and American imperialism loses none of its *objective* truth because it comes from a source which is in so many ways repellent and blind. To Pound it was a complex centered in England, a complex from which Germany and Italy sought to free themselves. But increasingly we can see that that complex is a parodic god whose center is everywhere and whose circumference is nowhere. The European wars of this century were mugs' games—like Russia, France, and England struggling with the Ottoman Empire at the end of the eighteenth century for control of Greece and the eastern Mediterranean trade routes. If Pound excepted Mussolini's Italy from the twentieth century's western ways—if he excepted himself, and if he sought to represent his exceptional condition in the *Cantos*—we may think or say that he failed. But the more important thought is that the *Cantos* finally imagined the failure it did not know—imagined it throughout, as a total form, though that imaginative form only began to raise the failure into a form of consciousness in the last twenty-five years of the work's production.

During those years—1945–1969—the academy began its quest to "understand" the *Cantos,* and to this day it has produced those two ways of reading the poem I have mentioned. Yet they will not do. The poem does not permit a distanced reading, and in this respect it carries out a definitive break with the Romantic Ideology of immanent form (the Kantian "aesthetic"). Immanent, "readerly" criticism, the last serious bastion of this Kantian norm, reestablished aesthetic space in the reader after Modernism in art began the labor to disestablish it from the work.

The *Cantos* is important, therefore, because—as a poem evidently included in history—it has explained once again, more clearly than at any time since the eighteenth century, that all poems and cultural

products are included in history, *including* the producers and reproducers of such works, the poets and their readers and interpreters.
But the *Cantos* is even more significant for its revelation of the meaning of history. To the historicist imagination, history is the past, or
perhaps the past as seen in and through the present; and the historical
task is to attempt a reconstruction of that past, including, perhaps,
the present of that past. But the *Cantos* reminds us that history includes the future and that the historical task involves as well the
construction of what shall be possible. Delivered through the world
over such a long and momentous period of time, the *Cantos* managed
to gather into itself, and then to foreground, parts of its own futurity.
History in this poem thereby revealed itself as the fullness of time—
a fullness whose shape(s) and direction(s) will never be known, though
they shall always be anticipated.

Poetical work, Aristotle said, is more philosophical than history.
If this is so then it is also more "historical" than history, as Nietzsche
argued, because the "history" which poems touch and re-present en-
compasses a far greater scale of possible, and therefore real, human
times and events than the most careful and scholarly historical text.
Indeed, the greatest of such texts—Herodotus, the Bible, Thucydides—have set themselves apart by actively embracing different types
of imaginative procedures. Poetical works are historically overdetermined—littered with incommensurate materials that grow only more
multiple when they are delivered over to further readings and uses.
What they do not know—which is a great deal, the abyss of their
ignorance—they will have imagined. The *Oresteia* and the *Cantos*
are unusual only because they have so graphically displayed this fault
line—ultimately catastrophic—of their nonconsciousness; in this respect they epitomize the resources of all poetical discourse, whose
knowledge is heterological.

When we read we construct our histories, including our futures.
In our day, this peculiar western moment, poetry's special contribution to that process—poetry's special form of "reading"—comes as
a set of complicating and undermining procedures. Calling into question all that is privileged, understood, and given, including itself, this
poetry operates under the signs of Difference and, most especially, of
Change. And this poetry has thereby set us our models for reading
the works which descend to us from "tradition." What is astonishing
here is the way our literary inheritance seems to have anticipated these
contemporary uses—seems, as it were, to have intended them.

Conclusion: The Loss of Poetry

At no time does a fortune serve to *shelter its owner from
need*. On the contrary, it functionally remains—as does its
possessor—*at the mercy of a need for limitless loss*.

Georges Bataille, "The Notion of Expenditure"

IN THE BEGINNING of his prose *Vision of the Last Judgment* (1810),
Blake wrote that "Plato confutes himself" in saying, through Socrates,
that "Poets & Prophets do not Know or Understand what they write
or Utter." Blake meant that Plato had a knowledge and an understanding of the things he wrote and uttered. What distinguishes any
"inferior Kind" of art from any superior kind is the level of knowledge
or understanding possessed by the poet.[1]

To Blake, Plato's remark is a most "Pernicious Falsehood," an
"Error" (as he would also call it) consequent upon the special character—the minute particulars—of Plato's own knowledge, or truth.
The execution of Plato's art is a revelation of its peculiar forms of
error and of truth. Indeed, this execution—an event which takes place
repeatedly throughout the (now so-called) reception history of every
work of art—is the perpetual Last Judgment which poetry brings into
the world, most immediately in relation to itself.

Blake's *Vision* is an explanation of the meaning of his picture by
the same title. The picture represents his special understanding that
the known world is an artistic and visionary reality. A meta-commentary
on the practice of poetry in general, both Visions appear to tell the
whole truth. Blake's work is, however, subject to the errors of its
special truths just as much as Plato's work. Blake knows this—he
even admits as much in his prose text[2]—but of course his admission

does not redeem his visionary work from all its errors. On the contrary in fact. Blake, for example, would never see the "error" in his theory and representation of the emanations. Nor is this error a merely localized limitation of his work; it affects every aspect of his art and can be properly seen—as it has been through recent feminist imaginations—as a "Pernicious Falsehood." In the same way, Blake's Christianity—a similar ideological deformation—introduced into his work a network of other, equally pernicious falsehoods.

In "the Productions of Genius," then, there is a necessary co-presence of truth and error (one form of which we now call blindness and insight). To Blake this reciprocal structure was a consequence of the material and temporal conditions within which all art is produced and reproduced. These conditions presented a recurrent problem for Blake, who continually shifted between a celebration of material reality and a denigration of its illusory and impermanent forms. A famous passage at the conclusion of his prose *Vision* declares that "Mental Things are alone Real; what is Calld Corporeal Nobody Knows of its Dwelling Place <it> is in Fallacy . . . Where is the Existence Out of Mind or Thought?"[3] But of course one might answer that Corporeal Existence is the imagination of Genius—of Chaucer, Shakespeare, and Lucretius as much as of Epicurus and Newton. And of course Blake would agree, though he would want to add—this is the burden of much of his work—that such Genius is infected with "Bad Art," the errors of corporeal vision, the ratios of Aristotle. "Some People flatter themselves that there will be No Last Judgment & that Bad Art will be adopted & mixed with Good Art . . . I will not Flatter them Error is Created Truth is Eternal. Error, or Creation, will be Burned Up & then & not till then Truth or Eternity will appear. It is Burnt up the Moment Men cease to behold it. I assert for my Self that I do not behold the Outward Creation & that to me it is hindrance & not Action it is as the Dirt upon my feet No part of me."[4] But in reality what Blake here calls "Bad Art" is always and necessarily married to what he calls "Good Art." The Last Judgment which he declares the foundation of artistic practice is a reciprocal event involving both a disappearance and an appearance. Furthermore, if error is created, then how are we to judge the (mortal, artistic) creations of Blake himself—his works, which he himself called creations? His own *Vision of the Last Judgment*? In fact these works judge themselves and call out for further judgment; in fact they are creations brought forth in and through their own truths and errors.

Blake is a crucial figure in the history of western poetry because he was one of the first to undermine the canons of poetic tradition. In his work the criteria for judging good art and bad art are radically destabilized. It is not merely that he epitomizes the collapse of the authority of inherited wisdom and the emergence of the authority of the individual imagination. More critically, Blake's work proposes a dynamic of art which, by undermining its own pretensions to authority and truth, forces one to regard all aspects of the experience in terms of the laws of change and transformation. This takes place because Blake's work no longer leaves any room for the traditional distinction between the ideal and the real, or worlds of permanence and worlds of change. Blake *says* that all reality is mental, but his work *shows* that this "mentality" comprehends a body of highly materialized and particular work. These works are not static "things," they are dynamic events in the field of human experience—more deeds of language and art than representations of things (whether "ideal" or "real"). Blake's term for "outward Creation" *properly conceived* is "Action" because he understands creation as something which takes place or is carried out. And being an event, creation is in continual flux and transformation.

This departure represented by Blake's work is graphically expressed in his imagination of the figure of Los, the giant form of poetic vision and practice as it operates in the world of time and space. One might expect Los to embody a set of unequivocal values and nonproblematic deeds, but this is far from being the case. Los is repeatedly involved in mistakes, errors, blindnesses of many kinds. Furthermore, the work of Los is regularly figured in terms of furnaces because Blake insists that this work—the actual practice of the various arts of imagination—is fundamentally, *eternally* an act of destruction, decreation, removal. That work produces—more accurately, that work *is*—the various cities and buildings of Los and of his many artificers: in fact, the cities and buildings of Loss (for such is the meaning of Blake's wordplay), all of which are bound for what Blake called "Eternal Death" and the perpetual unbuilding that accompanies a transformational experience.

THE HISTORICAL IMPORTANCE of Blake's work must also be emphasized. Poetry throughout the past two hundred years has been produced under the sign of those profound contradictions epitomized in Blake's work. As a consequence, our poetry has forced us to read the entire literary archive in the same unstable framework, to think hitherto unimaginable thoughts: for example, that Satan is not merely the hero of *Paradise Lost* but the moral superior of that poem's god; or—in Byron's twisted tale—that the murderer Cain is the victim crucified on the cross, on the dialectic, of righteousness and its offspring, sin.

Byronic heroes and gothic villains now seem relatively commonplace, like Blake's and Shelley's Romantic reading of Milton's epic. They are the familiar faces of poetry's recent preoccupation with the unfamiliar. That preoccupation, however, has not grown less intense with the passing of Romanticism. On the contrary, in fact, for as our disciplines of positive knowledge and technical control have advanced, our poetry has represented that accumulating world as a field of increasingly acute emergencies. Information is amassed and scientific technique acquires greater precision, yet in our correspondent poetic representations we observe the scandal of the dark reciprocals: long shadows of the unconscious and the nonconscious, everything we do not wish to know and much that we are completely unaware of. While powerful societies and their spokesmen look to gather and preserve the best that has been known and thought in the world, poetry increasingly returns from those quests with ruined fortunes, troubled reflections, and threatening looks.

Hence it is that we read and study poetical works: to acquire that creativity which is a function of their critical resources. The texts multiply insufficiencies in their passage through history, where they are subjected to repeated attempts to bring what is dark in them into the light. But the more we know about them the more silent they become; and their silence grows from their speech, ever more articulated and detailed, ever more defined and extended. All discourse is part of that labyrinth, but poetical discourse epitomizes it because poetry imagines complete worlds rather than partial or abstract structures. Yet poetry only approaches its completion via what Georges Bataille has called "the principle of insufficiency" and "the principle of loss." The former is expressed in the following aphorism: "The sufficiency of each being is endlessly contested by that of every other"; and the latter by the observation that "loss must be as great as possible in order for [human activity] to take on its true meaning." In poems, insufficiency and loss are increased, paradoxically, by their accumulation of forms and details that appear substantial and significant. To the degree that poems are forms of representation, they constitute, Bataille says, "vain efforts . . . to create pathways permitting the endless reattainment of that which flees."[5]

Considered merely as representation, then, or as "virtual reality," poetry is a dead loss, and this is true, Bataille argues, even when poetry gives its allegiance to the heterological:

> Poetry at first glance seems to remain valuable as a method of mental projection (in that it appears to accede to an entirely heterogeneous world). But it is only too easy to see that it is hardly less debased than religion. It has almost always been at the mercy of the great historical systems of appropriation. And insofar as it can be developed autonomously, this autonomy leads it onto the path of a total poetic conception of the world, which ends at any one of a number of aesthetic homogeneities. The practical unreality of the heterogeneous elements it sets in motion is, in fact, an indispensable condition for the continuation of heterogeneity: starting from the moment when this unreality immediately constitutes itself as a superior reality, whose mission is to eliminate (or degrade) inferior vulgar reality, poetry is reduced to playing the role of the standard of things.[6]

But when poetry is understood (and practiced) as a social activity, as an agenting form, Bataille's critique of its "practical unreality" loses its force. As a particular play or structure of language, poems will at most be conceived, and deployed, as those Buildings of Loss we might well call "self-consuming artifacts." But read for what they are—instances of a kind of social practice carried out through determinate material forms and institutions, and at particular places and times by many different people—poems emerge as the Buildings of Los[s].

Blake was among the first to understand this contradictory form of imaginative work. His conception of the poetical, however, cannot mean for us what it meant for him. Because his ideas were developed in a Christian framework and along a Romantic salient, he saw in poetry and "the human imagination" the vehicle for a literal redemption of the world. On the contrary, what poetry after Blake essays is the *descent* of all the gods and their spilled religions—or rather, their fall from the coasts of light. What one may aspire to imagine, therefore, is a world without redeemers, a world where redemption is as much at a loss as are all other human things.

Poetry, that is to say, must not be imagined as occupying a world elsewhere. The impulse to move "anywhere out of the world," to enter a "poetic" space redeemed from time and the agencies of loss, is simply one of the Buildings of Los[s] erected in a certain, by now familiar, vacant lot. Poems, therefore, should not be conceived as representations; they are *acts* of representation. Their forms are no more permanent than the forms of the gods, and they are to be found, like all the gods, in those human worlds where they are made and unmade repeatedly.

In our day poems are typically placed in the hands of academicians, who characteristically work to preserve them, or themselves, from ruin. Consequently, when poems are delivered into others' hands, they generally appear under various idealized forms: forms of permanence, abstraction, or objectivity. This is the death of the poetical event, but it becomes as well a fruitless death only when we do not register that institutional death deconstructively, as the loss that it is. And beyond the critique of deconstruction stands the poetical event itself—Blake's moment of "Eternal Death"—when all that is unique and particular, all that is begotten, born and dies, dances its Lucretian transformations.

Poems are not mirrors and they are not lamps, they are social acts— readings and writings which promote, deploy, and finally celebrate those processes of loss which make up the very essence of human living. In this sense poetry is best understood within the nexus of its many interesting histories: political and social histories, of course, but also the histories of productive institutions, ecclesiastical histories, the histories of scholarship and education, even the histories of ideas. All of these histories, being multiple and transformational, are at a loss, so far as the forms of human activity are concerned, including poetical activity; and within each of these historical frames we may glimpse, if we try, an indeterminate flux of conflicted and competing possibilities.

More than other types of discourse, poetry works to preserve our experience of these many forms of loss. Moving into the field of the poem, we come to endure its losses as our own. Initially—such is our mistaken prejudice about them—those losses may be consigned to the past and located in limbos of regret and nostalgia. But in fact loss is a universal and amoral experience falling to the just and the unjust alike. Furthermore, losses are not the exclusive privilege of the past.

If we say "the present is fleeting," we know that our futures disappear just as surely and just as swiftly. Losses are measured out uniformly across the field of temporality.

Yet among all these ruinations our moral interests move carefully about, looking for some to preserve in our selective and tributary memories and overlooking, ignoring, or mistaking the import of the others. Because this pattern is what Wittgenstein would call a "form of life," it is as well a way of reading and writing. Poetry is itself produced in this mode—it has, we say, its ideologies—but only with a significant difference. If poetry commits itself to totalization, its own frames of time show that it can never achieve the commensurability it may imagine. If you produce an interpretation of a poetical text, a "translation" of it, the new form of the text will be able to judge the old only as it opens itself to judgment in its turn, and these judgments can come from any quarter or direction. What comes "later," for example, may be judged by what comes "earlier"; and since both must be, in any case, multiplied and unstable forms, poetry gets carried out in the form of losses and incommensurates.

This is the eventuality of poetry—not its structure, but its fate; and such an eventuality explains why Bataille associated the poetic event with revolution. For Bataille the experience of perfect loss is the experience of "time released from all bonds; it is pure change."[7] Such a conception projects loss as a *catastrophic* event, the image and splendor of a world where everything hovers equally on the brink of the fully possible and the utterly impossible—for good and ill alike.

This does not mean, however, that all of poetry's possibilities and impossibilities are available to anyone at any time. The larger field of history within which poetry operates sets limits to its practical operations. In the United States today, for example, most poetry is carried out not in a revolutionary but in an imperialist mode; and even the poetry committed to revolution—the "reading" of Frederic Jameson, the "writing" of Ron Silliman—is executed within the limits set for it by American imperialism, simply because the larger historical field (America) has an imperialist and not a revolutionary character. Fortunately, this "American history"is neither global nor commensurate with itself. On the one hand, it operates within the reciprocal framework of the "second world"—equally threatening, equally imperialist—and the alternative framework of the "third," where the forms of change and catastrophe remain, for good and ill alike, real possibilities. On the other hand, its hegemony cannot even master the field of its own immediate dominion (its traditions and its current practices). There is a Third World which poetry finds even within the borders of America itself. There one glimpses those Buildings of Los which empty the sky of the buildings of the empire state.

Notes

Index

Notes

Introduction

1. In his laudatory essay on the work of Michael Riffaterre, de Man makes an interesting observation which clearly applies as much to himself as it does to Riffaterre. De Man remarks that Riffaterre's determination to keep his analytic interests closely tied to "reading" produces a critical "orientation which complicates and enriches his theoretical position." He then goes on immediately to add the following: "It may well have been the feeling of liberation felt by any European-trained interpreter of literature transposed to America in the late forties and discovering that close reading could be the most challenging part of any commentary, more challenging than the historical and philological information from which it cannot be dissociated." See "Hypogram and Inscription," in *The Resistance to Theory,* with a foreword by Wlad Godzich (Minneapolis, 1986), 33.

2. *Allegories of Reading* (New Haven, 1979), hereafter abbreviated *AR.*

3. D. F. McKenzie, *Oral Culture, Literacy and Print in Early New Zealand: The Treaty of Waitangi* (Wellington, New Zealand, 1985), 19.

1. Plato and the Dialectic of Criticism

1. Frank Lentricchia, *After the New Criticism* (Chicago, 1980), 10.

2. Geoffrey Hartman, *Criticism in the Wilderness: The Study of Literature Today* (New Haven, 1980).

3. J. G. Eichhorn, *Einleitung ins Alte Testament* (2d ed., 1787), II: 345 (my translation).

4. J. G. Herder, Sämmtliche Werke, ed. B. Suphan (Berlin, 1877–1909), XII: 23 (my translation).

5. Michel Foucault, *Language, Counter-Memory, Practice: Selected Essays and Interviews*, ed. Donald F. Bouchard (Ithaca, N.Y.: 1977), 156.

6. Paul Ricoeur, "The Model of the Text: Meaningful Action Considered as a Text," *Social Research* 38 (1971), 529.

7. Ibid., 532.

8. Ibid., 548.

9. See especially the "Postscript" to Pierre Bourdieu, *Distinction: A Social Critique of the Judgement of Taste*, trans. Richard Nice (Cambridge, Mass., 1984), 485–500.

10. Friedrich Nietzsche, *The Birth of Tragedy and The Genealogy of Morals*, trans. Francis Golffing (New York, 1956), 296.

11. Ibid., 290.

12. John Searle, "The Logical Status of Fictional Discourse," in *Expression and Meaning: Studies in the Theory of Speech Acts* (Cambridge, 1979), 61.

13. Ibid., 68, italics added.

14. For Searle's views see ibid., 58–75, as well as *Speech Acts: An Essay in the Philosophy of Language* (Cambridge, 1969), esp. 22–24. Stanley Fish's critique (*Is There a Text in This Class?* [Cambridge, Mass., 1980], esp. 231–245) of Searle's essay on fictional discourse argues that "one cannot make a clean break between the literary and the nonliterary" (233); nevertheless he does not dissent from its basic view that "there is a kind of discourse that is characterized by the suspension of the rules to which speech acts are normally held accountable" (235). The Auden quotation is from "In Memory of W. B. Yeats."

15. Searle, "Logical Status of Fictional Discourse," 74–75.

16. Michel Foucault, "The Discourse on Language," in *The Archaeology of Knowledge*, trans. A. M. Sheridan-Smith (New York, 1972), 229.

17. Ibid.

18. Ibid., 218.

19. See E. D. Hirsch, "Past Intentions and Present Meanings," *Essays in Criticism* 33 (1983), 79–98.

20. Jürgen Habermas, *The Theory of Communicative Action*, vol. I: *Reason and the Rationalization of Society*, trans. Thomas McCarthy (Boston, 1984).

21. Iris Murdoch, *The Fire and the Sun: Why Plato Banished the Poets* (Oxford, 1977).

22. My texts for Plato are taken from *Plato: The Collected Works*, ed. Edith Hamilton and Huntington Cairns (Princeton, 1961).

23. See *The Republic of Plato*, ed. James Adam, 2d ed., with introduction by D. A. Rees (Cambridge, 1963), II:434n. Socrates is also poking fun at Homer. The "tale to Alcinous told" which he will *not* tell—the "Apologos Alkinou"— was proverbial for "a long and tedious story." Thus Socrates wittily suggests that his story of Er will be a poem that Homer himself might rather have written.

24. For an interesting discussion of myth in Plato—it runs parallel to my own in certain respects—see Julius A. Elias, *Plato's Defense of Poetry* (London, 1984), esp. pt. 2.

25. See especially Jacques Derrida, "Plato's Pharmacy," in *Disseminations* (Chicago, 1981), 63–171.

2. Blake and the Aesthetics of Deliberate Engagement

1. Howard N. Fox, Miranda McClintic, and Phyllis Rosenzweig, *Content: A Contemporary Focus 1974–1984* (Washington, D.C., 1984), 9.

2. Ibid., 18.

3. Ibid., 96.

4. Ibid., 98.

5. Ibid., 19.

6. Ibid., 89.

7. Ibid., 21.

8. Ibid., 20.

9. Ibid., 27.

10. Ibid.

11. Charles Bernstein, "The Objects of Meaning," in *The L=A=N=G=U=A=G=E Book*, ed. Bruce Andrews and Charles Bernstein (Carbondale, Ill., 1984), 60. For further discussion of the L=A=N=G=U=A=G=E writers see Chapter 10.

12. Bernstein, "Semblance," in *L=A=N=G=U=A=G=E Book*, 115.

13. See Frederic Jameson, "Postmodernism, or the Cultural Logic of Late Capitalism," *New Left Review* 146 (1984), 53–92; Jean-François Lyotard, *The Postmodern Condition: A Report on Knowledge*, trans. Geoff Bennington and Brian Massumi (Minneapolis, 1984); Terry Eagleton, "Capitalism, Modernism, and Postmodernism," *New Left Review* 152 (1985), 60–73; see as well the important "Modernity and Postmodernity" issue, *New German Critique* 33 (1984).

14. *Kant's Critique of Aesthetic Judgement*, trans. and with introduction and notes by James Creed Meredith (Oxford, 1911), 41–42.

15. Kant's "Four Moments" set out four determinations of the Beautiful, of which the first and the third, and the second and the fourth, are nearly related. Moments one and three—which treat art as to its "quality" and its "relation"— deal with the aesthetic experience as a disinterested and autonomous event: the "quality" of the aesthetic experience is a disinterested one, and it is related to itself and its own integral purposiveness rather than to anything beyond itself (that is, it operates a *form* of finality rather than an actual one). Moments two and four—which treat art in relation to its "quantity" and its "modality"— focus on the aesthetic experience less as a particular than as a general phenomenon. The "quantity" of the experience is universal, and its "modality" is socially necessary. Categories one and three authorize the theoretical and critical traditions which treat the experience of art, and of the individual poem, as integral and autonomous; categories two and four authorize those related traditions which deal with poetry as an avenue to the apprehension of total or Ideal Form and as an expression which transcends the particular limits of time, place, circumstances.

16. Kant's subjective and psychological approach to the problem of art

applies equally to the work of the artist and of the critic. This fact defines the nature of the break with the "objectivist" aesthetics of Wolff and Baumgarten, and it places Kant at the source of the dominant modern tradition of "expressivist" theory (the "lamp" of M. H. Abrams's *The Mirror and the Lamp* [Oxford, 1953]). For a good discussion of these matters see Robert L. Zimmerman, "Kant: The Aesthetic Judgment," in *Kant: A Collection of Critical Essays,* ed. Robert Paul Wolff (South Bend, Ind., 1968), esp. 386, 395.

17. The rhetorical tradition which underpins Dryden's poem is excellently handled in John Hollander, *The Untuning of the Sky* (Princeton, 1961), chap. 4.

18. *Kant's Critique,* 75.

19. Ibid., 77.

20. In the case of works dominated by a Kantian/Coleridgean idea of imagination, although that faculty's operations are judged "incomprehensible," the *idea* of a noncognitive imagination is itself cognitive; that idea is, needless to say, basic to Romantic and much postromantic aesthetics.

21. William Wordsworth, "Preface," in *Lyrical Ballads,* ed. R. L. Brett and A. R. Jones (London, 1965), 259.

22. "A Defence of Poetry," in *Shelley's Poetry and Prose,* ed. Donald H. Reiman and Sharon B. Powers (New York, 1977), 503; see also 480–482.

23. William Hazlitt, *The Spirit of the Age,* ed. E. D. Mackerness (London, 1969), 141.

24. Ibid., 265–266.

25. Ibid., 270; see also 266.

26. George Crabbe, *Tales, 1812, and Other Selected Poems,* ed. Howard Mills (Cambridge, 1967), 370.

27. See *The Complete Poetical Works of William Wordsworth,* ed. Andrew J. George (Boston, 1904), 118; he contrasts "the imaginative influences which I have endeavoured to throw over common life with Crabbe's matter of fact style."

28. These remarks on Byron relate to the Egeria passage in *Childe Harold's Pilgrimage,* canto IV, stanzas 115–126.

29. *Jerusalem,* 24:24. The text is from the facsimile in Minna Doskow, *William Blake's Jerusalem* (Rutherford, N.J., 1982).

30. My text here is taken from the facsimile edition of *The Marriage of Heaven and Hell,* ed. with notes and commentary by Geoffrey Keyes (Oxford, 1975). It is important to realize that the minimal requirement in "reading" Blake is to work from facsimile editions. However useful the typographical editions are for various purposes (my quotations here are typographical), they seriously distort one's ability to grasp what Blake's work involves.

31. *Milton,* plate 2. My text here is the facsimile *William Blake: Milton,* ed. K. P. Easson and R. R. Easson (New York, 1978).

32. It is important to realize that earlier formulations of the autonomy of art, for example, Sidney's, are grounded in one or another realm of cognitivity. In Sidney the ground is Christian ideology. See Chapter 4.

33. As Barton Levi St. Armand has done in his exemplary *Emily Dickinson and Her Culture: The Soul's Society* (Cambridge, 1984).

3. The Dawn of the Incommensurate

1. *The Cantos of Ezra Pound* (New York, 1970), 5.

2. See *Literary Essays of Ezra Pound,* ed. T. S. Eliot (New York, 1954), 259, where Pound says he found Divus's translation in Paris "in 1906, 1908, or 1910."

3. D. S. Cairne-Ross, "Pound in the Classroom," *Boston University Journal* 21 (Winter 1973), 27.

4. "The Ruined Cottage," ll. 67–68.

5. See *Genesis,* trans. and ed. E. A. Speiser (Garden City, N.Y., 1964), 10–11.

6. See Nahum A. Sarna, *Understanding Genesis: The Heritage of Biblical Israel* (New York, 1970), 11–16.

7. See E. A. Speiser, "The Wife-Sister Motif in the Patriarchal Narrative," in *Biblical and Other Studies* (Cambridge, Mass., 1963), 15–28.

8. *Genesis,* 92.

9. Ibid., 93.

10. For discussion of these matters see Chapter 8.

11. Hans Frei, *The Eclipse of Biblical Narrative* (New Haven, 1974), is a thoughtful study of these matters.

12. See Walter Benjamin, *One-Way Street and Other Writings,* trans. Edmund Jephcott and Kingsley Shorter (London, 1979).

13. See Marshall Sahlins, *Islands of History* (Chicago, 1985), for a provocative reading of Cook's voyage to the Hawaiian Islands.

14. Benjamin, *One-Way Street,* 67.

15. Stephen Usher, *The Historians of Greece and Rome* (New York, 1970), 5.

16. *Herodotus: The Histories,* trans. Aubrey de Selincourt, with introduction and notes by A. R. Burn (Harmondsworth, 1972), 494. All quotations are from this translation and are cited by book and section number in the text.

17. Curiously, what comes closest to our understanding is the interpretation which Herodotus gives. The hermeneusis is basically allegorical, as we may see when we reflect on the iconic values to be associated with horse (war) and hare (timidity).

18. Samuel T. Coleridge, *Biographia Literaria,* ed. James Engell and W. Jackson Bate (Princeton, 1983), I: 279.

4. Poetic Ideology and Nonnormative Truth

1. *Sir Philip Sidney: An Apology for Poetry, or The Defense of Poesy,* ed. Geoffrey Shepherd (London, 1965), 129.

2. My quotations for the discussion of Matthew are taken from the King James version of the Bible. I have relied as well for various materials on the excellent scholarly text *Matthew,* trans. and ed. W. F. Albright and C. S. Mann (New York, 1971).

3. See *The Greek New Testament,* ed. from Ancient Authorities with Their

Various Readings in Full . . . by Samuel P. Tregelles (London, 1857–1879). The other passages referring to "their synagogues" include Matthew 4:23, 9:35, 12:9, 13:54.

4. My text here is *The Poems of Matthew Arnold*, ed. Kenneth Allott (London, 1965).

5. Arnold's two earlier books of poetry, aside from the prize poems *Alaric at Rome* (1840) and *Cromwell* (1843), were *The Strayed Reveller, and Other Poems* (1849) and *Empedocles on Etna, and Other Poems* (1852). See also T. B. Smart, *The Bibliography of Matthew Arnold* (London, 1892).

6. See, for example, the reviews by J. A. Froude (*Westminster Review*) and Coventry Patmore (*North British Review*), reprinted in *Matthew Arnold: The Poetry: The Critical Heritage*, ed. Carl Dawson (London, 1973), 85–95 and 114–124.

7. See Park Honan, *Matthew Arnold: A Life* (New York, 1981), 168.

8. See Smart, *Bibliography*, 3, and Dawson, *Matthew Arnold*, 6–10.

9. All the reviewers of the two early volumes call attention to their "scholarly" character, and several remark specifically on the small and "refined" audience which the poems appeal to. See Dawson, *Matthew Arnold, passim*.

10. See *Letters of Matthew Arnold 1848–1888*, collected and arranged by George W. E. Russell (London, 1895), 1: 34–35.

11. *Poems of Matthew Arnold*, 599.

12. Ibid., 595.

13. Ibid., 608.

14. Ibid., 595.

15. *Writers and Their Background: Matthew Arnold*, ed. Kenneth Allott (Athens, Ohio, 1976), 109.

16. Warren Anderson, *Matthew Arnold and the Classical Tradition* (Ann Arbor, 1965), 52.

17. Dawson, *Matthew Arnold*, 98.

18. Kenneth Allott's edition calls attention to the classical and Milton allusions, and notes as well many echoes of various other texts. See also Anderson, *Matthew Arnold and the Classical Tradition*, especially 53 and 238, for other classical allusions. Allott does not observe the recollection of Keats at lines 860–864 (compare the presentation of Saturn and Thea in *Hyperion* I: 72–92); but Leon Gottfried does; see *Matthew Arnold and the Romantics* (London, 1963), 117–118.

19. *Letters*, 1: 32.

20. See *The Letters of Matthew Arnold to Arthur Hugh Clough*, ed. H. F. Lowry (London, 1932), 145–146, and *Poems of Matthew Arnold*, 603.

21. See *Letters . . . to . . . Clough*, 145–146.

22. *Poems of Matthew Arnold*, 599.

5. Beginning Again

1. See Jürgen Habermas, *Legitimation Crisis*, trans. Thomas McCarthy (Boston, 1975); and Jean-François Lyotard, *The Postmodern Condition: Report on Knowledge*, trans. Geoff Bennington and Brian Massumi (Minneapolis, 1984).

McCarthy's introduction to *Legitimation Crisis* is a useful essay on the subject, as is his "Rationality and Relativism: Habermas' 'Overcoming' of Hermeneutics," in *Habermas: Critical Debates*, ed. John B. Thompson and David Held (Cambridge, 1982), 57–78; in the same volume see also Held's essay "Crisis Tendencies, Legitimation, and the State," 181–95.

2. "Personism: A Manifesto," in *The Selected Poems of Frank O'Hara*, ed. Donald Allen (New York, 1974), xiii.

3. The central problem facing criticism today, in my view, is to legitimate the study of the past and its products on their own terms, as well as within the general problematic raised by Marxist theory on the one hand and by the deconstructive critique on the other. This entails a critical account, and appropriation, of four hermeneutical traditions which normally stand in complex antithetical relations to each other: formalism, historicism, Marxism, and deconstruction.

4. For the collapse of "the authority of the exemplar," see especially Wayne C. Booth, " 'Preserving the Exemplar': or, How Not to Dig Our Own Graves," *Critical Inquiry* 3 (1977), 407–424. Abrams's article in the same issue (425–438) is also pertinent; and Graff's work in this area is well known, from *Literature against Itself* (Chicago, 1979) onward.

5. Geoffrey Hartman, "Literary Criticism and Its Discontents," *Critical Inquiry* 3 (1976), 216; see also Hartman, *The Fate of Reading and Other Essays* (Chicago, 1975), 3–19.

6. E. D. Hirsch, Jr., "Meaning and Significance Reinterpreted," *Critical Inquiry* 11 (1984), 202–225.

7. Paul de Man, *Blindness and Insight: Essays in Rhetoric and Contemporary Criticism*, 2d ed., rev., introduction by Wlad Godzich (Minneapolis, 1983); see, for example, 9–10, and chap. 7. Good discussions of de Man's work can be found in Frank Lentricchia's *After the New Criticism* (Chicago, 1980), chap. 8. See also *The Yale Critics: Deconstruction in America*, ed. Jonathan Arac, Wlad Godzich, and Wallace Martin (Minneapolis, 1983), esp. 23–24 and the essay by Stanley Corngold, "Error in Paul de Man," 90–108.

8. See especially Part II of *Is There a Text in This Class?: The Authority of Interpretive Communities* (Cambridge, Mass., 1980). There are good discussions of Fish's work in Jonathan Culler, *On Deconstruction: Theory and Criticism after Structuralism* (Ithaca, N.Y., 1982); William E. Cain, *The Crisis in Criticism: Theory, Literature, and Reform in English Studies* (Baltimore, 1984); and Jane Tompkins, ed., *Reader Response Criticism: From Formalism to Poststructuralism* (Baltimore, 1981); see also Walter A. Davis, "The Fisher King: *Wille zur Macht* in Baltimore," *Critical Inquiry* 10 (1984), 668–694, and Gerald Graff, "Interpretation on Tlön: A Response to Stanley Fish," *New Literary History* 17 (1985), 109–117.

9. De Man, *Blindness and Insight*, 50.

10. See "Criticism and Crisis," ibid., 3–19.

11. De Man's classic presentation of this position is "The Rhetoric of Blindness: Jacques Derrida's Reading of Rousseau," ibid., 102–41.

12. Corngold, "Error in Paul de Man," in *Yale Critics*. The essay first appeared in *Critical Inquiry* 8 (1983), 489–507, where de Man wrote a rejoinder ("A Letter from Paul de Man," 509–513). De Man's response maintained his

original position, that literary texts—*qua* literary—are open only to error, not to mistake. If they are "mistaken," or if critics make mistakes about them (as de Man argues that Corngold has been "mistaken" about de Man), these are events which "transform . . . the mistaking of error (for mistake) into the error of mistaking" (511).

13. Corngold, "Error in Paul de Man," 92.

14. Ibid.

15. De Man, *Blindness and Insight*, 50.

16. Ibid., 17.

17. Corngold, "Error in Paul de Man," 107.

18. I have been alluding to a pair of essays by de Man: "Phenomenality and Materiality in Kant," in *Hermeneutics: Questions and Prospects*, ed. Gary Shapiro and Alan Sica (Amherst, Mass., 1984), 121–144, and "Sign and Symbol in Hegel's *Aesthetics*," *Critical Inquiry* 8 (1982), 761–775. Several late papers and lectures which deal with Kant, Schiller, and Hegel have not yet been published, and I have not seen them.

19. De Man, *Blindness and Insight*, 228.

20. One of de Man's most revealing essays is that act of *hommage à* Riffaterre, "Hypogram and Inscription," reprinted in his *The Resistance to Theory*, foreword by Wlad Godzich (Minneapolis, 1986), 27–53. De Man's admiration for Riffaterre ("a technician addressing other technicians," 28) reflects many of his own basic commitments. The "Return to Philology" which de Man latterly called for (21–26) did not involve a return to history. On the contrary, it was a call for a rededication to a language-centered program of literary studies.

21. *Blindness and Insight*, 18.

22. Ibid.

23. Corngold, "Error in Paul de Man," 106.

24. Ibid.

25. Ibid.

26. De Man, *Blindness and Insight*, 19.

27. Fish, *Is There a Text in This Class?*, 321.

28. Ibid., 326.

29. Ibid., 336.

30. See Stanley Fish, "Consequences," *Critical Inquiry* 11 (1985), 433–458.

31. Ibid., 451.

32. De Man, *Blindness and Insight*, 288.

33. See *Paul Ricoeur: Hermeneutics and the Human Sciences*, ed. and trans. John B. Thompson (Cambridge, 1981), especially "Hermeneutics and the Critique of Ideology" (63–100); see also Thompson's *Critical Hermeneutics: A Study in the Thought of Paul Ricoeur and Jürgen Habermas* (Cambridge, 1981) and *Studies in the Theory of Ideology* (Berkeley, 1984), esp. "Action, Ideology, and Text" (173–204).

34. See "Hermeneutics and the Critique of Ideology" in *Paul Ricoeur*. Ricoeur gives a sufficient history of the debate between Gadamer and Habermas at 299.

35. Habermas, *Legitimation Crisis*, 98.

36. See especially Jean Baudrillard, *The Mirror of Production,* trans. and with introduction by Mark Poster (St. Louis, 1975) and *For a Critique of the Political Economy of the Sign,* trans. and with introduction by Charles Levin (St. Louis, 1981). For a thoughtful set of reflections on Baudrillard's work, see Arthur Kroker, "The Disembodied Eye: Ideology and Power in the Age of Nihilism," *Canadian Journal of Political and Social Theory* 7 (1983), 194–234; see as well Mark Poster, "Technology and Culture in Habermas and Baudrillard," *Contemporary Literature* 22 (1981), 456–476.

37. See M. M. Bakhtin, *The Dialogic Imagination,* ed. Michael Holquist, trans. Caryl Emerson and Michael Holquist (Austin, Tex., 1981); see also Chapter 11 for further discussion.

38. For example, we see that to the structural or deconstructive mind, historicism appears imprisoned in its empirical commitments, on the one hand, and in the illusion of recoverable past, on the other. To the historicist, however, the rational and theoretical modes of structuralism and deconstruction can seem airless and abstract. Other, correspondent conflicts develop between deconstruction and various kinds of formalism, as we all know; and all three propose, as well, their own *positive* virtues as interpretive strategies.

39. See Jean-Paul Sartre, *Search for a Method,* trans. Hazel Barnes (New York, 1968), esp. chap. 1; his views are elaborated in *Critique of Dialectical Reason,* trans. Alan Sheridan-Smith, ed. Jonathan Rée (London, 1976).

40. John B. Thompson, *Studies in the Theory of Ideology* (Berkeley, 1984), 4.

41. Marshall Sahlins, *Islands of History* (Chicago, 1985).

42. The work of Edward Said is obviously relevant here, perhaps especially his work *Orientalism* (New York, 1978). Besides that well-known book, see his recent "Orientalism Reconsidered," *Cultural Critique* 1 (1985), 89–107.

6. The Scandal of Referentiality

1. See Thomas E. Lewis's discussion of Umberto Eco, *A Theory of Semiotics* (Bloomington, Ind., 1976), in "Notes Toward a Theory of the Referent," *PMLA* 94 (May 1979), 460.

2. The antihistorical line of the New Criticism and, generally speaking, of its structuralist aftermath is well known. The same limitation applies to the principal work of the deconstructionists, at least in America: see *The Yale Critics: Deconstruction in America,* ed. Jonathan Arac, Wlad Godzich, and Wallace Martin (Minneapolis, 1983), esp. the summarizing "Afterword" by Arac. See also the similar critical exposition in Suresh Raval, *Metacriticism* (Athens, Ga., 1981), 208–238, esp. 220.

3. Jacques Derrida, "Structure, Sign and Play in the Discourse of the Human Sciences," in *The Language of Criticism and the Sciences of Man,* ed. Richard Macksey and Eugenio Donato (Baltimore, 1970), 264.

4. Samuel Taylor Coleridge, *Biographia Literaria,* ed. James Engell and W. Jackson Bate (Princeton, 1983), II:72–73 and n.

5. C. M. Wallace, *The Design of Biographia Literaria* (London, 1983), 113.

6. Coleridge, *Biographia Literaria*, II: 45–46.

7. See C. S. Lewis and E. M. W. Tillyard, *The Personal Heresy in Criticism* (Oxford, 1934), esp. essay 1, and Cleanth Brooks, *The Well Wrought Urn* (New York, 1947), app. 1.

8. Brooks, *Well Wrought Urn*, 227.

9. J. Hillis Miller, "Stevens' Rock and Criticism as Cure," *Georgia Review* 30 (1976), 29.

10. Ibid., 28–29.

11. Daniel Aaron, "The Treachery of Recollection," in *Essays in History and Literature*, ed. Robert H. Bremner (Athens, Ohio, 1976), 9.

12. Giambattista Vico, quoted by Marx in *Capital* (New York, 1967), I: 372.

13. Quoted by Wlad Godzich in Arac et al., *Yale Critics*, 39.

14. J. Hillis Miller, "The Critic as Host," *Critical Inquiry* 3 (1977), 443, 447.

15. I quote from the later, translated text published in Milman Parry, *The Making of Homeric Verse: The Collected Papers of Milman Parry*, ed. Adam Parry (Oxford, 1971), 2.

16. Ibid., 3, 2.

17. John M. Ellis, *The Theory of Literary Criticism: A Logical Analysis* (Berkeley, 1974), 136.

18. Ibid., 137, 154.

19. Miller, "Critic as Host," 458.

20. Ibid., 447.

21. Parry, *Making of Homeric Verse*, 411.

22. Ibid., 447. We are aware, of course, particularly from the work of Hayden White, that the construction of a "picture" by historians is a narrativizing act which embeds an interpretive structure. But the "great detail" which underlies this narrativizing whole always exercises a countermovement of more or less extreme resistance. The best historians and historical critics insist upon the significance of these details and matters of fact. See the discussion of incommensurate detail below, as well as in Chapter 3.

23. Ibid.

24. Ibid., 410, 413.

25. Ibid., 413.

26. Ibid.

27. The most complete analysis of the structures of human interests operating in culture and its products is set forth in Jürgen Habermas, *Knowledge and Human Interests,* trans. Jeremy J. Shapiro (Boston, 1971); see esp. chaps. 3 and 8 and app.

28. Throughout this chapter the distinction between poetical "works" and poetical "texts" is being preserved. The former refers to cultural products conceived as the issue of a large network of persons and institutions which operate over time, in numbers of different places and periods. "Texts" are those cultural products when they are viewed more restrictively, as language structures constituted in specific ways over time by a similar network of persons and institutions. Barthes's critique of the concept of the poetical "work" was a salutary move

against the naive idea of poems as stable and defined objects. His related effort to install the concept of "text" in literary discourse has much less to recommend it, since this concept—while it has promoted certain forms of dialectical thinking in criticism—has also broadened the gap between the empirical and the reflective dimensions of literary studies. See Roland Barthes, "From Work to Text," reprinted in *Textual Strategies: Perspectives in Post-Structuralist Criticism,* ed. Josué Harari (Ithaca, N.Y., 1979), 73–81.

29. *Sir Philip Sidney: An Apology for Poetry or The Defence of Poesy,* ed. Geoffrey Shepherd (London, 1965), 102.

30. Coleridge, *Biographia Literaria,* II: 72–73 and n.

31. Herbert A. Simon, *The Sciences of the Artificial* (Cambridge, Mass., 1969).

32. I take the concept of "subversive mimesis" from Michael Kahn, "Subversive Mimesis: Theodor W. Adorno and the Modern Impasse of Critique," in *Mimesis in Contemporary Theory,* I: *The Literary and Philosophical Debate,* ed. Mihai Spariosu (Philadelphia, 1984), 27–64.

33. Theodor Adorno, *Aesthetische Theorie,* in *Gesammelte Schriften,* 7 (Frankfurt, 1970), 264.

34. Ibid.

35. Adorno, *Noten zur Literatur,* in *Gesammelte Schriften,* 11: 429.

7. Some Forms of Critical Discourse

1. Michel de Certeau, *Heterologies: Discourse on the Other,* trans. Brian Massumi, foreword by Wlad Godzich (Minneapolis, 1986), 203. For some further discussion of narrativities and their antithetical forms, see Chapter 10.

2. Hayden White, "The Value of Narrativity in the Representation of Reality," *Critical Inquiry* 7 (Autumn 1980), 5–27. This entire issue of *Critical Inquiry* is devoted to explorations of "Narrative."

3. Ibid., 9.

4. For an excellent discussion of the antiquarian tradition, see Arnaldo Momigliano, "Ancient History and the Antiquarian," *Studies in Historiography* (New York, 1966), 1–39.

5. Chauncey Saunders, *An Introduction to Research in English Literary History* (New York, 1957), 228–229.

6. See Cleanth Brooks, "Keats's Sylvan Historian: History without Footnotes," in *The Well Wrought Urn: Studies in the Structure of Poetry* (New York, 1947), 151–166.

7. Thomas James Wise, *A Bibliography of the Writings in Verse and Prose of George Gordon Noel, Baron Byron, with Letters Illustrating His Life and Work, and Particularly His Attitude toward Keats,* 2 vols. (1933; reprint, London, 1963), 2:3–4.

8. Erich Auerbach, *Mimesis: The Representation of Reality in Western Literature,* trans. Willard R. Trask (New York, 1957), 10–11; J. Hillis Miller, introduction to Charles Dickens, *Bleak House,* ed. Norman Page (Harmondsworth, 1971), 34.

9. Stanley Fish, *Is There a Text in this Class? The Authority of Interpretive Communities* (Cambridge, Mass., 1980), 164.

10. The concept of adduction is treated by David Hackett Fischer in his *Historians' Fallacies: Toward a Logic of Historical Thought* (New York, 1970).

11. Harold Bloom, *The Anxiety of Influence: A Theory of Poetry* (New York, 1973), 5.

12. Ibid., 11.

13. Stanley Cavell, *The Claim of Reason: Wittgenstein, Skepticism, Morality, and Tragedy* (New York, 1979), viii.

14. See Michel Eyquem de Montaigne, *The Complete Essays of Montaigne,* trans. Donald M. Frame (Stanford, 1958), 19–20; page references to this work are given in parentheses in the text.

15. Geoffrey H. Hartman, "The Interpreter: A Self-Analysis," in *"The Fate of Reading" and Other Essays* (Chicago, 1976), 16.

16. See the similar critique of Hartman in Jonathan Arac's "Afterword" in *The Yale Critics: Deconstruction in America,* ed. Arac, Wlad Godzich, and Wallace Martin (Minneapolis, 1983), esp. 193: "I find a monumentalizing that deadens Hartman's historical prose. He writes that 'the political and economic unrest' of the 1930s 'made it important to protect art from imperious demands of an ideological nature, emanating from politics' . . . Perhaps historical sentences need not have human agents, but to avoid the monumental they must at least have interested parties. To whom was it important?"

8. The Idea of an Indeterminate Text

1. The information on the variances between and within the different copies of these Blake books, as well as the others discussed in this essay, are supplied in G. E. Bentley, Jr., *Blake Books* (Oxford, 1977), and his edition of *William Blake's Writings* (Oxford, 1978). I have, however, in the case of *The [First] Book of Urizen,* checked Bentley's descriptions against the facsimile copies of that work available in the Huntington Library.

2. Bentley, *William Blake's Writings,* I: 714.

3. Ibid., II: 1677.

4. Critics often assume, or believe, that Blake's Bible of Hell was also to include *Europe, America, The Song of Los,* and *The Visions of the Daughters of Albion.* I think, however, on the formatting evidence, that J. Middleton Murry was correct when he early included only the three printed in double columns: *William Blake* (London, 1933), 138.

5. Northrop Frye, *Fearful Symmetry: A Study of William Blake* (Princeton, 1947), 254.

6. Leslie Tannenbaum, *Biblical Tradition in Blake's Early Prophecies: The Great Code of Art* (Princeton, 1982), 203.

7. Ibid., 207.

8. I draw upon two works for the details of Geddes's life: Reginald Cuthbert Fuller, *Dr. Alexander Geddes: A Forerunner of Biblical Criticism,* 2 vols. (Ph.D. thesis, Cambridge University, 1968), and J. M. Good, *Memoirs of the*

Life and Writings of the Reverend Alexander Geddes LL.D. (London, 1803).

9. "The fact that over a third of the plates [in *Urizen*] are movable full page designs without a text, and that their order is different in each of the seven known copies of *Urizen*, suggests that this atemporal, antisequential quality is a deliberate formal device": W. J. T. Mitchell, *Blake's Composite Art: A Study of the Illuminated Poetry* (Princeton, 1978), 137.

10. Bentley, *William Blake's Writings*, I: 715.

11. Ibid.

12. Ibid.

13. Ibid., I: 716–717.

14. *The Poetry and Prose of William Blake*, ed. David V. Erdman (New York, 1965), 725.

15. The erasures are in certain proofs and copies A and G: see Bentley, *William Blake's Writings*, I: 239–240n.

16. *Poetry and Prose*, 676.

17. Ibid., 714.

18. Good, *Memoirs of the Life*, 192–194, gives a schedule of Geddes's reviews in the *Analytical*; they began in 1788 and ended in 1793.

19. Geddes, *Prospectus of a New Translation of the Holy Bible* (1786), 19.

20. See Fuller, *Dr. Alexander Geddes*, 187–192, for a discussion of the early responses to Geddes's work.

21. Albert J. Kuhn, "English Deism and the Development of Romantic Syncretism," *PMLA* 71 (1956), 1094–1095.

22. Blake's ideas on this matter may have shifted after 1800. His negative attitude toward pagan mythographic materials and his apparent privileging of the Christian corpus are not characteristic of the 1790s.

23. In a letter to me, Robert Essick noted several other parallel texts for the *Marriage*, plate 11. The most interesting of these is a passage from William Stukeley, *Stonehenge* (London, 1740), 59.

24. *Analytical Review* 18 (April 1794), 401.

25. Frye, *Fearful Symmetry*, chap. 1, and Peter Fisher, *The Valley of Vision: Blake as Poet and Revolutionary* (Toronto, 1961), chap. 4, present what has since become the dominant view—that Blake's work is a "visionary" response to the Enlightenment. But Blake's stance toward the eighteenth century was hostile to Reason as the norm of the human; he was not hostile to the Enlightenment's critical and emancipatory programs.

26. *Poetry and Prose*, 2–3.

27. Ruthven Todd, *Tracks in the Snow* (London, 1946), 41; see also Kathleen Raine, *Blake and Tradition*, 2 vols. (Princeton, 1968).

28. *Poetry and Prose*, 601.

29. Ibid., 603.

30. Ibid.

31. Ibid., 604.

32. Ibid., 605.

33. Ibid.

34. Ibid., 544.

35. *Dr. Geddes' Address to the Public on the publication of the First Volume of his Translation of the Bible* (London, 1793), 2.

36. Blake and Geddes are not deploying an allegorical structure here but an antiallegorical one. The cleansing of the surface removes the overlay of priestly meanings ("forms of worship") in order to reveal the clear text ("poetic tales"). Like Geddes's, Blake's is essentially a bibliographical rather than an allegorical operation. Blake's hostility to allegory is, of course, well known: see in particular his *Vision of the Last Judgment*.

37. *Dr. Geddes' Address*, 1.

38. F. B. Curtis, "The Geddes Bible and the Tent of the Eternals in *The Book of Urizen*," *Blake Newsletter* 6 (1973), 93–94.

39. Geddes, *Prospectus of a New Translation*, iii.

40. Ibid., iv.

41. Ibid.

42. Ibid., xi.

43. Ibid., xii.

44. *The Chief Works of Benedict de Spinoza*, ed. R. H. M. Elwes (New York, 1955), I: 135.

45. Ibid., I: 100.

46. Ibid.

47. Geddes, *Prospectus of a New Translation*, xx.

48. Ibid., xix.

49. See Johann Severin Vater, *Commentar über den Pentateuch . . .* , 3 Theile (Halle, 1802–1805).

50. Robert Essick, "Variation, Accident, and Intention in William Blake's *The Book of Urizen*," *Studies in Bibliography* 39 (1986), 230–235.

51. W. H. Stevenson, in *The Poems of William Blake* (London, 1971), 284, notes that Los and Urizen "are not consistent" with each other: "In *Urizen* [lines 196ff.] Los has already been working at his anvil for some time, and has created the spine which he here [*Los* line 133] discovers." For other parallels compare *Urizen* chaps. 2–3 and *Los* chap 1; *Ahania* plate 4: 41–42 and *Urizen* plate 28: 9–10; and compare *Los* chaps. 3–4 with *Urizen* chaps. 8–9.

9. Ulysses as a Postmodern Work

1. See the discussions of Lachmann's *Zwanzig alte Lieder von der Nibelungen* (1840) in Peter F. Ganz, "Lachmann as an Editor of Middle High German Texts," in *Probleme Mittelalterlicher Überlieferung und Textkritik*, ed. Peter F. Ganz and Werner Schröder (Berlin, 1968), 12–30, and in Lee Patterson, "The Logic of Textual Criticism and the Way of Genius . . . ," in *Textual Criticism and Literary Interpretation*, ed. Jerome J. McGann (Chicago, 1985), esp. 82–84.

2. Joseph Bédier, "La tradition manuscrite du *Lai de L'Ombre*," *Romania* 54 (1928), 161–196, 321–356.

3. W. W. Greg, "The Rationale of Copy-Text," *Studies in Bibliography* (1950–51), 19–36. Greg's is a culminant statement for the movement known as

the "New Bibliography"; an account of the movement may be found in F. P. Wilson, "Shakespeare and the 'New Bibliography,' " *The Bibliographical Society 1892–1942: Studies in Retrospect,* ed. F. C. Francis (London, 1945), 76–135.

4. *Ulysses: A Critical and Synoptic Edition,* Hans Walter Gabler with Wolfhard Steppe and Claus Melchior (New York, 1984), 3 vols. Further references to pages of this work are given in parentheses in the text.

5. See *Piers Plowman: The B Version,* ed. George Kane and E. Talbot Donaldson (London, 1975), and Patterson's incisive discussion of its significance in "The Logic of Textual Criticism." The single best introduction to the revolution in Shakespearean textual studies is probably the following collection of essays: Gary Taylor and Michael Warren, eds., *The Division of the Kingdoms: Shakespeare's Two Versions of King Lear* (Oxford, 1983).

6. *Ulysses: A Facsimile of the Manuscript,* with a critical introduction by Harry Levin and bibliographical preface by Clive Driver (New York, 1975), 3 vols.; *The James Joyce Archive,* ed. Michael Groden et al. (New York, 1977–1979), 63 vols.

7. An important critique of some of the technical aspects of the edition was recently presented in a paper by John Kidd, "Errors of Execution in the 1984 *Ulysses,*" at the meetings of the Society for Textual Scholarship (April 1985) in New York City. Scholars have yet to assess fully the lines of criticism which Kidd's paper has opened up.

8. In a letter to me Gabler writes that he would prefer to call these base texts or copytexts "the 'assembly texts' for the continuous manuscript text." For Gabler the latter is his edition's "copytext." My argument here is simply that in calling the continuous manuscript text his "copytext," Gabler has altered the traditional meaning of the term. For an excellent discussion of the "copytext" issues in relation to Gabler's edition, see Anthony Hammond's review in *The Library,* 6th ser., 8 (December 1986): 382–390, esp. 386–387.

9. *TLS* (13 July 1984), 771. Kenner's misunderstanding, in this instance, seems to be widespread among Joyce scholars. See, for example, Michael Groden, "Editing Joyce's 'Ulysses': An International Effort," *Scholarly Publishing* (October 1980), esp. 38–39. Unlike Gabler, Groden does not grasp what is involved in the choice and deployment of copytext by editors.

10. In his important article "The Synchrony and Diachrony of Texts: Practice and Theory of the Critical Edition of James Joyce's *Ulysses,*" *Text* 1 (1984), 305–326, Gabler himself misleadingly remarks that "the text of the first edition" is "teeming with transmissional errors—2000? 4000? 6000? 8000? we shall know when the [Gabler] edition is completed" (318).

11. This distinction between the writer and the author is a specifically postmodern one. For a convenient discussion of the context and meaning of the distinction see Roland Barthes's essay "From Work to Text," Michel Foucault's "What is an Author?" and Edward Said's "The Text, the World, and the Critic," all collected in *Textual Strategies: Perspectives in Post-Structuralist Criticism,* ed. and with introduction by Josué Harari (Ithaca, N.Y., 1979).

12. See Gabler's admirable discussion of the theoretical significance of his edition in "Synchrony and Diachrony of Texts," n. 7. One particularly notes the summary statement of his "theoretical premise": "that the work of literature

possesses in its material medium itself, in its text or texts, a diachronic as well as a synchronic dimension . . . The synchronous and diachronous structures combine to form the literary work in the totality of its real presence in the documents of its conception, transmission and publication" (325).

13. Indeed, this "continuous productive text" (if I may so call it) seems to me the one which Gabler's own theory ought to have led him to reconstruct. See again "Synchrony and Diachrony of Texts," esp. the conclusion, where he says that "the basic assumption" of his edition is that the object of "critical analysis and study" is "not the final product of the writer's art alone, but . . . the totality of the Work in Progress" (325).

14. For a discussion of the significance of the pirated editions of *Don Juan*, see Jerome J. McGann, *The Beauty of Inflections* (Oxford, 1985), 115–117. For Byron's manner of dealing with his publishers, see *Lord Byron: The Complete Poetical Works*, ed. Jerome J. McGann (Oxford, 1980–), I: xxxvi–xxxvii, and V: "Introduction"; see also the chronicle of publication set forth in vol. I of *Don Juan: A Variorum Edition*, ed. T. G. Steffan and W. W. Pratt (Austin, Tex., 1957).

15. See *Byron: Complete Poetical Works*, III: 406–413. The best single example from Tennyson is probably in the publishing history of *The Princess*; for a general view of the subject, see June Steffansen Hagen, *Tennyson and His Publishers* (University Park, Pa., 1979).

16. See Hershel Parker, "Melville and the Concept of Author's Final Intentions," *Proof* 1 (1971), 156–168, and Jerome J. McGann, *A Critique of Modern Textual Criticism* (Chicago, 1983), 86–89.

17. Reprinted, along with the important sequel "Interpreting 'Interpreting the *Variorum*'" in *Is There a Text in This Class?* (Cambridge, Mass., 1980), 147–173 and 174–180. Further references to this book are given in parentheses in the text.

18. See his *Principles and Practice of Textual Analysis* (Berkeley, 1973) as well as G. Thomas Tanselle's important comments in "Classical, Biblical, and Medieval Textual Criticism and Modern Editing," *Studies in Bibliography* 36 (1983), esp. 29–35.

19. For a discussion of the "text" as the ideal object of immanentist criticism of the last two generations, see my *Beauty of Inflections*, esp. 92–99 and 112–114.

20. The key editions which illustrate this new development in European studies are the following: *Friedrich Gottlieb Klopstock: Werke und Briefe*, ed. Horst Gronemeyer, Elisabeth Höpker-Herberg, Klaus Hurlebusch, and Rosemarie Hurlebusch (New York, 1974–); *Friedrich Hölderlin: Sämtliche Werke*, ed. D. E. Sattler (Frankfurt, 1975–); *Franz Kafka: Schriften, Tagebücher, Briefe*, ed. Jürgen Born et al. (Frankfurt, 1982–); *Corpus flaubertianum*, 1 *Un Coeur simple*, ed. Giovanni Bonnacorso et al. (Paris, 1983); *Marcel Proust: Matinée chez la Princesse de Guermantes*, Cahiers du *Temps retrouvé*, ed. Henri Bonnet and Bernard Brun (Paris, 1982).

21. Christine Froula, *To Write Paradise: Style and Form in Pound's Cantos* (New Haven, 1984), 176.

10. Contemporary Poetry, Alternate Routes

1. Black and Feminist writings in the United States often confine the focus of their political engagements to a more restricted national theater. Not always, of course; besides, even in these cases engagement is necessarily carried out within the global framework I have sketched above.

2. *The New American Poetry 1945–1960*, ed. Donald M. Allen (New York, 1960), xi.

3. Robert von Hallberg, *American Poetry and Culture 1945–1980* (Cambridge, Mass., 1985), 228. While I disagree with von Hallberg's criteria for poetry, his book is by far the best account yet written of the post–Second World War poetry scene in America. Also its readings of a number of poets—especially Lowell and Dorn—are impressive and important. Criteriological differences aside, its only notable deficiency is its failure to observe the development of L=A=N=G=U=A=G=E Writing through the seventies and eighties. See also Robert Pinsky, *The Situation of Poetry* (Princeton, 1976). The best academic discussion to date of L=A=N=G=U=A=G=E Writing and its traditions are in Marjorie Perloff's *The Dance of Intellect* (Cambridge, 1985) (see esp. chap. 10); and Lee Bartlett, "What Is Language Poetry?" *Critical Inquiry* 12 (Summer 1986), 741–752.

4. In a letter to me Ron Silliman suggested that this work be designated *Language* (rather than L=A=N=G=U=A=G=E) Writing because the latter term is associated with a specific journal (which began relatively late in the day, so far as this movement was concerned), and because the name calls attention to institutional rather than stylistic matters. Though the first point is important and persuasive, I disagree with the second, in this sense: I think the institutional character of this movement should be emphasized. One of the most salient characteristics of the movement has been its determination to disseminate itself outside the traditional institutional structures (outside the New York publishing centers, on the one hand, and the academic network, on the other). L=A=N=G=U=A=G=E Writing developed its own infrastructure in reading centers and publishing ventures in various locations, but having as its two chief points of reference New York and San Francisco. These social and institutional networks have been painstakingly constructed from approximately 1970 to the present.

5. The literature on the question of postmodernism is now quite large. The best account of the debate—an essay at once descriptively acute and critically significant—is Andreas Huyssen's "Mapping the Postmodern," *New German Critique* 33 (Fall 1984), 5–52. The argument is sometimes made that postmodernism, though outwardly accommodational, mounts an *implicitly* critical comment upon contemporary society. But no one who has taken part in this debate, with the (qualified) exception of Frederic Jameson, has discussed the postmodernism of the L=A=N=G=U=A=G=E writers, who are aggressively and openly oppositional in their political stance. See the following discussion.

6. For a good "languaged" reading of Ashbery, see Bruce Andrews's "text"

on *The Tennis Court Oath,* "Misrepresentation," reprinted (from 1980) in *In the American Tree,* ed. Ron Silliman (Orono, Maine, 1986), 520–529.

7. The best (critical) account of the Yale school is in *The Yale Critics: Deconstruction in America,* ed. Jonathan Arac, Wlad Godzich, and Wallace Martin (Minneapolis, 1983).

8. Barrett Watten, "Method and Surrealism: The Politics of Poetry," *L=A=N=G=U=A=G=E* IV, ed. Bruce Andrews and Charles Bernstein (Open Letter, Fifth Series no. 1), 129.

9. Richard Rorty, "Solidarity or Objectivity," in *Post-Analytic Philosophy,* ed. John Rajchman and Cornel West (New York, 1985), 3.

10. See Michel de Certeau, "La fiction de l'histoire," *L'écriture de l'histoire* (Paris, 1978), 312–358, and "History: Science and Fiction," in *Heterologies: Discourse on the Other,* trans. Brian Massumi, foreword by Wlad Godzich (Minneapolis, 1986), 199–221. Robert Scholes has a good discussion of the ways "post-modernist anti-narratives" move antithetically against the continuities of narrativity, in "Language, Narrative, and Anti-Narrative," *Critical Inquiry* 7 (Autumn 1980), 211; see also Nelson Goodman's "Twisted Tales" in the same issue (103–120). Some of the more general forms of non-narrative and antinarrative are treated in Chapter 7.

11. The image appears in both *Milton* and *Jerusalem;* see, for example, *Milton* 27:9–10.

12. For information on the different copies of *The Marriage of Heaven and Hell,* see *William Blake's Writings,* ed. G. E. Bentley, Jr. (Oxford, 1978) I: 692–695.

13. Reprinted in the important *The L=A=N=G=U=A=G=E Book,* ed. Bruce Andrews and Charles Bernstein (Carbondale, Ill., 1984), 50–51. This is a generous selection of pieces from volumes I–III of the journal *L=A=N=G=U=A=G=E.* Unless otherwise indicated, all prose citations from writers in the L=A=N=G=U=A=G=E orbit are to this book, and page numbers are given in parentheses in the text.

14. Alan Davies and Nick Piombino, "The Indeterminate Interval: From History to Blur," *L=A=N=G=U=A=G=E* IV, 31–39.

15. Ibid., 37.

16. Edward Said, *Beginnings* (Baltimore, 1975), 58, 48.

17. Charles Bernstein, *Controlling Interests* (New York, 1980), 48.

18. Ron Silliman, *Tjanting,* with introduction by Barrett Watten (Berkeley, 1981), 11.

19. Charles Bernstein, "Narrating Narration: The Shapes of Ron Silliman's Work," *The Difficulties,* Ron Silliman Issue II, no. 2 (1985), 93.

20. Ibid.

21. Silliman, *Tjanting,* 12.

22. Ibid.

23. The following prose quotations are from Silliman's two important essays "Disappearance of the Word, Appearance of the World" and "If By Writing We Mean Literature," in *L=A=N=G=U=A=G=E Book.*

24. Bernstein, "Narrating Narration," 94.

25. Ibid., 95.

26. Ibid.

27. "Interview [with Ron Silliman]," *Difficulties,* 35.

28. Ibid. Silliman's interest in the Fibonacci numbers may well have been generated through his reading of Charles Olson's "The Praises," or—alternatively—through a reading of the book which was the chief source for Olson's poem: Matila Ghyka's *The Geometry of Art and Life* (New York, 1946). See Robert von Hallberg, *Charles Olson: The Scholar's Art* (Cambridge, Mass., 1978), 21–23 and nn.

29. "Interview," 36.

30. The poem appeared in *Poetry* 125 (November 1974), where it took up the entire issue. The text here is the longer book version (New York, 1976). Numbers in parentheses indicate page references in Hollander's book.

31. Bernstein, *Controlling Interests,* 48–49.

32. Davies and Piombino, "Indeterminate Interval," 39.

11. *The Third World of Criticism*

1. Frantz Fanon, *The Wretched of the Earth,* preface by Jean-Paul Sartre, trans. Constance Farrington (New York, 1968), 105.

2. Ibid., 106.

3. Walter Benjamin, *Illuminations,* ed. Hannah Arendt, trans. Harry Zohn (New York, 1969), 256.

4. Ibid., 257.

5. Fanon, *Wretched of the Earth,* 222.

6. Ibid., 222–223.

7. Ibid., 240.

8. I mean to recall here Marshall Sahlins's *Islands of History* (Chicago, 1985), which demonstrates how an imperial culture encounters, and mistakes, the histories in which it is involved.

9. The best single presentation of the historical and political context of the *Oresteia* is in Anthony J. Podlecki, *The Political Background of Aeschylean Tragedy* (Ann Arbor, 1966), chap. 5.

10. See George Grote, *A History of Greece* (New York, 1881), vol. II, chaps. 45–46.

11. I use here Richard Lattimore's translation of the *Oresteia* (Chicago, 1953).

12. See, for example, James C. Hogan, *A Commentary on the Complete Greek Tragedies: Aeschylus* (Chicago, 1984), 31, 159–160.

13. See Grote, *History of Greece,* 411.

14. From Shelley's preface to *Prometheus Unbound,* in *Shelley's Poetry and Prose,* ed. Donald H. Reiman and Sharon B. Powers (New York, 1977), 133.

15. See Thucydides, *The Peloponnesian War,* II, sec. 63.

16. From "Defence of Poetry," *Shelley's Poetry and Prose,* 502–503.

17. For information on the provenance histories of Blake's works, see Gerald Bentley, Jr., *Blake Books* (Oxford, 1977).

18. See Gerald Bentley, Jr., *Blake Records* (Oxford, 1969). My texts of

Blake are taken from *The Poetry and Prose of William Blake,* rev. ed., ed. David V. Erdman, with commentary by Harold Bloom (Berkeley, 1982).

19. See Kenneth Scott Latourette, *A History of Christianity in the 19th and 20th Centuries,* vol. 2 (Grand Rapids, Mich., 1969), chaps. 16–19.

20. See Anne K. Mellor, "Blake's Portrayal of Women," *Blake: An Illustrated Quarterly* 16 (Winter 1982–83), 148–165.

21. For Byron's plans to have Juan executed in the Reign of Terror, see *Byron: The Poetical Works,* ed. Jerome J. McGann (Oxford, 1986), vol. 5, Introduction.

22. For the bibliographical history of the *Cantos* see Donald Gallup, *Ezra Pound: A Bibliography* (Charlottesville, Va., 1983). A good discussion of the bibliography can be found in Alan Durant, *Ezra Pound: Identity in Crisis* (London, 1981), chap. 3.

23. George Kearns, *Guide to Ezra Pound's Selected Cantos* (New Brunswick, N.J., 1980), 149.

24. For the Byron text Pound is recalling, see *Byron: The Poetical Works,* IV: 33–35 ("Stanzas to [Augusta]").

25. The second is the way Michael Bernstein has proceeded in his excellent *The Tale of the Tribe: Ezra Pound and the Modern Verse Epic* (Princeton, 1980). His book is at the same time a conscious critique of all readings of the *Cantos* which operate as if the poem were transparent to itself.

Conclusion: The Loss of Poetry

1. *The Poetry and Prose of William Blake,* rev. ed., ed. David V. Erdman, with commentary by Harold Bloom (Berkeley, 1982), 554.

2. See ibid., 563.

3. Ibid., 565.

4. Ibid.

5. George Bataille, *Visions of Excess: Selected Writings 1927–1939,* ed. with introduction by Allan Stoekl (Minneapolis, 1985), 172, 118, 241.

6. Ibid., 97.

7. Ibid., 134.

Index

Aaron, Daniel, 120

Abrams, M. H., 15, 97, 253n16, 257n4

Adam, James, 252n23

Adorno, Theodor, 130, 151

Aeschylus: *Oresteia*, 224–230, 232–233, 240; *Prometheus Bound*, 230; *Prometheus Unbound*, 230

Albright, W. F., 255n2

Allegory, 164, 264n36

Allen, Donald, 198

Allott, Kenneth, 87, 256nn4,15,18

Allott, Miriam, 87

Analytical Review, 158, 161, 163, 263n18

Anderson, Warren, 87, 256nn16,18

Andrews, Bruce, 210, 253n11, 268nn8,13, 267n6

Antinarrative. *See* Discourse, forms of

Arac, Jonathan, 257n7, 259n2, 262n16, 268n7

Arendt, Hannah, 269n3

Aristotle, 73, 127, 128, 240, 242

Arnold, Matthew, 30, 107, 108, 147. Works: *Alaric at Rome*, 256n5; *Cromwell*, 256n5; "Empedocles on Etna," 85; *Empedocles on Etna, and Other Poems* (1852), 256nn5,9; "Memorial Verses," 84; *Poems* (1853), 83, 84–85, 86, 91; "Preface" to *Poems* (1853), 85;

"Sohrab and Rustum," 82–91, 152, 256n18; *The Strayed Reveller, and Other Poems* (1849), 256nn5,9

Array. *See* Critical discourse, forms of

Art: postmodern, 32–35, 48; and Kant's aesthetic, 35–36, 38, 73; dynamic of and Blake, 241–243. *See also* Content exhibition

Ashbery, John, 198, 199–200. Works: *As We Know*, 200; *Houseboat Days*, 200; *The Tennis Court Oath*, 199, 267n6; *Three Poems*, 199; *Vermont Notebook*, 200

Auden, W. H., 183, 199; "In Memory of W. B. Yeats," 20, 252n14

Auerbach, Erich, 140, 141–144, 150

Austin, J. L., 20

Bakhtin, Mikhail, 73, 112, 232, 259n37

Barnes, Hazel, 259n39

Barthes, Roland, 4, 260n28; 265n11

Bartlett, Lee, 267n3

Bataille, Georges, 195, 241, 244–245, 247

Bate, W. Jackson, 255n18, 259n4

Baudelaire, Pierre Charles, 239

Baudrillard, Jean, 111, 259n36

Baumgarten, Siegmund Jacob, 253n16

Bayle, Pierre, 161, 162

Bédier, Joseph, 173

Benjamin, Walter, 6, 63–64, 173, 222, 224, 238

Bennington, Geoff, 253n13, 256n1

Bentley, G. E., Jr., 145, 153, 156, 157, 262n1, 268n12, 269nn17,18

Bernstein, Charles, 34, 209, 212, 215, 268nn8,13; "For Love has such a Spirit that if it is Portrayed it Dies," 210–211, 219

Bernstein, Michael, 270n25

Bible: ideological dimension of, 56–57, 81–82, 240; and textual methodology, 57, 59–61, 63, 64, 81–82, 169; interpretation of earlier texts in, 58–60, 79; performativity in, 59, 77–82; versions of, 88, 159, 160, 263n20; documentary and fragmentary hypotheses about, 154–155, 168, 169; Geddes and Spinoza on state of texts of, 158–160, 167–170. *See also* Genesis

Blake, William, 9, 122, 145, 201, 246; on order of imagination, 42–44, 46, 205–206; alternative poetics of, 42–49, 241–244, 245; production processes of, 44, 47, 62, 76, 77, 153, 232; and Milton, 47, 126, 153–154; and L=A=N=G=U=A=G=E Writing, 48, 219; and biblical criticism, 62, 152–172 *passim*; and the incommensurable, 72; unstable texts of, 152, 155, 170–171, 205, 262n1; facsimile editions of, 157, 205, 254n30, 262n1; and Geddes's influence, 158, 160, 164–167, 170–172; and myth, 159, 160–167, 171, 172, 263nn22,25; and allegory, 164, 264n36; history and futurity in, 230, 231–232, 233, 234–236; reception history of, 232, 233–234, 236, 269n17; provenance of works of, 233, 269n17; on knowledge in literature, 241–243. Works: *All Religions are One,* 162–163; *America,* 262n4; "The Bible of Hell," 62, 77, 153, 154, 158, 159, 160, 162, 167, 170, 171–172, 262n4; *The Book of Ahania,* 62, 153, 154, 155, 166, 171–172; *The Book of Los,* 62, 153, 154, 155, 166, 171–172, 264n51; *Europe,* 262n4; *The [First] Book of Urizen,* 62, 77, 152, 153–154, 155–158, 160, 164–167, 170–172, 263nn9,15;

264n51; *Jerusalem,* 11, 32, 132, 152, 155, 206, 254n29, 268n11; *The Marriage of Heaven and Hell,* 6, 44–45, 47, 62, 77, 126, 153, 155, 161–162, 164, 171, 197, 203, 204–206, 207, 232, 254n30, 268n12; *Milton,* 45–46, 47, 152, 155, 203–204, 206, 234–235, 268n11; *The Song of Los,* 262n4; *Songs of Innocence and of Experience,* 77, 152, 157–158, 204, 205, 207; *The Vision of the Daughters of Albion,* 262n4; *Vision of the Last Judgment,* 241–242, 264n36

Bloom, Harold, 1, 141–144, 150, 269n18, 270n1

Boehme, Jacob, 163

Bohr, Niels, 102

Bonnacorso, Giovanni, 266n20

Bonnet, Henri, 266n20

Bonneville, Nicholas, 162; *De l'Esprit des Religions,* 161

Booth, Wayne C., 97, 257n4

Born, Jürgen, 266n20

Bouchard, Donald F., 252n5

Bourdieu, Pierre, 18–19

Bowdler, Dr. Thomas, 182

Bowers, Fredson, 173

Bremner, Robert H., 260n11

Brett, R. L., 254n21

British Critic, 160

Brooks, Cleanth: *The Well Wrought Urn,* 50–51, 54, 118–119, 135, 260n7

Brown, John, 221

Browning, Robert, 153; "How It Strikes a Contemporary," 217

Brun, Bernard, 266n20

Bryant, Jacob, 52, 161, 162, 165

Burn, A. R., 255n16

Byron, George Gordon, Lord, 42, 46, 48, 76, 182, 183, 221, 233. Works: *Childe Harold's Pilgrimage,* 236–237, 254n28; *Don Juan,* 76, 97, 125, 126, 136–138, 139, 140, 183, 203, 236–237, 266n14, 270n21; *The Giaour,* 62, 152, 179, 183; *Manfred,* 95; "Stanzas to [Augusta]," 238

Cain, William E., 257n8

Cairne-Ross, D. S., 53

Cairns, Huntington, 252n22

Cassity, Turner, 200

Cavell, Stanley, 146–147, 151

Chatterton, Thomas, 62, 172
Chaucer, Geoffrey, 242
Child, Abigail, 207
Christian Remembrancer, The, 87
Clough, Arthur Hugh, 84
Coleridge, J. D., 87
Coleridge, Samuel Taylor, 30, 40, 43, 46, 72, 117–118, 125, 143, 237. Works: "Aeolian Harp," 38; *Biographia Literaria,* 35, 39, 73, 74, 127, 255n18, 259n4; *Lyrical Ballads,* 91; "The Rime of the Ancient Mariner," 62, 152
Content exhibition (Hirshhorn Museum), 32–34, 48
Corngold, Stanley, 101, 257n7, 258nn23,24,25
Crabbe, George, 41–42, 254n27. Works: *The Borough,* 41; "Delay Has Danger," 41; "Infancy," 41–42; *Tales,* 41
Critical discourse, forms of, 134–135; dialectic, 19–22, 64, 131, 133, 145, 146–149, 151; narrative, 132–133, 140–145, 149–150; array, 133, 136–140, 145, 151; narrative/array hybrid, 145–146; narrative/dialogic hybrid, 150. *See also* Discourse, forms of
Critical Review, 160
Criticism, literary: and legitimation crisis, 98, 99, 257n3; as antithetical, 222–224, 269n8
Criticism, techniques of: empirical, 1–2, 5–6, 16; close reading, 2, 251n1; computer-based word processing, 174, 188, 192, 193; sociohistorical, 182–189. *See also* Deconstructionism; Formalism; Hermeneutics; Historicism; Kant, Immanuel; Marx, Karl; Modernism; New Criticism; Philology; Postmodernism; Poststructuralism; Romanticism; Structuralism; Texts, literary; Yale school
Culler, Jonathan, 257n8
Cumberland, George, 233
Curtis, F. B., 164

Dante Alighieri, 89
Darragh, Tina, 207–208, 209, 216
Davidson, Thomas, 136, 137
Davies, Alan, 209, 219, 220
Davis, Walter A., 257n8
Dawson, Carl, 256nn6,8,9,17
De Certeau, Michel, 132, 133, 268n10
Deconstructionism, 5, 13, 18, 115, 257n3,

259n2; and referentiality, 5–6, 119, 128, 129–130; defined, 18–19; cognitive function of and poetical discourse, 30–31; and nihilism, 110, 122; as technology, 112–114, 257n3, 259n38; and Miller, 119–121; vs. modern textual studies, 130, 131; Hartman on, 150, 262n16; and Yale school, 200; and Ashbery, 200; and L=A=N=G=U=A=G=E Writing, 219. *See also* De Man, Paul; Derrida, Jacques; Miller, J. Hillis
De Man, Paul; and deconstructionism, 1–5, 51, 258n20; blindness/insight dynamic of, 2–3, 101–103, 108–109, 257nn11,12; and referentiality, 5–6; and hermeneutics, 99, 100–101, 257n11; on interpretation, 104–110
Derrida, Jacques, 2, 15, 18, 31, 104, 105, 117, 120
De Selincourt, Aubrey, 255n16
Dialectical forms. *See* Critical discourse, forms of
Dickinson, Emily, 48–49
Discourse, forms of, 20–22; narrative, 132, 133–134, 135, 202, 203–204, 210–211, 268n10; nonnarrative, 203, 204–207, 210, 211–212, 214, 219; antinarrative, 203–204, 205, 207, 210, 211, 219–220, 268n10; and L=A=N=G=U=A=G=E Writing, 207–220 *passim. See also* Critical discourse, forms of
Divus, Andreas, 52–53, 54, 194, 255n2
Donaldson, E. Talbot, 174
Donato, Eugenio, 259n3
Donne, John, 76, 107
Dorn, Edward, 267n3
Doskow, Minna, 254n29
Driver, Clive, 265n6
Driver, Samuel Rolles, 130
Drummond, Sir William, 161
Dupuis, Charles-François, 161, 162
Duncan, Robert, 198
Durant, Alan, 270n22

Eagleton, Terry, 253n13
Easson, K. P., 254n31
Easson, R. R., 254n31
Eco, Umberto, 115
Egoist, and text of Joyce's *Ulysses,* 176
Eichhorn, J. G., 14, 57, 62, 152, 158, 172, 173; and documentary theory of biblical texts, 154, 167, 168, 169–170

Elias, Julius A., 252n24
Eliot, T. S., 255n2; *The Waste Land*, 153
Ellis, John M., 121–122
Elwes, R. H. M., 264n44
Emerson, Caryl, 259n37
Engell, James, 255n18, 259n4
Enuma Elish, 58–60
Erdman, David V., 157, 269n18, 270n1
Essick, Robert, 170, 263n23

Fanon, Frantz, 221–224, 229, 230
Farrington, Constance, 269n1
Fellowes, B., 83, 84
Feminist studies, 6, 116, 242, 267n1
Fenwick, Isabella, 42
Fibonacci numbers, 215, 216, 218, 269n28
Firdausi: *Shah Nameh*, 88
Fischer, David Hackett, 141, 262n10
Fish, Stanley, 51, 99–101, 109–110, 111, 184–186, 188, 252n14, 257n8
Fisher, Peter, 263n25
Fitzgerald, Edward: *Rubaiyat*, 219
Flaubert, Gustav, 187
Foreman, Richard, 207
Formalism, 107, 112–114, 116, 257n3, 259n38; and referentiality, 116
Foucault, Michel, 4, 16, 19, 20–22, 189, 232, 252n5, 265n11
Frame, Donald M., 262n14
Francis, F. C., 264n3
Fraser's Magazine, 84
Frei, Hans, 255n11
Frost, Robert, 199
Froude, J. A., 256n6
Froula, Christine, 193, 266n21
Frye, Northrop, 153, 263n25; *Anatomy of Criticism*, 13–14
Fuller, Reginald Cuthbert, 262n8, 263n20

Gabler, Hans Walter: edition of Joyce's *Ulysses*, 173–182, 184, 186–194, 265nn7,8,9,10
Gabler, J. P., 152, 158, 167
Gadamer, Hans Georg, 111, 124, 258n34
Gallup, Donald, 270n22
Ganz, Peter F., 264n1
Geddes, Dr. Alexander: biblical scholarship of, 62, 63, 158–173 *passim*; influence of on Blake, 152, 158–159, 160, 164–167, 170–172, 264n36; fragment hypothesis of, 154–155, 167, 169–172;

reviews by, 158, 263n18; on state of biblical texts, 158–159, 167–170; and myth, 159, 160–161, 162. Works: *Critical Remarks*, 160; *Dr. Geddes' Address to the Public*, 264nn35,37; Preface to translation of Bible, 164; *Prospectus of a New Translation of the Holy Bible*, 159–160
Genesis: and historicism, 14, 15; formative history of, 57–60, 144, 153–154, 168–169; and *Enuma Elish*, 58–60; Blake's parody of in *Urizen*, 153–154, 165–166, 171; history in, 230. *See also* Bible
George, Andrew J., 254n27
Ghyka, Matila, 269n28
Gilchrist, Alexander, 233
Glück, Louise, 199
Godzich, Wlad, 257n7, 258n20, 259n2, 261n1, 262n16, 268nn7,10
Golffing, Francis, 252n10
Good, J. M., 262n8, 263n18
Goodman, Nelson, 268n10
Gottfried, Leon, 256n18
Graff, Gerald, 97, 257nn4,8
Gray, Thomas, 88
Greg, W. W., 173, 177
Griesbach, Johann Jacob, 172
Groden, Michael, 265nn6,9
Gronemeyer, Horst, 266n20
Grote, George, 123, 124, 269nn10,13
Guston, Philip, 33

Habermas, Jürgen, 5, 22, 57, 95, 111, 130, 258n34, 260n27
Hagen, June Steffanson, 266n15
Hamilton, Edith, 252n22
Hammond, Anthony, 265n8
Harari, Josué, 260n28, 265n11
Hardy, Thomas: "The Convergence of the Twain," 99
Hartman, Geoffrey, 13, 97, 115, 116, 142, 150, 262n16
Hazlitt, William: *The Spirit of the Age*, 41–42
Hecht, Anthony, 198
Hegel, Georg Wilhelm Friedrich, 15, 133–134, 236, 237; *Aesthetics*, 104, 258n18
Heidegger, Martin, 147, 150
Heijinian, Lyn, 197, 219
Heisenberg, Werner, 102
Held, David, 256n1

Herder, J. G., 14–15

Hermeneutics, 17–18, 38, 39, 61–62; and legitimation crisis, 98, 99, 257n3; and de Man, 99, 100–109, 110, 111, 257nn11,12, 258nn18,20; and Fish, 99–101, 109–110, 111, 257n8; and theory of meaning, 104–106; traditions of, 112–113, 130, 131, 257n3, 259n38; model for, 112–114

Herodotus, 25, 56, 81, 82, 88, 240, 257n17; *Histories,* 7, 64–72, 255n16

Hesiod, 21

Heyne, C. G., 62, 152, 158

Hirsch, E. D., Jr., 21, 98

Historicism, 1–2, 5, 14–17, 97, 115–118, 257n3, 260n22; and Parry, 7, 15, 121, 122–124; and Nietzsche, 14–16, 232, 240; vs. deconstructionism, 107–108; as technology, 112–114, 257n3, 259n38; failure of, 123–124; and referentiality, 123–124, 129–130

Hölderlin, Friedrich, 187

Höpker-Herberg, Elisabeth, 266n20

Hogan, James C., 269n12

Hollander, John, 199; *Reflections on Espionage,* 216–219, 269n30; *The Untuning of the Sky,* 254n17

Holquist, Michael, 259n37

Homer, 29, 48, 53, 56, 57, 63, 161, 227; Plato on, 19–22, 23, 31, 252n23; Thucydides on, 25; and Pound, 52, 54, 193–194; and Arnold, 87, 88, 89–90, 256n18. Works: *Iliad,* 27, 88, 144; *Odyssey,* 24, 27, 52, 54, 141, 144, 252n23

Honan, Park, 256n7

Howe, Susan, 219

Howard, Richard, 198–199

Huebler, Douglas, 33, 34

Hurlebusch, Klaus, 266n20

Hurlebusch, Rosemarie, 266n20

Huyssen, Andreas, 267n5

Imagination, concept of: in Romanticism and Kantian aesthetic, 38, 39–42, 254n20; and Blake, 42–44, 46, 205–206

Jameson, Frederic, 35, 247, 267n5

Jenney, Neil, 33

Jephcott, Edmund, 255n12

Jesus, parables of, 30, 77–81, 82

Jones, A. R., 254n21

Jones, David, 153

Johnson, Joseph, 158, 161

Joyce, James: *Finnegans Wake,* 1; *Ulysses,* 97; Gabler's edition of, 173–182, 184, 186–194, 265nn7,8,9,10, 265n12, 266n13; and Rosenbach manuscript, 174, 176, 178, 265n6; texts of, 174–176, 177, 180, 192, 265n10; composition vs. production text of, 175–184, 188–192, 265nn8,9,10, 266n13; production processes of, 265n12

Justice, Donald, 198

Juvenal, 75

Kafka, Franz, 187

Kahn, Michael, 261n32

Kane, George, 174

Kant, Immanuel, 15; aesthetic of, 18, 19, 30, 36–37, 38–39, 42–46, 73, 74, 104, 231, 236, 237, 239, 253–254n16, 254n20; *Critique of Judgment,* 35–37, 40, 117; "Four Moments" of aesthetic pleasure, 37, 253n15; categorical imperative of, 129

Kearns, George, 270n23

Keats, John, 48, 76, 86, 88. Works: *Hyperion,* 62, 90, 153, 256n18; "The Fall of Hyperion," 62, 90, 153; "La Belle Dame sans Merci," 75; "Ode on a Grecian Urn," 50; "On First Looking into Chapman's Homer," 63

Kenner, Hugh, 180, 265n9

Keyes, Geoffrey, 254n30

Kidd, John, 265n7

Klopstock, Friedrich Gottlieb, 187

Kroker, Arthur, 259n36

Kuhn, Albert J., 263n21

Lachmann, Karl, 173

Lai de L'Ombre, 173

Lamb, Charles, 182

Langland, William: *Piers Plowman,* 174

L=A=N=G=U=A=G=E Writing: theory and practice of, 34, 189, 207–220 *passim;* and Blake, 48, 207; and politics, 197, 198–199, 200, 201, 202, 207, 210, 215–216, 217, 267n5; and poetic experimentation, 199, 207–210

Latourette, Kenneth Scott, 270n19

Lattimore, Richard, 269n11

Lentricchia, Frank, 251n1, 257n7

Levin, Charles, 259n36
Levin, Harry, 265n6
Lewis, C. S., 118
Lewis, Thomas E., 259n1
Linnell, John, 233
Little Review, 176, 191
Locke, John: *An Essay Concerning Human Understanding,* 36
Longmans (publisher), 84
Lowell, Robert, 198, 200, 267n3; *History,* 197; *Lord Weary's Castle,* 197
Lowry, H. F., 256n20
Lowth, Bishop Robert: *Lectures,* 162
Lucretius, 87, 173, 179, 242; *De rerum natura,* 82
Lyotard, Jean-François, 35, 95, 130

McCarthy, Thomas, 252n20, 256n1
McClintic, Miranda, 253n1
McEvilley, Thomas, 33
McGann, Jerome J., 76, 264n1, 266nn14,16,19, 270n21
McKenzie, D. F., 8–9
Mackerness, E. D., 254n23
Macksey, Richard, 259n3
McMichael, James, 200
Macpherson, James, 62, 172
Mann, C. S., 255n2
Marlowe, Christopher, 143
Martin, Wallace, 257n7, 259n2, 262n16, 268n7
Marx, Karl: and literary criticism, 19, 98, 112–114, 116, 124, 213–214, 257n3; eleventh thesis on Feuerbach, 49; *The Eighteenth Brumaire,* 133
Massumi, Brian, 253n13, 256n1, 261n1, 268n10
Matthew, performativity in, 59, 77–82. *See also* Bible
Mayer, Bernadette, 208, 216
Melchior, Claus, 265n4
Mellor, Anne K., 270n20
Melville, Herman: *Moby-Dick,* 183
Meredith, James Creed, 253n14
Michaelis, J. D., 158
Miller, J. Hillis, 119–121, 124, 140
Mills, Howard, 254n26
Milton, John, 143, 231, 236; and Blake, 47, 126, 153–154; Arnold's imitation of, 87–88, 90, 256n18. Works: *Comus,* 184; *Lycidas,* 184; *Paradise

Lost,* 47, 88, 153–154, 231, 234–235, 244
Mitchell, W. J. T., 263n9
Modernism, 35; and Pound's *Cantos,* 51–52; and referentiality, 128
Mohl, Jules, 88
Momigliano, Arnaldo, 261n4
Montaigne, Michel Eyquen de: *Essais,* 147–149; "That Intention Is Judge of Our Actions," 147, 148; "That Our Happiness Must Not Be Judged until after Our Death," 147–148; "Of the Power of the Imagination," 148
Monthly Review, 160
Morris, Robert, 32, 34
Morris, William, 152
Murdoch, Iris, 22
Murry, J. Middleton, 262n4
Myth: Plato on, 24–27, 29–31, 252n24; and Geddes, 159, 160–161, 162; and Blake, 159, 160–167, 171, 172, 263nn22,25

Narrative. *See* Critical discourse, forms of; Discourse, forms of
New Bibliography movement, 264n3
New Criticism, 2, 13–14, 35, 101, 105, 115, 181, 200; and referentiality, 118, 119, 259n2; vs. traditional philology, 130, 131
New York Review of Books, 174
Nice, Richard, 252n9
Niebelungenlied, 173
Nietzsche, Friedrich Wilhelm, 3, 48, 102, 121, 151; and deconstructionism, 6, 19–22, 104; and historicism, 14–16, 232, 240. Works: *The Genealogy of Morals,* 19; *On the Advantage and the Disadvantage of History for Life,* 123; *On the Use and Abuse of History,* 15; *Untimely Meditations,* 15, 21
Nonnarrative. *See* Discourse, forms of

O'Hara, Frank, 96–97, 198
Olson, Charles, 198; "The Praises," 269n28

Page, Norman, 261n8
Paine, Thomas, 161, 163, 164
Parker, Hershel, 266n16
Parker, John William, Jr., 84

Parry, Adam, 260n15

Parry, Milman, 7, 15, 121, 122–124, 260n15

Patmore, Coventry, 256n6

Patterson, Lee, 264n1, 265n5

Perloff, Marjorie, 267n3

Petre, William Joseph, Lord, 159

Philology: and modern textual studies, 1, 5, 14–16, 57, 61–63, 173–174; Nietzsche on, 15–16; and legitimation crisis, 50–51; and Arnold's "Sohrab and Rustum," 89–90, 152; vs. immanent criticism, 130, 131; and biblical scholarship, 152, 154–172 *passim;* and Romanticism, 152–153. *See also* Hermeneutics

Pinsky, Robert, 198, 199, 200, 267n3

Piombino, Nick, 209, 220

Plato, 48, 56, 80; on Homer, 19–22, 23, 31, 252n23; on status of poetry, 19–31 *passim,* 73, 241; and myth of Socrates' life, 21, 29–31; on truth in poetry, 21–31; and myth of Er, 24–27, 29, 252n24; logocentrism of, 30, 31. Works: *Apology,* 29; *Dialogues,* 27; *Euthyphro,* 29; *Ion,* 23; *Laws,* 23–24; *Lesser Hippias,* 27–29; *Phaedrus,* 17, 26; *Protagoras,* 26; *Republic,* 19, 22–23, 24, 26; *Symposium,* 27, 31

Podlecki, Anthony J., 269n9

Poetic theory: classical vs. Kantian aesthetic, 19–31, 38–39, 43; and Shelley, 40–41, 269n16; and Blake, 42–49, 241–244, 245; and Sidney, 73–74; and ideology, 74–75 , 85, 86–89, 90–91; and representation, 117–118, 126–128, 130

Poetry: as form of discourse, 9–10; post-structural definition of, 19; as performative, 55; post-World War II American, 197–199, 267n3; ways of reading, 238–239. *See also* L = A = N = G = U = A = G = E Writing; entries for specific poets

Ponge, Francis, 207

Pope, Alexander, 76, 87, 129

Poster, Mark, 259n36

Postmodernism, 33, 34–35; and Blake, 48; and Gabler's edition of *Ulysses,* 174, 188–189, 192; and textual instability, 187; and L = A = N = G = U = A = G = E Writing, 199–200, 267n5; and anti- and nonnarrative discourse, 203

Poststructuralism, 100, 106, 199, 207; vs. Frye, 13, 14; definition of poetry, 19; and legitimation crisis, 98, 99, 257n3; and referentiality, 128; and textual instability, 181, 187

Pound, Ezra: *The Cantos,* 51–55, 63, 95, 153, 270nn22,25; production processes in, 183, 192–194, 237, 238; vs. Byron's *Don Juan,* 236–237; history and futurity in, 237, 238–240; reception history of, 238–239

Powers, Sharon B., 254n22, 269n14

Pratt, W. W., 266n14

Proust, Marcel, 187

Raine, Kathleen, 163

Rajchman, John, 268n9

Raval, Suresh, 259n2

Realism, 63

Rée, Jonathan, 259n39

Rees, D. A., 252n23

Reiman, Donald H., 254n22, 269n14

Richmond, George, 233

Ricoeur, Paul, 17–18, 111

Riffaterre, Michael, 251n1, 258n20

Rochester, John Wilmot, second earl of, 76

Romanticism, 15, 254n20; and imagination, 39–42, 254n20; and modern textual studies, 62–63; elements of, 90, 152, 153

Rorty, Richard, 202, 207

Rosenzweig, Phyllis, 253n1

Rossetti, Dante Gabriel, 48, 76, 86; *The Early Italian Poets,* 75; *House of Life,* 219

Rousseau, Jean Jacques, 104; Second Preface to *Julie,* 3–5

Russell, George W. E., 256n10

Sahlins, Marshall, 114, 255n13, 269n8

Said, Edward, 259n42, 265n11, 268n16

St. Armand, Barton Levi, 254n33

Sarna, Nahum A., 255n6

Sartre, Jean-Paul, 13, 113, 269n1

Sattler, D. E., 266n20

Saunders, Chauncey, 261n5

Scholes, Robert, 268n10

Schröder, Werner, 264n1
Searle, John R., 19–20, 21, 22, 252n14
Shakespeare, William, 90, 143, 144, 182, 242; and modern textual studies, 174, 264n3, 265n5
Shapiro, Gary, 258n18
Shapiro, Jeremy J., 260n27
Shelley, Percy Bysshe, 6, 46, 88, 129, 229, 231, 232, 233, 244. Works: "A Defence of Poetry," 40–41, 269n16; "Epipsychidion," 219; "Life of Life," 219; *Prometheus Unbound,* 62, 230
Shepherd, Geoffrey, 255n1, 261n29
Sheridan-Smith, A. M., 252n16, 259n39
Shorter, Kingsley, 255n12
Sica, Alan, 258n18
Sidney, Sir Philip: *An Apology for Poetry,* 73–74; *Defence of Poesie,* 127, 254n32
Silliman, Ron, 211–215, 219, 247, 267n4, 267n6, 269n28; *Tjanting,* 211–215, 216, 220; *Ketjak,* 214–215
Simon, Herbert A., 261n31
Simonides, 26
Simpson, Louis, 198
Smart, T. B., 256nn5,8
Socrates. *See* Plato
Spariosu, Mihai, 261n32
Speiser, E. A., 60–61, 255n5
Spenser, Edmund, 143
Spinoza, Benedict de: *Theologico-Political Treatise,* 167–168
Steffan, T. G., 266n14
Stein, Gertrude, 199
Stella, Frank, 33
Steppe, Wolfhard, 265n4
Stevens, Wallace, 199
Stevenson, W. H., 264n51
Stoekl, Allan, 270n5
Structuralism, 106, 259n2
Stukeley, William, 263n23
Suphan, B., 252n4

Tannenbaum, Leslie, 153
Tanselle, G. Thomas, 266n18
Tatham, Frederick, 233
Taylor, Gary, 265n5
Tennyson, Alfred, Lord, 88, 90, 183; *The Princess,* 266n15
Texts, literary: blindness/insight dialectic, 2, 99, 241–242; cognitive functions of, 2–4, 6–7, 18, 26–27, 30, 36, 72, 98–99, 241, 243; textuality in and de Man, 3–5; performativity of, 5, 7–9, 19–20, 21, 42–49, 55, 75–92 *passim,* 103, 243–244; and referentiality, 5–6, 115–131 *passim,* 213–214, 259n2; production processes of, 6, 74–75, 76–77, 83–85, 91, 117; reproductive history of, 6, 125, 135, 137, 229–230, 241; history and futurity in, 14, 51–56, 60–62, 222, 223–224, 225–240 *passim,* 247–248, 269n9; legitimation crisis and, 50–51, 54, 95–114 *passim,* 130–131, 257n3; and incommensurability, 65–66, 69–70, 71–72, 77, 85, 86–89, 90–91, 128, 129, 130, 229, 246–247; and ideology, 74–75, 85, 86–89, 90–91, 107–108, 111, 113, 124, 129, 199, 200, 247; grammatological, productive, and documentary codes of, 74–85 *passim;* and theory of copytext, 173, 177–178, 264n3, 265n8; composition vs. production of, 175–184, 188–192; writer as distinct from author, 181, 265n11; instability of, 181–192 *passim;* as distinct from document, 185–186; as self-contradicted, 228–229, 231, 236, 238, 240, 243, 248; knowledge in, 241–242; as distinct from "works," 260n28
Thompson, John B., 256–257n1, 258n33, 259n40
Thoreau, Henry David: *Walden,* 151
Thucydides, 65, 240; *History of the Peloponnesian War,* 25, 65, 66, 67, 70, 269n15
Times Literary Supplement, 174
Todd, Ruthven, 161, 163
Tolstoy, Leo: "What Is Art?" 37
Tompkins, Jane, 257n8
Trask, Willard R., 261n8
Tregelles, Samuel P., 255n3
Trotsky, Leon: *History of the Russian Revolution,* 145

Unger, Roberto, 50
Usher, Stephen, 65

Vater, Johann Severin, 169
Vendler, Helen, 199
Vico, Giambattista, 120
Volney, Constantin François de: *Les Ruines,* 163

Von Hallberg, Robert, 198, 199, 267n3, 269n28

Wallace, C. M., 259n5
Warren, Austin, 118
Warren, Michael, 265n5
Watson, Bishop Richard, 163–164
Watten, Barrett, 200, 201, 268n18
Wechel, Christian, 53, 54
Wellek, René, 97, 118
West, Cornel, 268n9
White, Hayden, 133–134, 135–136, 140, 141, 260n22
Wilbur, Richard, 198
Wilson, F. P., 264n3
Wise, Thomas James, 140, 261n7
Wittgenstein, Ludwig, 27, 115, 146, 147, 151, 247

Wolf, F. A., 15, 62, 130, 152, 173; *Prolegomena ad Homerum,* 63
Wolff, Robert Paul, 253n16
Wordsworth, William, 41–42, 118, 143, 182, 201, 231, 254n27. Works: "Lucy Gray," 42; *Lyrical Ballads,* 91; "Peele Castle," 42; "Preface" to *Lyrical Ballads,* 40, 127; *The Prelude,* 52, 183; "The Ruined Cottage," 57, 172; "Tintern Abbey," 39–40, 4⌐

Yale school, 35, 200, 207, 268n7
Yeats, William Butler, 199

Zimmerman, Robert L., 253–254n16
Zohn, Harry, 269n3
Zukofsky, Louis, 199